D1197514

Remembering Heart Mountain

Essays on Japanese American Internment in Wyoming

**Donated by the
Sonoma County
chapter of the
Japanese American
Citizens League**

Remembering Heart Mountain

Essays on Japanese American Internment in Wyoming

Edited and Contributions by
Mike Mackey

A Western History Publications Book
Western History Publications
P. O. Box 291
Powell, Wyoming 82435

Printed by
Mountain States Lithographing
Casper, Wyoming

Cover design by Tina Faxon

Cover photo courtesy of the Buffalo Bill Historical Center
Cody, Wyoming

ISBN 0-9661556-1-0

Table of Contents

Dedication

This book is dedicated to the memory of my friends,

Sam Fujishin

and

Frank T. Inouye.

My life is better for having known them.

Acknowledgments

The Heart Mountain symposium and this publication were made possible through the participation and generosity of several organizations and institutions. The Heart Mountain project would not have moved beyond the planning stage had it not been for a generous grant from the Wyoming Council for the Humanities. With numerous groups applying for dwindling funds, the Council saw merit and potential in this project. However, in spite of Humanities Council funding, this program would not have succeeded without important contributions from the History Department at Northwest College in Powell, Wyoming, Paul Fees and the Buffalo Bill Historical Center in Cody, Wyoming, the use of facilities at Northwest College and financial support from Dick Nelson and the First National Bank of Powell, Wyoming.

In an effort to save money in the early stages of development, this program was, for the most part, a two-man operation carried out by Northwest College history professor Steven Thulin and myself. As conference time grew near we were able to insure the program's success by imposing upon faculty and staff from Northwest College. Laurel Vredenburg handled the design and printing of the pamphlet announcing the conference; Nickie Proffit did an excellent job of promoting the conference nation wide; professors Winifred Wasden and Charlotte Patrick acted as emcees and enforcers, insuring that the program moved along on schedule; professor Mike Masterson handled the sound and lighting duties at the auditorium; numerous Northwest College staff in housing, food services, transportation and maintenance worked through the weekend to insure the success of the symposium; a number of Northwest College and Powell High School students also volunteered their services, and my daughters, Traci and Erin Mackey worked ten to twelve hour days taking care of book sales at the conference. These individuals, and many others, contributed not only to the success of the Heart Mountain symposium, but also to this publication and I want to offer them my most sincere thanks. I must also extend a special thanks to Steven Thulin without whose help this conference would not have succeeded.

A number of individuals were directly involved in the production of this publication. Melanie Lennon spent many hours transcribing the conference proceedings. Arthur Hansen at California State University at Fullerton solicited articles from contributors who did not participate in the conference but whose works give this book some semblance of balance. Frank Van Nuys at the University of Wyoming pushed me to complete this project and helped with a good deal of the editing. Steven Thulin handled the copy editing chores for the conference papers appearing in *Peace & Change*. I must also thank Blackwells Publishing and *Peace & Change* for allowing me to reprint those papers in this book. Winifred Wasden accepted the copy editing duties for this publication. When I decided to include a few photographs at the last minute, Liz Holmes at the Buffalo Bill Historical Center came through on a moment's notice. I want to thank all of these individuals for their contributions and for making this process easier.

The articles that follow represent a great deal of work on the part of the contributors. I want to thank all of those whose papers appear in this publication for their effort. Though many people participated in this project, I accept full responsibility for any errors which the scrutinizing reader may find.

Preface

During April of 1994 I was approached by an old high school classmate who suggested that I organize a conference on the Heart Mountain Relocation Center. Since I had written my MA thesis on Heart Mountain I felt the idea worth further consideration. I ran the proposal past my friend Steven Thulin, a history professor at Northwest College in Powell, Wyoming. By July of 1994 preparations for a three day symposium were underway. The program was to be held on the Northwest College campus twelve miles east of the Heart Mountain Relocation Center historic site. While I wrote grant proposals and organized a group of presenters, Thulin took on the less glamorous, yet more important job, of organizing housing, meals, bus schedules to and from airports, registration and promotion of the conference.

Ten short months later, on May 19-21, 1995, a symposium titled, "Japanese American history: The Heart Mountain Experience," was underway. The program featured presentations by this country's top scholars in the area of Japanese American History, former Heart Mountain internees, and residents who lived in the area when Heart Mountain was the third largest population center in Wyoming. With the closest major airport located one hundred miles north of Powell in Billings, Montana, I was pleasantly surprised when the symposium was attended by more than 330 people from twenty-two different states.

Following the completion of the symposium, and a well deserved rest, Thulin and I edited five of the papers presented at the conference into a special spring 1998 issue for the journal, *Peace & Change*. This volume, *Remembering Heart Mountain*, is the final phase of the symposium project. Twelve of the sixteen articles that appear in this publication are versions of papers which were presented at the May 1995 conference. Four additional papers were solicited to give the book balance. Part one of this collection is designed to give the reader some understanding of the anti-Japanese movement that existed in California prior to World War II and an overview of the politics behind the relocation process. Parts two through five focus primarily on aspects of the Heart Mountain experience. Finally, parts six and seven look at a re-reading of the archives, future research on this subject, the long-term health effects of internment, and the importance of commemorating events such as Japanese relocation.

Papers from three of the more provocative symposium presentations by Bacon Sakatani, Jack Tono and Raymond Uno, do not appear in this collection. The structure of both the papers and the presentations by these individuals led to difficulties in attempting to include the works in this collection. However, these presenters deserve mention and my thanks for the interest their presentations generated in the audience. Of the articles which do appear in this book, I should point out that I feel the authors, whether scholars or non-scholars, had something important to say and interesting ways of saying it. For that reason these papers were only lightly edited. Those who find fault with this approach can place the blame squarely on me.

It is my feeling that this volume contains something for everyone. A good number of the articles will be of interest to the scholar studying various aspects of Japanese American history in general, and the Heart Mountain experience in particular. It is hoped that all of the articles will be of interest to the student and general reader looking for a better understanding of different aspects of the Heart Mountain experience and this dark chapter in American history.

Mike Mackey
Powell, Wyoming
March, 1998

About the Authors

Scott L. Bills is a professor of history at Stephen F. Austin State University. He served as co-editor of the journal *Peace & Change* from 1994-1997. Dr. Bills is the author of *The Libyan Arena* (1995) and *Empire and Cold War* (1990). In addition, Bills has written extensively on the Kent State shootings of May 1970 and the emergence of the May 4th movement.

Eric Bittner is an archive specialist at the National Archives—Rocky Mountain Region in Denver, Colorado and is a member of the Heart Mountain Foundation. Among his earlier writings is a piece on the Heart Mountain draft resisters which appeared in the fall issue of *Prologue* (1991).

Roger Daniels is the Charles Phelps Taft Professor of History at the University of Cincinnati. Publications by Dr. Daniels include numerous works about Japanese Americans and other immigrant and ethnic groups. His most recent book is titled, *Not Like Us: Immigrants and Minorities in America, 1890-1924* (1997).

Louis Fiset is affiliate associate professor of dentistry at the University of Washington. One of the results of Dr. Fiset's interest in Japanese relocation is his recent book, *Imprisoned Apart: The World War II Correspondence of an Issei Couple* (1997). Fiset's other writings on relocation include articles on Japanese Americans in the state of Washington and health care issues at the Topaz camp in Utah.

Sam Fujishin was originally interned at Tule Lake in California where he received his high school diploma. The Fujishin family was later moved to the Heart Mountain Relocation Center where Sam became the first man drafted out of the camp. He was awarded the Bronze Star for valor while serving with the famed, 442nd Regimental Combat Team. Following the war he homesteaded in southeast Oregon where he farmed and raised his family. Sam Fujishin died in 1997.

Arthur Hansen is a professor of history and Director of the Japanese American Oral History Program at California State University at Fullerton. Dr. Hansen has published widely on the subject of Japanese American history. One of his most recent projects has involved the editing of Japanese American newspaperman James Omura's memoirs.

Lane Hirabayashi is a professor in the Department of Ethnic Studies at the University of Colorado. His latest anthology, *Teaching Asian America: Diversity and the Problem of Community* (1998), reflects more than fifteen years of work in the classroom. Dr. Hirabayashi has also published, *Cultural Capital: Mountain Zapotec*

Migrant Association in Mexico City (1993) and two books dealing with the Japanese American Evacuation and Resettlement Study at Poston.

Bill Hosokawa is a former Heart Mountain internee and founding editor of the *Heart Mountain Sentinel*. Following the war he worked for both the *Denver Post* and *The Rocky Mountain News*. Hosokawa has authored numerous books dealing with the Japanese American experience, the best known of which is *Nisei: The Quiet Americans*. His most recent book is, *Old Man Thunder: Father of the Bullet Train* (1997).

Frank T. Inouye was a Heart Mountain internee who left the camp to attend college. He earned his Ph.D. at the University of Southern California and was professor of history at the University of Hawaii. Dr. Inouye's last major project involved the co-authoring of a book dealing with the history of the University of Hawaii. Frank Inouye died in 1995.

Mamoru Inouye is a former Heart Mountain internee and recently retired NASA research scientist. His recent book, *The Heart Mountain Story: Photographs by Hansel Mieth and Otto Hagel of the World War II Internment of Japanese Americans,* was written and designed in conjunction with his photo exhibit which is scheduled for display in California, Wyoming and Pennsylvania and is booked through the year 2000.

Gwenn Jensen, after working for twenty years as an oil industry geologist, received her Ph.D. in medical anthropology from the University of Colorado in 1997. Dr. Jensen has presented papers at meetings of the American Anthropological Association and the Oral History Association. She is currently working on two books related to her dissertation, "The Experience of Injustice: Health Consequences of the Japanese American Internment."

Velma Kessel is a retired nurse living in Powell, Wyoming. She worked as a registered nurse at the Heart Mountain Hospital from fall, 1942 through spring, 1945. The diary she kept while employed by the WRA at Heart Mountain has been edited into a book which depicts various aspects of her life both inside and outside the Heart Mountain Relocation Center.

Mike Mackey is a native of Powell, Wyoming who has worked on a number of writing projects and film documentaries dealing with the Heart Mountain Relocation Center. He has also published a number of works looking at various aspects of Wyoming's history.

Philip J. Roberts is an associate professor of history at the University of Wyoming. Dr. Roberts is a Wyoming native who has written numerous articles and books dealing with the history of Wyoming and the American West. In addition, he is the editor of *Wyoming Almanac* and the State Historical Society's journal, *Annals of Wyoming*. Roberts is also involved in the organization and development of the University of Wyoming Press.

Peter K. Simpson is a Wyoming native and member of the politically involved Simpson family. Dr. Simpson served as president of Sheridan Community College in Sheridan, Wyoming and recently retired as vice-president of the University of Wyoming Foundation.

Frank Van Nuys is a lecturer at the University of Wyoming. Dr. Van Nuys' research on the Progressive era has resulted in numerous publications. He is currently conducting research on the Americanization movement in the West during World War I and the 1920's. He is also developing his dissertation, on the same subject, into a book.

Part I

The Seeds of Internment and the Relocation Process

One of nine guard towers on the perimeter of the Heart Mountain Relocation Center. All photographs in this publication are courtesy of the Jack Richard collection, Buffalo Bill Historical Center, Cody, Wyoming.

Sowing the Seeds of Internment:
James D. Phelan's Anti-Japanese Crusade, 1919-1920

Frank Van Nuys

Once permitted to leave the camp in 1945, many, if not most, of the Heart Mountain internees returned to their former homes on the West Coast, this in spite of the unbridled zealousness with which so many of their white neighbors in those states had turned them out. It is instructive to consider the well-documented xenophobia regarding Japanese-born and Japanese American residents on the West Coast in the early years of the twentieth century. I hope to shed some light on the salient forces at work in one state—California—that sowed the seeds for internment in 1942.

At the center of these developments were California progressives and specifically the career of California's premier Democratic progressive, an individual who bears a considerable amount of responsibility for fomenting and exacerbating white hatred and fear of the Japanese and Japanese Americans. Although he died eleven years before Pearl Harbor, Senator James D. Phelan, in his re-election campaign of 1919-1920, personified California's forty year campaign to harass, dispossess, stereotype and otherwise bully its inhabitants of Japanese birth and descent. Phelan's opportunism and irresponsibility set an ignoble example eagerly followed by contemporaries and subsequently, and tragically by many Californians, Wyomingites and other white Americans in the 1940s.

James Duval Phelan was born April 20, 1861 in San Francisco. His Irish father, James Phelan, came into California during the gold rush and quietly grew rich selling general merchandise to miners. The elder Phelan also helped found San Francisco's wildly lucrative wheat export trade of the 1860s and 1870s and subsequently settled into banking. The younger Phelan graduated from St. Ignatius College (the present-day University of San Francisco) in 1881 and attended the Hastings Law School of the University of California. He entered the family banking firm in 1884 and then assumed control upon the death of his father in 1892. Phelan served as Mayor of San Francisco from 1897 to 1902 and was Chairman of Relief and Red Cross Funds in 1906 after the great earthquake. He also played a key role in the approval of the Hetch Hetchy project that created a municipal water supply for San Francisco out of the Hetch Hetchy Valley in Yosemite National Park.[1]

Historian Kevin Starr describes Phelan as "a smallish dapper man, his beard kept well-trimmed, his tailoring impeccable, a lifelong, very ardent and discreet wooer of the ladies."[2] He also ardently and not always discreetly wooed those interests that could further his political career. As Mayor of San Francisco, for instance, Phelan cultivated labor support by endorsing minimum wage and maximum hour regulations for city workers and appointing a powerful labor leader to a newly formed Civil Service Commission. The Irish had long been a dominant force in San Francisco labor unions, so Phelan, both of whose parents had emigrated from Ireland, could appeal to the working men along ethnic, if not class lines. A crucial element in this appeal involved the disparagement of immigrants from Asian countries, mainly the Chinese before exclusion began in 1882, and subsequently the growing numbers of Japanese, who were derided as cheap labor imported by unscrupulous capitalists to undermine native white workers.

Yet, the millionaire banker could not have hoped to construct a political base upon the labor movement. A member of the state Democratic Party executive committee since the late 1880s, and regularly selected as the party's finance chairman, Phelan's closest associates and supporters were fellow capitalists and reformers. Try as he might to befriend the laboring man, he was an elitist to the core. From childhood, Phelan had desired above all else to join the ultimate "millionaire's club," the United States Senate. Unfortunately, the California legislature, responsible for selecting the State's Senators, remained a Republican bailiwick.

In May 1900, Phelan delivered a keynote address at an anti-Oriental rally in San Francisco, a mass meeting which, while focused on a renewal of the 1882 Chinese Exclusion Act, also sounded ominous warnings to the Japanese. Mayor Phelan summed up the purposes of the convention with an ode to California's responsibility to the rest of the nation:

> If there be one thing that the people of California have done worthy of the commendation of the nation [Phelan declared] it is that California forced Congress to adopt the exclusion act and protected the United States from the dreadful effects of Oriental social, moral, commercial, and intellectual ideals. California owes it again to the nation to insist upon the enforcement of the Chinese exclusion act and to demand the enactment of an exclusion act against the Japanese.[3]

The Japanese immigrants whom Phelan wished to exclude comprised a laughingly small proportion of California's total population in 1900, a situation little changed by 1910, even after 130,000 more Japanese had arrived in the United States. Compared to the numbers of European immigrants during the same period, Japanese immigration was but a trickle. Moreover, unlike the "new immigrants" from eastern, central, and southern Europe, the Japanese could not become American citizens. Most of the immigrants were males, and most came from four predominantly agricultural prefectures in southwestern Japan. Perhaps one-half of the Japanese who resided in California in 1910 were involved in agriculture. Most of the first generation of Japanese immigrants—the Issei—who began life as farm laborers ended life as farm laborers. Few became land owners or lessees. Nonetheless, white farmers, both large-scale growers and small operators, felt increasingly threatened. Agitators would proclaim repeatedly that the incoming Japanese "hordes" would soon snap up the state's prime agricultural holdings.[4]

The anti-Japanese movement, effectively given life by Phelan and others in

1900, ebbed and flowed throughout the first decade of the new century. An attempt by the San Francisco school board to segregate Japanese school children in 1906 precipitated a diplomatic crisis which President Theodore Roosevelt presumably ironed out the following year. Shortly afterwards, Japan and the United States negotiated a Gentlemen's Agreement designed to prevent the further immigration of Japanese laborers. Quiet diplomacy spelled spinelessness to anti-Japanese agitators, however, who insisted on absolute exclusion.

The movement also found new grievances, most notably the "picture bride" practice. A variation upon a centuries-old Japanese tradition of families arranging marriages for their children, single laborers hoping to find a wife sent photographs to their families in Japan to aid in negotiations. The suitors also received a photograph of the prospective bride, and if both parties expressed satisfaction, then a proxy marriage would be conducted in Japan. Upon the wife's arrival in the United States, a second ceremony usually occurred immediately. Between 1900 and 1920, about five-thousand "picture brides," representing approximately one-fourth of all Japanese women immigrants during the period, came to the United States. While hardly the invasion that agitators depicted, the "picture bride" controversy symbolized the ineffectiveness of the Gentlemen's Agreement and helped to strengthen the anti-Japanese movement.[5]

The Japanese in California did not remain passive in the face of growing animosity. Shortly after the rally in 1900, Japanese community leaders in San Francisco formed the Japanese Deliberative Council of America. As anti-Japanese agitation expanded, the organization eventually became the Japanese Association of America. It is good to keep in mind that, while this paper chiefly concerns the role of James D. Phelan in events affecting Japanese immigrants, the immigrants themselves were organized in their own defense.[6]

While considerations of space preclude a more detailed examination of the course of the anti-Japanese movement in California up to 1920, it is essential that we very briefly consider the 1913 Alien Land Act. The rise of the anti-Japanese movement coincided with the emergence of Progressive Republicans (remembering that Phelan was a progressive Democrat), who swept into power in 1910 with the election of Hiram Warren Johnson as Governor. In 1911, the California progressives instituted a wide-ranging reform program. Meanwhile, Johnson quashed the now customary anti-Japanese legislation on behalf of the federal government, which feared a diplomatic breach with Japan. In 1913, though, with a Democratic President, Woodrow Wilson, newly inaugurated, Governor Johnson changed direction and backed a discriminatory alien land law clearly aimed at the Japanese. President Wilson, in an unprecedented move of international diplomacy, sent William Jennings Bryan, the Secretary of State, to Sacramento to consult with Johnson and the legislature. Bryan failed to convince the Californians to reverse their course, and the Alien Land Act was signed into law by Governor Johnson. The main section of the Act referred to the right of "aliens eligible to citizenship" to own agricultural land; this, of course, implicitly denied such rights to the Japanese. In a small concession (that would loom large in 1920), "aliens ineligible to citizenship" were allowed to lease land for up to three years.[7]

While Hiram Johnson and the progressive Republicans were shaking things up in Sacramento, James D. Phelan signed on, in late fall 1911, as a supporter of the progressive Democratic presidential candidate, Woodrow Wilson.[8] During the 1912 presidential campaign Phelan performed yeoman duties on the stump in an extremely close contest in California between the former President and Progressive Party candidate, Theodore Roosevelt, and Wilson. Then, with the 1913 ratification of the seventeenth amendment providing for the direct election of United States Senators, James D. Phelan's great opportunity to realize his dream finally arrived. After an easy primary victory, Phelan entered the three-way race in 1914 as the frontrunner. He emphasized his long service to California and, to avoid alienating the Wilson administration, backed away from the Japanese issue. Phelan outdistanced Progressive Republican Francis J. Heney by 28,000 votes, thus becoming the first Senator from California to be sent to Washington by popular vote.

Ironically, Phelan accomplished little in his running battle against Japanese immigration and expansion during his Senatorial career.[9] In fact, he came to be perceived by many political observers as more of a showhorse than workhorse. The elaborate entertainments at his Washington home won more fame for the Senator than his achievements in the Senate chamber. Never having served in a legislative post before, Phelan's parliamentary tactics were amateurish, his attendance spotty, and aside from the Japanese question, he exhibited little sustained interest in issues. A review of his performance reveals a somewhat lazy and inept Senator who was typically opportunistic and publicity-conscious rather than principled and public-spirited. Phelan's ineffectual efforts in Washington, combined with Woodrow Wilson's declining prestige and the rapprochement in Republican ranks, suggested an extremely difficult reelection battle ahead in 1920.

To win, Phelan had to gather significant non-partisan support and needed an issue that could cut across party lines. He believed that issue to be the League of Nations and, in his speeches in early 1919, emphasized the importance of an international body to check Japan's ambitions in the Pacific. Audiences and newspaper reports ignored the League but responded enthusiastically to Phelan's warnings about the Japanese. Soon the League took a back seat to the "Japanese menace." The issue was all the more appealing since the Alien Land Law of 1913 had not appreciably affected Japanese land-holding in California. During the six ensuing years, the amount of land owned and leased by Japanese aliens had actually increased. Phelan's obsession with Japanese expansion fit nicely with his constituents' concerns about the land law. Phelan had the issue which he believed would return him to the Senate.

Of course, the increases in the amount of landholdings and in the number of Japanese in the state, which rose from 41,000 in 1910 to 72,000 in 1920, were major irritants to exclusionists.[10] Natural increase accounted for about half of the expansion in population because a significant portion of Japanese arrivals in California were picture brides. Phelan seized upon the phenomenon and began a highly visible campaign against the picture bride practice in March 1919. After visiting the federal immigration facilities at Angel Island in San Francisco Bay, he declared the picture brides a "decided menace to the country." He considered the practice "a mere subterfuge to defeat the spirit and intent of the immigration restriction" and lectured that "action should be taken at once."[11] Taking alarm, the Japanese consul in San Francisco advised his government to discontinue the practice and also compelled the executive board of the Japanese Association to disavow it as well. Local Japanese associations and other central bodies on the coast were angered by the consul's actions but were powerless in the face of growing hysteria.[12] In December 1919, the Japanese government promised to discontinue granting passports to picture brides.

An unsatisfied Phelan dismissed the gesture as irrelevant, since there were, he alleged, enough children of immigrants to eventually own all of California. He assailed the Japanese concession as "camouflage designed to draw the attention of the American people away from the main issue in the Asiatic situation," which, according to Phelan, was the Japanese attempt to gain control of the land. In a contradiction of his usual statements about Japanese women and Japanese land ownership, Phelan held that the elimination of picture brides had no bearing on the land question.[13] When opening his campaign against the picture brides, which in effect was the beginning of his campaign for reelection, Phelan asserted that California was fated to become a colony of Japan unless Japanese were prevented from acquiring land through their children. "The evil," he said "consists in the nonassimi[l]ability of the Japanese, which, if tolerated, would produce a mongrel and degenerate population."[14]

On March 31, 1919, having grabbed headlines for several weeks, Phelan appeared before a joint session of the State legislature. The United States was then in the midst of the Red Scare, a period of anti-foreign and anti-radical hysteria which erupted after the World War ended. It was the latest in a long tradition of periodic nativist attacks upon groups considered to be "un-American," such as the Irish in the 1840s and Catholics throughout the nineteenth century. The Red Scare focused primarily on alleged sympathizers with Russian and other European Communists, or Bolsheviks. However, any foreign influence, be it European or Asian, fueled the hysteria. According to Senator Phelan in his speech to the legislators, the influx of picture brides, smuggling of laborers, and evasion of land laws threatened the creation and perpetuation of "American communities which are the units of national greatness." Playing off Red Scare fears, Phelan foresaw that "despair will be followed by resentment, and those conditions will breed I.W.Wism, Bolshevism and all the modern evils of a deranged economic system."[15] He also conjured up visions of the lately concluded war against imperial aggression. Referring to the Japanese as the "Germans of the Orient," he lambasted the federal government for repeatedly caving in to Japan and warned of that nation's imperial designs.[16]

Just a few weeks later, in June 1919, hearings conducted by the House

Committee on Immigration and Naturalization in Washington, in the words of the contemporary political scientist Raymond Leslie Buell, "gave Senator Phelan and others an opportunity to harp *ad nauseum* on the Japanese menace to the country."[17] In his testimony, Phelan struck a blow for the theory of a propaganda campaign directed from Japan, stating that "The People of the State of California . . . have been overawed, or, in the language of the street, they have been 'buffaloed' by the Japanese Government, through its numerous agents and representatives in this country." He also got in a poke at the Wilson Administration, from which Phelan hoped to dissociate himself in his reelection effort. Referring to "the administration itself on various occasions," Phelan criticized Washington for warning California against "legislating [its] own preservation." The now former Secretary of State, William Jennings Bryan, was charged with going soft on the Japanese in 1913. Speaking of meeting with Bryan at Governor Johnson's mansion during the land law crisis, Phelan remarked that the Secretary's "principle concern was to draft a law in such language, dulcet and sweet, that it would give no offense to the Japanese."[18]

The Senator was on a roll. He repeated favorite allegations concerning the smuggling of Japanese laborers into California via Mexico and Japanese fishing fleets at San Diego and Los Angeles. He also developed a "twofold" theory about the rationale behind the picture bride practice. "The woman coming and taking up the duties of wifehood becomes a mother in due course, and a child born upon the soil is entitled to own land," Phelan helpfully informed the Committee. But "These women are not only wives but they are laborers" and Phelan had photographs and had seen these women working side by side with their husbands, often with a baby on their back. "So they accomplish the dual purpose of defeating the law (by which he presumably meant the Gentlemen's Agreement) by getting in actual laborers and in defeating the land law by getting in by the birth route persons eligible to hold land."[19] Clearly, to those not so sentimental as to believe Japanese women had babies because they liked children, it was obvious that the Japanese were procreating at an alarming rate with the express purpose of flooding the state with Japanese land-owners.

Near the end of his testimony, Phelan sighed, "I got so much of this stuff I can not read it all."[20] Indeed he did. Subscribing religiously throughout his career to newspaper clipping services, Phelan kept a file on the Japanese question from at least 1908 until 1929, the year prior to his death. In addition to several scrapbooks of clippings devoted to the issue, he collected reams of magazine articles and pamphlets treating every aspect of the problem. This massive amount of information did not preclude, and in fact may have expedited, his tendency to devolve into cornucopias of generalizations. For instance, at one point in his statement, Phelan shifted to a favorite theme, that of Japanese loyalty to the homeland. "Their allegiance is to the Mikado," he insisted, "and that vast number of Japanese on the western coast now would rise as a man in case of conflict between the United States and Japan . . . ."[21] Rambling on, he briefly referred to an immigration quota system such as that ultimately incorporated in the 1924 National Origins Act. "I would not consent to the admission of 1 percent or one-half percent or one-fourth percent under any scheme to mollify them," Phelan blustered. "I regard them in their economic destructiveness, their competitive ability as enemies to be rejected, to keep away from as a plague of locusts, not to be compromised with but to be eliminated." Following another journey through the florid fields of his imagination, Phelan spelled out the dreary alternative: ". . . you can well imagine that if a state is abandoned to an alien race, the white people would resent it, and ultimately and certainly drift away from a love of country and turn next to resentment and then to violence and crime."[22]

A few months later, Phelan aided in a reorganization of the anti-Japanese movement. The old Asiatic Exclusion League formed by San Francisco labor leaders had gradually fizzled out after peaking in 1909. The revived entity, the California Oriental Exclusion League, coordinated the on-going anti-Japanese efforts of such established groups as the American Legion, Native Sons and Daughters of the Golden West, and the State Federation of Labor. A five-point program declared the new organization's uncompromising attitude toward Japan and Japanese immigrants. It demanded an end to the Gentlemen's Agreement, exclusion of picture brides, rigid enforcement of exclusion laws, a ban forever on the naturalization of "Asiatics," and an amendment to the Constitution to deny naturalization to the children of "Orientals," even if born in the United States.[23] Phelan, impressed with the publicity value of that last addition to the exclusionist program, later introduced a joint resolution in the Senate to contravene certain provisions of the Fourteenth Amendment that guaranteed the right of citizenship to children of Asian immigrants. Playing to the continuing post-war fears of foreign influence, Phelan told his colleagues that his amendment was "appropriate and timely for the reason that the Congress is engaged in the work of Americanization."[24] His resolution died in committee but Phelan benefited by pleasing the most radical segments of the anti-Japanese movement.

In his speech to the legislature in March 1919, Phelan had proposed an amendment to remove leasing privileges from the land law. The legislature proved uninterested, so pressure mounted to draft an initiative to put before the voters in 1920. Besides barring leases, the initiative measure forbade any transfer of land to Japanese; prohibited land-holding, through lease or purchase, by corporations controlled by Japanese, and outlawed guardianships by Issei on behalf of their citizen offspring. With the American Legion and the Native Sons and Daughters procuring many of the petition signatures, the measure was placed on the general election ballot.[25]

Meanwhile, supporters of the Japanese had an opportunity to counter the propaganda of Phelan and the exclusionists when a subcommittee of the House Committee on Immigration journeyed to California for a series of hearings in July 1920. At the first hearing held in San Francisco, long-time state Democratic party leader John P. Irish heatedly answered a Phelan charge that he was receiving money from Japanese sources. Irish stormed that he was speaking out on behalf of Japanese farmers and farm laborers as "An act of justice and to maintain the honor of my State and my country . . . . This initiative measure denies them the primitive rights of humanity."[26] Kiichi Kanzaki, secretary of the Japanese Association, later scolded Phelan and his cohorts for their wild speculations on Japanese population growth, religion and other issues. "A sympathetic attitude, not antagonistic dealings," Kanzaki declared, "is the only reliable key to the permanent solution of the problem . . . . Why should the Californians make so much out of the insignificant problem of Japanese agricultural pursuits," he asked, "in a state which possesses such a vast amount of unimproved land . . . ?"[27]

Unfazed by the criticism, Phelan declared the investigation by the subcommittee "highly gratifying." Indeed, with the initiative campaign in need of just a few more petitions to be turned in, the hearings occurred at a most propitious time. All of the finger-wagging by opponents of the exclusionists had the typical result of raising enthusiasm for the amendment. Phelan noted with pride that subcommittee members had witnessed "the arrival of a cargo" of picture brides and had "also learned of the surreptitious entry of numberless Japanese over the border." Phelan also pointed out that the committee could better appreciate how rapidly California's farm land was "passing . . . into the hands of aliens." Again, it had been proven that the Japanese alien "lives in colonies and is non-assimilable;" that Japanese children crowded country schools and attended Japanese schools "before and after regular school hours;" that California had seventy-six Buddhist temples, which, Phelan mistakenly announced, "taught Shintoism, which is Emperor worship;" that all of the Japanese residing in the state owed their first allegiance to the Mikado; that "they are not made of the stuff from which American citizens are made."[28]

After the hearings, Phelan began campaigning for the November 2 election. His Republican opponent, Samuel Shortridge, had lost out to Joseph R. Knowland for that party's nomination in 1914. Factors that made Shortridge undesirable six years before—his arch-conservatism, corporate ties, and dubious ethics—no longer bothered voters in 1920. As unappealing as Phelan appeared to those put off by his pandering to the anti-Japanese bloc, Shortridge promised to be an extremely bitter pill to swallow. Stanford University president David Starr Jordan informed Fresno newspaper editor Chester Rowell "that strongly as I disapprove of much that the present junior senator [actually Phelan was the senior senator and former Governor Hiram Johnson the junior senator] has said and done, I shall vote for him in preference to his unspeakable opponent. Phelan is, at any rate, 'speakable,' whatever that may be."[29] In a state in which registered Republicans outnumbered Democrats by a two to one ratio, Phelan would need many voters to find him at least "speakable." Therefore, from the outset, his efforts were focused on a non-partisan appeal and a dissociation from Wilson and the League of Nations as well as the Democratic nominee for President, James M. Cox. However, as Rowell, who also backed Phelan, conceded, "A year in which Harding is possible may be a year in which Shortridge is also possible."[30]

Both candidates participated in another general gathering of anti-Japanese organizations. On September 2, in a meeting called by Phelan, the Japanese Exclusion League was organized at Native Sons Hall in San Francisco. Whereas the California Oriental Exclusion League formed the previous year had been designed to coordinate the statewide effort to stop Japanese immigration and thwart efforts to evade the land law, the new organization added a pledge to launch a national campaign. Displaying again the formidable unity of the anti-Japanese movement, a coalition emerged that included the American Legion, California Federation of Women's Clubs, Loyal Order of Moose, Native Sons and Daughters, the State Federation of Labor, and the State Grange. Phelan and Shortridge served together on a five-man committee set up to foster a permanent organization.[31]

Both Senatorial campaigns utilized the Japanese issue, and practically every candidate for national, state, or local office followed suit. Yet, Phelan, newspaper magnate V. S. McClatchy, the Hearst papers, and the Japanese Exclusion League led the way. The American Legion sponsored a film entitled *Shadows of the West*, which dramatized all of Phelan's favorite anti-Japanese themes. One Japanese villain was shown tapping out vegetable prices on a wireless transmitter from a secret location, controlling the state's markets. In his speeches, Phelan would tell of how a "Japanese sits at the telephone board and dictates prices throughout that region . . . telling people of that section what they shall pay for their vegetables."[32] In an article published after the campaign, Phelan asserted that "no influence that may be brought to bear will swerve a Japanese from the course which is dictated by his leaders."[33] In *Shadows of the West*, this assumed monolithic Japanese mindset was portrayed by innumerable Japanese spies and a secret government. At the film's climax, two fair white maidens, abducted by the treacherous Japanese, are saved from a fate presumably worse than death by heroic American Legionnaires.[34]

Anti-Japanese films and literature kept public enthusiasm for the initiative high. Senator Phelan attempted to generate fervor for his own campaign through a frenetic schedule of personal appearances (between September 3 and November 2) and an absolute blizzard of propaganda from his campaign headquarters in San Francisco. In 1914, he ran as a Wilson Democrat, admonishing voters to support their President by sending him an agreeable Senator. In 1920, however, Phelan essentially repudiated his party and ran the one-issue campaign for which he had seemingly prepared his entire career. His campaign slogan was "Keep California White."[35] (On a swing into southern California, Phelan and his subordinates found a fair number of black and Mexican voters attending the rallies. The slogan in that section of the state became "Keep California American.")[36]

Courting the votes of small farmers, Phelan embraced agrarianism during the campaign as enthusiastically as if he had been raised on a homestead and not among the San Francisco elite. "Our American farmer leads a happy life," Phelan stated confidently, "no matter if he is on the large tract or on his small ranch of a few acres."[37] He greatly feared, Phelan told his audiences, the surrender of the white races as tillers of the soil." In answering the critics who warned of economic disaster if

Japanese farm labor was lost, Phelan believed that California "could well afford a slight interruption" because patriotic whites would flock into the fields and take up the slack in production at high wages. He also proposed a land settlement plan which would allow the state to buy tracts from "Orientals" and place "favorable citizens" upon them. "If the Orientals will not sell," the candidate said, "then the power of eminent domain might be properly invoked."[38] The fundamental solutions, as always, lay in exclusion and an amendment to deny the rights of citizenship to children of Japanese immigrants. Land legislation, vital to Californians, was but a small part of a great national program.

Faced with the bipartisan assault on Japanese immigrants, which obviously precluded any significant opposition to the initiative by the press, the Japanese and their white supporters did the best they could to balance the rhetoric of Phelan and the exclusionists. Eastern liberals churned out pamphlets decrying the latest manifestation of West Coast xenophobia. In California, the Japanese Association, led by potato grower George Shima and Kiichi Kanzaki, went to great lengths to prove the assimilability and Americanization of the Japanese immigrants. John P. Irish formed the American Committee of Justice to agitate against Phelan and the land law measure.[39] In a pamphlet published by the Committee, the irascible Irish compared the anti-Japanese movement to a Russian pogrom and verbally lacerated Phelan. "He has made no record of any benefit to the State in the Senate;" Irish declared, "so he must divert attention from his uselessness as a senator by attacking the Japanese and trying to stampede the state by lying about them . . . . They [Phelan's lies] are as thick in his record as cooties in a battle trench," and the time has come, according to Irish, to stop "Phelan's pogrom gang."[40]

John P. Irish was a quotable old pol, but he had a negligible impact on public attitudes about the Japanese. Such was not the case, obviously, with the California press. Phelan enjoyed considerable newspaper support, from the Democratic Hearst papers to old Progressive sheets such as the *Fresno Republican* and the *San Francisco Bulletin*.[41] The latter urged its readers to vote for Phelan, "the progressive statesman and not for the professional reactionary," Shortridge, because the incumbent stood "in the estimation of both America and Japan as the acclaimed leader of California against the Japanese."[42] On the other side, the *San Francisco Chronicle* jealously asserted its claim that it and not Phelan originated the anti-Japanese movement. Where was he, the *Chronicle* asked, on the Japanese issue those six years in the Senate? Another editorial castigated Phelan for deserting Democratic principles while a subsequent article chided him for distancing himself from Cox and support for the League of Nations. His 1914 victory by "an inconsiderable plurality" over the divided Republicans further indicated Phelan's weakness.[43]

In the end the *Chronicle* was correct. Many unregenerate Progressives heeded the Senator's non-partisan call. Even so, more held their noses and cast their ballots for Shortridge. Phelan lost by 76,000 votes. The outcome of the initiative vote was never in doubt, yet supporters were somewhat surprised that it carried by only a three-to-one margin. Nonetheless, the next crucial step toward exclusion had been taken.[44]

James D. Phelan's legacy on the Japanese question had tragic consequences for the Japanese residents in California. The hysteria he helped stir up in 1920—the hatred for which he and his cohorts hold considerable responsibility—festered until 1942, when, after the attack on Pearl Harbor, white Californians finally drove the Japanese from the land and the cities and into internment camps and relocation centers. Phelan disregarded the basic civil rights of the immigrant farmers and other Japanese. To him they were a faceless horde of potential adversaries—the "enemy . . . within the gates," each a "trained soldier"[45]—and to manipulate their presence for political purposes was a legitimate undertaking.

"Once a Japanese always a Japanese is axiomatic"[46] he asserted, and upon this foundation, Phelan believed, Japan conspired to dominate the Pacific and ultimately the United States. "If foreigners come en mass [sic] and settle as foreigners and maintain their racial status and fail to blend with the population wherever they locate, as in the case of the Japanese," Phelan pointed out, "that would practically be the territory of Japan." Furthermore, to allow the naturalization of Japanese residents in the United State was but "a further step in the Japanese program" to undermine the country from within.[47] Exclusion and preparedness could solve the racial problem of Japanese immigration and the diplomatic problem of the Japanese threat. When it was impossible to live together peaceably, then "Each should live in a house of his own," he concluded.[48]

Ignoring American mistreatment of Japanese and other Asian immigrants, Phelan did all that he could to assure that it was indeed impossible for white Americans and Japanese immigrants and their children to coexist in California. While historians make judgements at the constant risk of misrepresenting historical figures who could not have known better, an objective evaluation of Phelan's anti-Japanese rhetoric and actions reveal his opportunistic and paranoid fear-mongering. True, hundreds of thousands of his fellow Californians were predisposed to believe everything he said about the Japanese immigrants and perhaps did not really need a James D. Phelan to rile them up. On the whole, white Americans in 1920 relied upon many racist assumptions as foundations for their world views, and Phelan's nativist pronouncements seemed perfectly sensible to most, especially in California. Nonetheless, regardless of the historical context, Phelan's behavior and rhetoric are indeed shameful. I do not wish to deny this individual his attributes as a generous patron of the arts and a well-intentioned reformer. His legacy has its noble side as well. Yet, sowing the seeds of internment, Phelan and his ilk subverted, perhaps unwittingly, American ideals of civil liberties and tolerance in their opportunistic campaign to divest the Japanese in California of their livelihoods and accomplishments. Although James D. Phelan could not foresee the humiliating and tragic implications of his words and deeds, let him remain, obscure as he is to most Americans, an object-lesson in the triumph of bigotry and paranoia represented at Heart Mountain.

Notes

1. Dorothy Kaucher, *James Duval Phelan, A Portrait 1861-1930* (Saratoga, California: Gallery Committee of the Montalvo Association, 1965); Robert E. Hennings, *James D. Phelan and the Wilson Progressives of California* (New York: Garland Publishing, Inc., 1985), *passim*; James P. Walsh, "James Phelan: Creating the Fortune, Creating the Family," *Journal of the West* 31 (April 1992): 17-23; Walsh and Timothy J. O'Keefe, *Legacy of a Native Son: James Duval Phelan & Villa Montalvo* (Forbes Mill Press, 1993) *passim; San Francisco Chronicle,* August 30, 1930.

2. Kevin Starr, *Inventing the Dream: California Through the Progressive Era* (New York: Oxford University Press, 1985), 242.

3. *San Francisco Call,* May 8, 1900. For a close analysis of Phelan's anti-Japanese rhetoric, see Martha Walrath Riley, "A Rhetorical Biography of Senator James D. Phelan of California Concentrating on the Ways in Which His Rhetoric Constructed Images and Ideas About Asian Immigrants to the United States" (Ph.D. diss., University of Pittsburgh, 1992).

4. Recent historiographical literature on Japanese immigration includes Hilary Conroy and T. Scott Miyakawa, eds., *East Across the Pacific: Historical and Sociological Studies of Japanese Immigration and Assimilation* (Santa Barbara: ABC-CLIO Press, 1972); Yuji Ichioka, *The Issei: The World of the First Generation Japanese Immigrants* (New York: The Free Press, 1988); Ronald Takaki, *Strangers From a Different Shore: A History of Asian Americans* (Boston: Little, Brown and Company, 1989); and Robert A. Wilson and Bill Hosokawa, *East to America: A History of the Japanese in the United States* (New York: William Morrow and Company, Inc., 1980). For Japanese immigrant agriculture, see, in addition to the works cited above, Eiichiro Azuma, "Japanese Immigrant Farmers and California Alien Land Laws: A Study of the Walnut Grove Japanese Community," *California History* 73 (Spring 1994): 14-29; Don and Nadine Hata, "George Shima: The Potato King of California," *Journal of the West* 25 (January 1986): 55-61; Robert Higgs, "Landless By Law: Japanese Immigrants in California Agriculture to 1941," *Journal of Economic History* 38 (March 1978): 205-25; Masakazu Iwata, "The Japanese Immigrant in California Agriculture," *Agricultural History* 36 (January 1962): 25-37.

5. On the anti-Japanese movement in California, see Roger Daniels, *The Politics of Prejudice: The Anti-Japanese Movement in California and the Struggle for Japanese Exclusion* (Berkeley: University of California Press, 1962). For the school segregation controversy, see Thomas A. Bailey, *Theodore Roosevelt and the Japanese-American Crisis* (Stanford: Stanford University Press, 1934). The Gentlemen's Agreement is discussed in Ichioka, *Issei,* 71-72 and "picture brides" in Wilson and Hosokawa, *East to America,* 54-56.

6. Daniels, *Politics of Prejudice,* 23, 26; Yuji Ichioka, "Japanese Associations and the Japanese Government: A Special Relationship, 1909-1926," *Pacific Historical Review* 29 (August 1977): 409-37.

7. Descriptions and analyses of the 1913 Alien Land Law are numerous: Thomas A. Bailey, "California, Japan and the Alien Land Legislation of 1913," *Pacific Historical Review*1 (1932): 36-59; Madelon Berkowitz, "The California Progressives and Anti-Japanese Agitation" (M.A. thesis, University of California, Berkeley, 1966); Paolo E. Coletta, "'The Most Thankless Task': Bryan and the California Alien Land Legislation," *Pacific Historical Review* 36 (May 1967): 163-87; Daniels, *Politics of Prejudice*; Jun Furuya, "Gentlemen's Disagreement: The Controversy Between the United States and Japan Over the California Alien Land Law of 1913" (Ph.D. diss., Princeton University, 1989); Higgs, "Landless by Law;" Teruko Okado Kachi, *The Treaty of 1911 and the Immigration and Alien Land Law Issue Between the United States and Japan, 1911-1913* (New York: Arno Press, 1978); James B. Kessler, "The Political Factors in California's Anti-Alien Land Legislation, 1912-1913" (Ph.D. diss., Stanford University, 1958); Herbert Lepore, "Hiram Johnson, Woodrow Wilson, and the California Land Law Controversy of 1913," *Southern California Quarterly* 61 (Spring 1979): 99-110; Spencer C. Olin, "European Immigrant and Oriental Alien: Acceptance and Rejection by the California Legislature of 1913," *Pacific Historical Review* 35 (August 1966): 303-15; Frank W. Van Nuys, "California Progressives and Alien Land Legislation, 1913-1924" (M.A. thesis, California State University, Chico, 1993); and Van Nuys, "A Progressive Confronts the Race Question: Chester Rowell, the California Alien Land Act of 1913, and the Contradictions of Early Twentieth-Century Racial Thought," *California History* 73 (Spring 1994): 2-13.

8. The remainder of this section, which treats Phelan's career between 1911 and 1920, is based primarily on Hennings, *Phelan and Wilson Progressives*, 32-177.

9. See Hennings, *Phelan and Wilson Progressives*, passim; Van Nuys, "California Progressives and Land Legislation," 147-48.

10. Not surprisingly, estimates and enumerations of the Japanese population in California varied from source to source. The federal census population schedules, once revised and published in 1922, listed 71,952 Japanese residents. A March 1920 count by the Japanese Association estimated over 78,000 while the State Board of Control, which did not undertake an enumeration, claimed 87,000. Hennings, *Phelan and Wilson Progressives*, 182; Payson J. Treat, "California and the Japanese," *Atlantic Monthly*, April 1921, 539; California State Board of Control, *California and the Oriental: Japanese, Chinese, and Hindus* (Sacramento: California State Printing Office, 1922; reprint San Francisco: R and E Research Associates, 1970), 25.

11. *San Francisco Bulletin*, March 6, 1919.

12. Ichioka, *Issei,* 173-75.

13. *San Francisco Bulletin*, December 18, 1919.

14. *New York Times,* March 22, 1919.

15. *San Francisco Chronicle*, April 1, 1919.

16. *Sacramento Bee*, April 1, 1919. On the Red Scare, see John Higham, *Strangers in the Land: Patterns of American Nativism, 1860-1925* (New Brunswick, New Jersey: Rutgers University Press, 1955), 222-33.

17. Raymond Leslie Buell, "The Development of the Anti-Japanese Agitation in the United States," Part II, *Political Science Quarterly* 38 (March 1923): 68.

18. Statement of Hon. James D. Phelan of California Before the Committee on Immigration and Naturalization, House of Representatives, Friday, June 20, 1919 (Washington: Government Printing Office, 1920), 3, 7-8, in James D. Phelan Papers, Bancroft Library, University of California, Berkeley. Cited hereafter as Phelan Statement.

19. Phelan Statement, 8-9.

20. Phelan Statement, 23.

21. Phelan Statement, 12. Phelan and other anti-Japanese agitators based many of their dire predictions upon the testimony of the extraordinary Homer Lea. Only five feet tall and born a hunchback, Lea parlayed a fascination with military history into participation in the Boxer Rebellion in China, a commission as a Lieutenant General with Chinese forces attempting to overthrow the Manchu Dynasty, and a role as one of Dr. Sun Yat Sen's advisors. After spending time in Japan, Lea became convinced that the country's military rulers were bent on world conquest. In 1909, now residing in Long Beach, Lea published *The Valor of Ignorance*, which predicted a Japanese attack on Hawaii and the Philippines as well as an invasion of the Pacific Coast. A second volume, entitled *The Day of the Saxon*, published in 1912, foresaw a Japanese assault on British possessions in the Far East. Lea died that same year at age thirty-six. While some critics disputed his claims, Lea's influence, particularly on the West Coast, was significant. Marco R. Newmark, "Homer Lea," *Historical Society of Southern California Quarterly* 37 (June 1955): 177-84; Charles Van Doren, ed., *Webster's American Biographies* (Springfield, Mass.: G. and C. Merriam and Company, 1979), 614; Higham, Strangers in the Land, 172.

22. Phelan Statement, 15-16.

23. Daniels, *Politics of Prejudice*, 84-87; Berkowitz, "California Progressives and Anti-Japanese Agitation," 81; Buell, "Development of Anti-Japanese Agitation," Part II, 68-69; Hennings, *Phelan and Wilson Progressives*, 179-80. Phelan was also on the Executive Committee of the California Joint Immigration Committee, a coalition of immigration reform organizations.

24. *Congressional Record*, 66th Cong., 2nd sess., 1920, 59, pt. 1: 1815-1816.

25. Hennings, *Phelan and Wilson Progressives*, 75-76, 192; "Amendments to Constitution and Proposed Statutes with Arguments Respecting the Same to be Submitted to the Electors of the State of California at the General Election on Tuesday, November 2, 1920" (Sacramento: Department of State Printing, 1920), pamphlet in Japanese File, 1920, Carton 15 Phelan Papers.

26. *San Francisco Chronicle*, July 13, 1920; House Committee on Immigration and Naturalization, *Japanese Immigration: Hearings on Immigration and Naturalization*, 66th Cong., 2d sess., July 12-14, 1920, 34, 51-52. See same, 3-34, for Phelan's statement and testimony, which opened the hearings.

27. Kiichi Kanzaki, *California and the Japanese* (San Francisco: Japanese Association of America, 1921; reprint, San Francisco: R and E Research Associates, 1971), 16, 59; House Committee, *Japanese Immigration*, 695.

28. "By Senator James D. Phelan," undated statement in Japanese File, 1920, Carton 15, Phelan Papers; House Committee, *Japanese Immigration*, 33. Tied to all of his allegations about the Japanese residents of California was the overriding concern with the nation of Japan. To Phelan, every indication, from the Japanese immigrants' "mastery of the land" to "their great fecundity" revealed "their plans to establish a little Japan permanently in California, which would ultimately colonize the entire Pacific coast." Stop the influx at once and the threat of Japanese expansion beyond her own immediate sphere would be halted. See "By Senator Phelan."

29. David Starr Jordan to Chester Rowell, 23 September 1920, Chester H. Rowell Papers, Bancroft Library, University of California, Berkeley.

30. Chester H. Rowell, "The Campaign in California," *New Republic*, October 13, 1920, 165. See Hennings, *Phelan and Wilson Progressives*, 195-200.

31. Daniels, *Politics of Prejudice*, 147n; Hennings, *Phelan and Wilson Progressives*, 193; *San Francisco Chronicle*, September 3, 1920.

32. "Advance Copy of Senator Phelan's Speech," typed copy in 1920 campaign folder, Box 16, in Phelan Papers.

33. James D. Phelan, "The False Pride of Japan," *Atlantic Monthly*, March 1921, 399.

34. Buell, "Development of Anti-Japanese Agitation," Part II, 71; Carey McWilliams, *Prejudice: Japanese-American, Symbol of Racial Intolerance* (Boston: Little, Brown and Company, 1944), 60; Daniels, *Politics of Prejudice*, 90; Berkowitz, "California Progressives and Anti-Japanese Agitation," 82.

35. Hennings, *Phelan and Wilson Progressives*, 194,198-99.

36. Berkowitz, "California Progressives and Anti-Japanese Agitation," 82.

37. James D. Phelan, "The Ethics of the Japanese Problem," *Overland Monthly*, November 1920, 12.

38. "By James D. Phelan United States Senator for California," undated typed statement in Japanese File, 1920, Carton 15, Phelan Papers.

39. Kanzaki, *California and the Japanese*, 26-30; Berkowitz, "California Progressives and Anti-Japanese Agitation," 95-96; Hennings, *Phelan and Wilson Progressives*, 193-94. Appealing for "Fair Play," the Committee nonetheless called for "a constructive immigration policy to safeguard the State against further influx of Oriental labor." The American Committee of Justice, "Fair Play," handbill in Japanese File, 1920, Carton 15, Phelan Papers.

40. Colonel John P. Irish, "The Anti-Japanese Pogrom: Facts Versus Falsehoods of Senator Phelan and Others," n. p. n. d. in Japanese Pamphlets, vol. 3, California State Library, Sacramento. The pamphlet was also inserted as an exhibit in House Committee, *Japanese Immigration*, 5-7. See the same source for Phelan's attempts to discredit Irish's allegations.

41. Hennings, *Phelan and Wilson Progressives*, 197, 199, 201-202.

42. *San Francisco Bulletin*, November 1, 1920.

43. *San Francisco Chronicle*, September 29 and October 26, 31, 1920.

44. For the perspectives of those affected and subsequent legal proceedings during the 1920s, see Yuji Ichioka, "The Japanese Immigrant Response to the 1920 California Alien Land Law," *Agricultural History* 58 (April 1984): 157-78.

45. James D. Phelan, "Should Not the Legislature Act on the Japanese Question," article enclosed with letter to Hiram Johnson, February 9, 1911, Box 26, Phelan Papers.

46. Phelan, "Ethics of the Japanese Problem," 11.

47. Phelan, "Should Not the Legislature . . . ."

48. Phelan, "False Pride in Japan," 403.

Incarcerating Japanese Americans: An Atrocity Revisited

Roger Daniels

The round-up, expulsion and incarceration of more than a hundred thousand Japanese Americans in the months following the outbreak of the Pacific War between the United States and Japan is a major blot on the record of American democracy, an ironic counterpoint to a war that was fought to preserve and establish what Franklin D. Roosevelt called the Four Freedoms.[1] The event attracted little attention during the war, and, in the decades immediately following it, was generally written off as an aberration, or, as one scholar put it, America's "worst wartime mistake,"[2] and the mistreatment and abuse suffered by the West Coast Japanese American civilian men, women and children, more than two-thirds of them native-born American citizens, was usually ignored by the nation's historians.[3] Since the early 1970s, however, historians and others have placed this wartime atrocity squarely in the historical canon so that almost every textbook carries at least a brief and usually a condemnatory account.[4] And, beginning in 1980, the federal government itself began a process which resulted in the passage of the Civil Liberties Act of 1988, entailing a payment of 20,000 tax-free dollars to each of the more than sixty-thousand Japanese American survivors, and apologies from both Congress and the president for war-time wrongdoing.[5] The investigative body which made the recommendations on which the government acted in the 1980s reported that the incarceration of Japanese Americans:

> was not justified by military necessity . . . . The broad historical causes . . . were race prejudice, war hysteria, and a failure of political leadership. Widespread ignorance of Japanese Americans contributed to a policy conceived in haste and executed in an atmosphere of fear and anger at Japan. A grave injustice was done to American citizens and resident aliens of Japanese ancestry who, without individual review or any probative evidence against them, were excluded, removed, and detained by the United States during World War II.[6]

More recently, in a speech commemorating the fiftieth anniversary of the Pearl Harbor attack, President George H. W. Bush acknowledged that "the internment of Americans of Japanese ancestry was a great injustice" and vowed that "it will never be repeated."[7] In this paper I will briefly recapitulate the relevant events of 1941-42, attempt to explain the changes in the climates of opinion which caused Americans to reevaluate the significance of the wartime incarceration, and attempt to answer the haunting question—could such a thing happen again?

*****

According to the census of 1940 there were almost 127,000 persons of Japanese birth or ancestry in the continental United States, constituting less than one-tenth of one percent of the population. Some forty-seven thousand of these were persons who had immigrated from Japan before 1925 and were, like other Asians, "aliens ineligible to citizenship."[8] Their children born in the United States, the Nisei[9], were, thanks to the Fourteenth Amendment to the Constitution, citizens of the United States with, in theory, all the rights and privileges of that citizenship.[10] In fact, however, their citizenship was, at best, second class. This was nowhere more true than in California and other West Coast states where almost nine of ten Japanese Americans then lived. In these coastal states, where the incidence of Japanese in the population was never as high as one in fifty, a whole panoply of discrimination in employment, housing and education was imposed upon them and other Asian Americans.[11] The all but universal prejudice against people of color was the chief cause of discrimination in America, but for Japanese Americans there was the added factor of the trans-Pacific rivalry between Japan and the United States and, in the decades after World War I, what most Americans saw as Japan's unjustified aggression in China. And, after war came, Americans were much more hostile to Japanese than to German soldiers. For example, in testing American soldiers during WW II, Army psychologists reported that thirty-eight to forty-eight percent indicated agreement with the statement: "I would really like to kill a Japanese soldier," whereas only five to nine percent indicated agreement to the statement: "I would really like to kill a German soldier."[12]

Some Japanese Americans imagined that they might become pawns in a future war between America and Japan. To cite just one example of such fears, a Nisei student at the University of California at Berkeley asked, four years before Pearl Harbor:

> . . . what are we going to do if war does break out between United States and Japan? . . . In common language we can say "we're sunk." Even if the Nisei wanted to fight for America, what chances? Not a chance! . . . our properties would be confiscated and most likely [we would be] herded into prison camps—perhaps we would be slaughtered on the spot.[13]

Although this horrific vision was not generally shared—many of the Nisei believed that although things would be very difficult for their alien parents, their own citizenship would protect them from drastic federal action—most Japanese Americans knew that their futures would be threatened in the event of a Pacific war.

American leaders had been seriously preparing for war since the spring of 1940. Many were all too painfully aware of the shocking violations of civil liberties that had taken place during World War I and some were determined to avoid them if and when war came again. The president himself made this very clear. In a public letter to a conference of law enforcement officials in the summer of 1940 Franklin D. Roosevelt wrote:

[Our] common defense should be through the normal channels of local, state and national law enforcement. The untrained policeman is as ineffective as the untrained soldier. The amateur detective soon becomes a fussy and malicious busybody. We must be vigilant, always on guard, and swift to act. But we must also be wise, and cool-headed, and must not express our activities in the cruel stupidities of the vigilante.[14]

In one sense this goal was achieved. The anti-German hysteria which swept America in 1917-18 was largely avoided.[15] Legal historians concerned with individual rights in the United States have often noted with pride that there were fewer violations of civil liberty during the Second World War, when the government prosecuted only twenty-six indictments under federal security statutes as opposed to more then twenty-five hundred during World War I.[16]

Still it is now quite clear that the federal government in general and its naval and military intelligence agencies in particular spent an inordinate amount of time and effort trying to monitor the Japanese American population, sometimes deliberately violating American law to do so. In addition various individuals within the government, from President Roosevelt down, at one time or another expressed a desire to round-up very large numbers of "Japanese." However there is no evidence of any pre-war planning to do so as far as "ordinary" persons, whether alien or citizen were concerned. What the intelligence agencies did do, with approval at the highest levels of government, was to prepare lists of dangerous aliens of various nationalities who were to be interned at the outbreak of war. All in all some eight-thousand Japanese nationals, and thus enemy aliens, were interned. Although many, and perhaps most, of the individual internments were ill-advised, and some persons were even put behind barbed wire as a result of mistaken identity, the internment of enemy aliens was traditional and well within the usages of nations. If some of the internments, such as those of elderly and infirm Buddhist priests, were stupid, they were consonant with the provisions of American law.[17] But what happened to most of the rest of the Japanese Americans can only be described as lawless, even though it was eventually sanctioned by a majority of the justices of the United States Supreme Court.[18]

Much has been written—and properly so—about the shock of Admiral Isoruku Yamamoto's surprise raid on Pearl Harbor, but not enough has been written about the numbing series of defeats which followed as Imperial Japanese forces "ran wild," as Yamamoto put it, in Southeast Asia and the Central Pacific. While it is now clear that American forces were simply unprepared to resist effectively, some American officials and many politicians, journalists and broadcasters were quick to claim that sabotage by resident Japanese was instrumental in the disaster at Pearl Harbor. Secretary of the Navy Frank Knox, in a Los Angeles press conference held on his return from Hawaii just eight days after the Pearl Harbor attack, claimed that there had been "treachery" in the Islands and insisted, mendaciously, that much of the disaster was caused by "the most effective fifth column work that's come out of this war, except in Norway."[19]

Journalists and politicians were already sowing seeds of suspicion. The day after the attack the *Los Angeles Times*, one of the leading papers of the region, invoked California's vigilante tradition, calling, editorially, for:

> alert, keen-eyed civilians [who could be] of yeoman service in cooperating with the military authorities against spies, saboteurs and fifth columnists. We have thousands of Japanese here. . . . Some, perhaps many, are . . . good Americans. What the rest may be we do not know, nor can we take a chance in the light of yesterday's demonstration that treachery and double-dealing are major Japanese weapons.[20]

Other West Coast newspapers, broadcasters and some nationally-syndicated columnists kept up a drum beat of stories and commentaries, often with invented tales about Japanese espionage and fifth column activities.[21] These covered the political spectrum from right-wing gutter journalists such as Westbrook Pegler to the editorial stalwarts of the *Communist People's Daily World* of San Francisco. A rising liberal star of the airwaves, Edward R. Murrow, told a Seattle audience that: "I think its probable that, if Seattle ever does get bombed, you will be able to look up and see some University of Washington sweaters on the boys doing the bombing."[22]

It was all chimerical. Not one single case of espionage or sabotage by an ethnic Japanese was ever detected in the United States after war came, but few American officials or political leaders chose to make this point,[23] which is what the 1981 presidential commission report meant by "a failure of political leadership." Added to that, some important federal officials fanned the fires of prejudice. Fiorello La Guardia, an outstanding liberal who served for a time as the director of the Office of Civilian Defense, made appeals for decent treatment of German and Italian aliens, but pointedly omitted to ask for tolerance toward Japanese.[24] To be sure, Francis Biddle, Roosevelt's fourth attorney general, asked for calmness and fair play, but his voice was easily drowned out.[25] In retrospect, only the president himself might have been heard above the patriotic racist roar, but he was silent. Franklin Roosevelt was not prepared either to risk rupturing wartime unity by taking an unpopular stand or, as we shall see, to oppose the political pressures for incarceration that came from within his own government.

Those pressures began to build in December and early January. Their most persistent sources were West Coast politicians, certain second-echelon military officials, particularly Maj. Gen. Allen W. Gullion, the Army's Provost Marshal General, and, after some hesitation, Lt. Gen. John L. De Witt, in charge of the Western Defense Command, the ranking military officer on the West Coast. The latter, after a good deal of backing and filling, supported proposals for mass evacuation that had been drawn up by Gullion and his subordinate, Karl R. Bendetsen, who rose from major to colonel in a few months. The civilian heads of the army, Assistant Secretary John J. McCloy and War Secretary Henry L. Stimson, were persuaded in early February that there was a "military necessity" which justified mass evacuation. The great fear was sabotage of the West Coast aircraft factories whose output was crucial to American war plans, as both contemporary archival documents and Stimson's personal diary demonstrate. That there had been absolutely no sabotage either before or after Pearl Harbor seemed irrelevant. Stimson sent to Roosevelt a draft executive order to authorize the military to move civilians without declaring martial law. The more realistic top military leadership—Chief of Staff George C. Marshall and his planners—did not think that a mass evacuation was necessary but did not actively oppose Stimson's decision.

At the same time congressional pressure—in part abetted by prodding from the Provost Marshal's men—mounted. The senior West Coast Senator—Hiram W. Johnson who had represented California since 1917—organized the entire congressional delegations of California, Oregon and Washington, which unanimously forwarded a recommendation to the president on February 13 stating:

> the immediate evacuation of all persons of Japanese lineage and all others, aliens and citizens alike, whose presence shall be deemed dangerous or inimical to the defense of the United States from all strategic areas . . . . such areas [should] be enlarged . . . until they encompass the entire strategic areas of the states of California, Oregon and Washington, and the Territory of Alaska.[26]

On February 19, 1942, Franklin Roosevelt signed an executive order, numbered 9066, in the form that the Army had submitted it to him. The executive order, based on a war powers act passed in 1918 and amended in 1940 and 1941, was a sweeping grant of power. It authorized "the Secretary of War, and [subordinate] Military Commanders" to designate "military areas" from which "any or all persons may be excluded" and to provide "such transportation, food, shelter, and other accommodations as may be necessary." No ethnic group was named and in theory any American, anywhere, could have been affected by it. We know that some in the military considered using it on the East Coast and against large numbers of German and Italian aliens, but that was never done. Although *individual* German and Italian aliens on the West Coast were forced to move,[27] the order and almost all of the subsequent execution of it was directed against Japanese Americans living on the West Coast. As defined by the United States Army it affected all persons of Japanese birth or ancestry living in California, the western halves of Oregon and Washington, and a small portion of Arizona. A few thousand Japanese Americans—both native and foreign-born—living east of the excluded zone were left in nervous liberty throughout the war. After the summer of 1942 they were joined there by tens of thousands of others who were first incarcerated and then selectively released.[28] And, ironically, the largest Japanese American community—the 150,000 living in Hawaii who constituted about a third of its population—was not affected by E.O. 9066, although a few individuals had been interned earlier.[29]

Roosevelt did not initiate the incarceration of Japanese Americans. Stimson, McCloy and the paperwork soldiers who egged them on were self-starters. But, of course, the ultimate responsibility was the president's. He never explained why he did it, although he was willing later to mitigate his order in a number of ways. Roosevelt shared, at least in part, some of the national prejudice against Japanese, but a much more important causal factor, I believe, was that indulging in "revenge" against Japanese Americans was good politics. This helps to explain, but does not exculpate, FDR's willingness to let his subordinates round up the West Coast Japanese Americans. We must also remember just how badly the Pacific War was going. The United States and its allies were suffering a terrible series of defeats in the Far East. Hong Kong, Wake and other mid-Pacific islands fell to Imperial Japanese forces in December; they took Manila in early January and overran Malaya and much of what is now Indonesia later that month. In early February Japanese troops landed on the island of Singapore, on New Britain, and were menacing Burma and Australia; most of the American forces in the Philippines were hemmed in on the Bataan peninsula and on the fortress island of Corregidor. Thus Roosevelt gave the green light to Stimson during a brief telephone call. As McCloy later retold the conversation to his colleagues, the President's only proviso was to "be as reasonable as you can."

But the mid-February executive decision could not be rapidly translated into action. No detailed plans had been made by the Army, and its lawyers soon discovered that positive legislation was necessary before citizens could be forced to move. The War Department drafted a statute which made it a crime punishable by a year in jail and a $5,000 fine for a citizen to fail to obey a military order and a compliant Congress passed it without a dissenting vote on March 19 and FDR signed it into law two days later. On March 24, General DeWitt issued his first two restrictive orders. Public Proclamation No. 3[30] established an 8 p.m. to 6 a.m. curfew on the West Coast for all alien Japanese, Germans and Italians and "all persons of Japanese descent" (i.e. United States citizens, although the Army almost never used that term. It sometimes referred to them as "non-aliens.") It also forbade "any person of Japanese ancestry" from possessing or using firearms or other weapons of war, ammunition, bombs, explosives, short-wave radio receiving sets, radio transmitters, signal devices, codes, ciphers or cameras.

The other order was a "Civilian Exclusion Order," ominously numbered "1."[31] It applied to only some fifty Japanese families living on Bainbridge Island in Puget Sound directly west of Seattle, Washington. The Bainbridge Islanders, given five days notice, were ordered to report to the ferry slip on March 29 bringing only what they could carry. Although they were not told where they were going most adults assumed, correctly, that they were en route to some kind of concentration camp, although, to be sure, the Army never used that term, but created the euphemisms "Assembly Centers" and "Relocation Centers" instead.[32] The

Bainbridge Islanders were surrounded by soldiers armed with bayonetted rifles, ferried to the mainland, loaded onto railway carriages, and shipped more than 1,000 miles to Southern California. Other Seattleites would later be sent to the nearby fairgrounds at Puyallup, but in March there was no Assembly Center in Washington.

We can now see that it was a dress rehearsal. Using punch cards supplied, contrary to law, by the Bureau of the Census, the army bureaucrats with the help of an expert on loan from the census, divided the area to be cleansed of Japanese Americans into 107 other "Exclusion Areas"— geographic units calculated to contain about one-thousand Japanese—some 250 families—each.[33] Although the deportations began in March, large-scale movements continued into June to the sixteen Assembly Centers, consisting mostly of fairgrounds, race tracks and other facilities originally intended to house livestock.[34] These camps were only temporary way stations, located reasonably close to where most Japanese Americans lived. Most of those from San Francisco, for example, went to nearby Tanforan, a race track. Despite the continued use of armed soldiers the army bureaucrats assumed, correctly, that its victims were law abiding persons who would obey orders. In each exclusion area a control point for registration was established, notices were placed in prominent places, ethnic community leaders were notified, and the persons affected reported as they were ordered, usually five days after the notices went up.[35] Only a handful of Japanese Americans in an evacuation area even attempted to hide and just a few resisted.[36] The exodus to Assembly Centers, although traumatic, was orderly.

While this initial removal was going on, the federal government created a civilian agency, the War Relocation Authority,[37] to administer and supervise the more permanent camps, which the government called Relocation Centers.[38] Unlike the Assembly Centers, the more permanent camps were far away in desolate locations, where almost no one had lived before and where no one lives now. Even the two camps on Indian reservations in Arizona, were located in their unpopulated portions. Two other camps were in eastern California, two were in Arkansas, and there was one each in Idaho, Utah, Colorado and Wyoming. While some Japanese spent the whole war, and more, in camps—the last camp (Tule Lake, California) closed only on March 20, 1946—many thousands were released beginning in the summer of 1942. By the first week of January 1945, thanks to the Supreme Court ruling in *Ex Parte Endo*, "loyal" Japanese American citizens could return to the formerly forbidden West Coast over the protests of California Governor Earl Warren and other western politicians.

*****

During and immediately after the war, the incarceration of most of the Japanese Americans was a popular move. Indeed, many politicians complained about "coddling Japs," and public opinion polls indicated not only support for what the government had done, but a willingness to support even more draconian actions, such as the post-war expatriation of all ethnic Japanese. This obviously did not happen, although a little-known post-war program did result in sending some forty-seven hun-

23

dred Japanese persons to Japan, more than three-thousand of them American citizens.[39]

But even before the war was over, the improvement of the image of the Japanese Americans had begun, promoted largely by civilian liberals within the government.[40] Agencies such as the Office of War Information and the War Relocation Administration issued reams of pro-Japanese American propaganda, stressing the wartime heroism of Japanese American troops in Italy and the quiet good-citizenship of the Nisei generally. In addition, even though the United States fought World War II with segregated armed forces, the notion was beginning to prevail that equal opportunity—or something approaching it—ought to have a place on the national agenda. Eight months before he issued E.O. 9066, Franklin Roosevelt had put out E.O. 8802 establishing a Fair Employment Practices Committee "to encourage full participation in the national defense program by all citizens regardless of race, creed, color, or national origin."[41]

In July 1946 Roosevelt's successor, Harry S. Truman, who as a senator had silently acquiesced in the incarceration, held a special ceremony on the Ellipse behind the White House for members of the 442nd Regimental Combat Team composed of Japanese Americans and told them that they had "fought not only the enemy, but [also] prejudice—and you have won."[42] Nineteen months later, he sent Congress a ten-point civil rights message whose last three points were of special concern to Japanese Americans. Point eight called for Hawaiian (and Alaskan) statehood, point nine for dropping racial bars in naturalization, and point ten for providing some compensation for economic losses Japanese Americans had sustained when they were forced to abandon their property.

The last point was quickly achieved. The president pointed out that "more than one hundred thousand Japanese-Americans were evacuated from their homes in the Pacific states solely because of their racial origin"—he made no mention of the fictitious "military necessity"—and urged Congress to pass legislation which was already before it.[43] On July 2, 1948 Truman signed the Japanese-American Claims Act which appropriated $38 million to settle all property claims, a figure which almost all commentators now agree was not nearly enough.[44]

The other objectives took longer. Full equality in naturalization came first. The first turn of the tide had occurred back in 1943 when Congress repealed the fifteen separate pieces of legislation which had enforced Chinese exclusion and granted Chinese persons naturalization rights. Separate pieces of legislation in 1946 had made similar grants to Filipinos and "natives of India," but other Asians remained "aliens ineligible to citizenship" until 1952. In that year Congress enacted the McCarran-Walter Act over Truman's veto. The president's veto message praised those parts of the law which made naturalization color blind but found "this most desirable provision . . . embedded in a mass of legislation which would perpetuate injustice."[45] The admission of Hawaii as the 50th state was delayed even longer, until near the end of Dwight D. Eisenhower's term in 1959. It was significant for Japanese and other Asian Americans because the heavy Asian American majority in the new state made Asian American legislators in Washington a certainty.[46]

Although much has been written "explaining" the practical benefits Truman sought to gain from his general civil rights program, it is difficult to imagine what domestic political gains he can have hoped for by advocating legislation to benefit Japanese and other Asian Americans.[47] The president himself gave two reasons which can be taken at face value. He said that he believed in it as a matter of justice and fairness *and* as he put it:

> If we wish to inspire the peoples of the world whose freedom is in jeopardy, if we wish to restore hope to those who have already lost their civil liberties, if we wish to fulfill the promise that is ours, we must correct the remaining imperfections in our practice of democracy.[48]

Thus, both a desire to improve democracy at home and certain cold war imperatives explain the steps that the United States took in the post-war decades to improve the status of Japanese Americans.

To explain the passage of the Civil Liberties Act of 1988 other reasons must be considered, although a continuing struggle for ethnic equality is a constant. The combined effects of Lyndon Johnson's Great Society programs of the mid-1960s and of the eventual rejection of the misbegotten war in Vietnam contributed to a climate of opinion in which the acts of the 1940s could be reconsidered. In 1976 President Gerald R. Ford, hardly a radical, repealed FDR's Executive Order 9066 and, in a proclamation noting that the nation was celebrating its two-hundredth birthday, insisted that "an honest reckoning" must take account "of our national mistakes as well as our national achievements." The president continued:

> We know now what we should have known then—not only was that evacuation wrong, but Japanese Americans were and are loyal Americans. On the battlefield and at home, Japanese Americans . . . have been and continue to be written into our history for the sacrifices and contributions they have made to the well-being and security of this, our common Nation.[49]

Four years later, at the urging of Japanese American activists and ethnic organizations, and with the guidance of Japanese American legislators, Congress passed and President Jimmy Carter signed legislation creating the Presidential Commission on the Wartime Relocation and Internment of Civilians (CWRIC) whose mission was to "review the facts and circumstances surrounding" E.O. 9066 and its sequelae and to "recommend appropriate remedies."[50] A detailed investigation confirmed what most scholars had been saying since 1959,[51] and a series of hearings held in Washington and in midwestern and far western centers of Japanese American population produced unexpected and unprecedented displays of anger and other emotions by survivors and their descendants nearly forty years after the event. In 1983 the

CWRIC, as noted above, recommended a tax-free payment of $20,000 to each survivor and a formal apology. Five years later Congress enacted, and President Ronald W. Reagan signed, the Civil Liberties Act of 1988, but it was not until well into the Bush Administration that payments were actually made. After nearly half a century the legal and legislative ramifications of Executive Order 9066 seemed to have been played out.

*****

What, however, of the future? Could it happen again, or was what happened to Japanese Americans, as George Bush believed, something that "will never be repeated?" Prediction is not the historian's primary task, but those of us who study the past have learned that although the precise circumstances which trigger any specific historical situation are unique, similar forces acting within a society can produce similar results. Racist and xenophobic forces still exist in American (and most other) societies. An extended external or internal crisis somehow associated with a minority group, whether political or ethnic, could produce similar results. Rather than trying to imagine what such future crises might be, I will note several separate occasions since the end of World War II in which the United States has seemed to be on the verge of effecting mass incarceration.

At the height of the Cold War, Congress passed the Emergency Detention Act, which after a great deal of rhetoric about a monolithic worldwide Communist conspiracy, authorized the president to declare, by executive order, an "Internal Security Emergency." In such a circumstance, the attorney general was then empowered to "apprehend and . . . detain . . . each person as to whom there is reason to believe that such person probably will engage in, or probably will conspire with others to engage in, acts of espionage or espionage." The statute also provided for the creation of a number of stand-by concentration camps. Although the law was clearly aimed at ideological rather than ethnic "enemies" of the republic, it was distinctly modeled on the procedure, upheld by the Supreme Court, under which the Japanese Americans had been incarcerated.[52] The statute, although never utilized, remained on the books until 1969 when it was repealed.[53]

Every recent American administration has at least considered some kind of massive incarceration of individuals. During the hostage crisis growing out of the seizure of the American embassy in Teheran the Carter administration took preliminary steps against Iranians—mostly college students—living in the United States. When the Immigration and Naturalization Service's filing system proved so chaotic that it could not provide the White House with even approximate numbers, much less names and addresses, the administration instructed the nation's colleges and universities to provide them and most complied. Happily, no mass incarceration resulted, but it is clear that the White House was at least contemplating some punitive action. There was also sporadic mob violence against Iranians.

The Reagan administration caused the detention of large numbers of illegal Haitian immigrants—while welcoming illegal Cubans with open arms—although some of the worst aspects of their treatment were modified by federal judges unconstrained by a war-time crisis. Partly to avoid both federal courts and immigration lawyers the Bush administration set up a camp for Haitian refugees inside the American military base at Guantanamo Bay, Cuba, a policy the Clinton administration continued and used for Cubans as well.

The Bush administration, just before and during the brief hostilities in the Persian Gulf in 1990-91, had some of its agents interrogate Arab American leaders, both citizen and alien. When spokespersons for Arab communities and some civil liberties organizations protested, the interrogations were stopped; the government made the lame excuse that the federal agents were only trying to protect those whom they had questioned. And there was sporadic violence against Arab American individuals and businesses.

These events, spread across nearly half a century, do not amount to very much when compared to what was done to Japanese Americans. But, similarly, no crisis comparable to World War II has occurred. All of these instances were violations of the spirit of the Constitution and they did happen even in a society in which both racial prejudice and xenophobia have been reduced. What might have happened had they been accompanied by some great crisis or outrage—suppose, for example, that Iran had decided to execute the American hostages on television, say at the rate of one a day—is frightening to contemplate. But these "minor" events do demonstrate an on-going American propensity to react against "foreigners" in the United States in times of crisis, especially when those foreigners have dark skins. Despite the amelioration of American race relations, there are still huge inequities between whites and non-whites, and potentially explosive emotions exist in both the oppressing and the oppressed populations. While optimists claim that American concentration camps are a thing of the past—and I certainly hope that they are—many Japanese Americans, the only group of citizens ever incarcerated *en masse* because of their genes, would argue that what has happened in the past can happen again. This student of Japanese American history can only agree with them.

Notes

1. Roosevelt first enunciated the "four essential human freedoms," - freedom of speech and expression, freedom to worship God, freedom from want, and freedom from fear - in his January 6, 1941 annual message, printed in Samuel I. Rosenman, comp. *The Public Papers and Addresses of Franklin D. Roosevelt* (New York: MacMillan, 1941), 1940 volume, 672.

2. Eugene V. Rostow "Our Worst Wartime Mistake," *Harper's Magazine* 191 (1945): 489-533.

3. Roger Daniels, "American Historians and East Asian Immigrants," *Pacific Historical Review*,43 (1974): 448-72.

4. The most recent general account, Roger Daniels, *Prisoners Without Trial: Japanese Americans in World War II* (New York: Hill and Wang, 1993), contains an up-to-date historiographical essay.

5. See Roger Daniels, "Redress Achieved, 1983-1990." in Daniels, Sandra C. Taylor, and Harry H.L. Kitano, eds, *Japanese Americans: from Relocation to Redress*, 2nd ed. (Seattle: University of Washington Press, 1991), 219-23, and Leslie T. Hatamiya, *Righting a Wrong: Japanese Americans and the Passage of the Civil Liberties Act of 1988* (Stanford: Stanford University Press, 1993).

6. Commission on the Wartime Relocation and Internment of Civilians, *Personal Justice Denied* (Washington, DC: GPO, 1982), 18.

7. As quoted, *New York Times*, December 8, 1991.

8. The phrase, "aliens ineligible to citizenship," was often used in American state and federal legislation to describe Asians. The naturalization statute of 1870 limited the right of naturalization to "white persons," and "persons of African descent."

9. The terms issei, nisei, sansei, etc. are used to differentiate the generations of Japanese immigrants. They are based on the Japanese words for one, two, three,—ichi, ni, san—etc. A Nisei, thus, is a person born in the United States—or elsewhere outside of Japan—of immigrant parents.

10. The 14th Amendment to the Constitution of the United States, adopted in 1868 specifies that "all persons born or naturalized in the United States," are "citizens of the United States and the State wherein they reside." Designed to protect the former slaves, it protected many of the rights of second-generation immigrants from Asia.

11. For a recent summary of such discrimination see Harry H.L. Kitano and Roger Daniels, *Asian Americans: Emerging Minorities,* 2nd ed. (Englewood Cliffs, New Jersey: Prentice Hall, 1995).

12. Ronald H. Spector, *Eagle Against the Sun: The American War with Japan* (New York: Free Press, 1985), 410. See also John W. Dower, *War Without Mercy: Race and Power in the Pacific War* (New York: Pantheon, 1986).

13. *Campanile Review* (Berkeley), Fall, 1937.

14. Samuel I. Rosenman, comp, *The Public Papers and Addresses of Franklin D. Roosevelt* (New York: Macmillan, 1941), 1940 volume, 315-17.

15. For American WW I excesses see, for example, Joan M. Jensen, *The Price of Vigilance* (Chicago: Rand McNally, 1968); Donald Johnson, *Challenge to American Freedoms: World War I and the Rise of the ACLU* (Lexington: University of Kentucky Press, 1963); and Harry N. Scheiber, *The Wilson Administration and Civil Liberties* (Ithaca: Cornell University Press, 1960). Wartime and postwar hysteria often made it impossible for orchestras to program the

music of long-dead German composers such as Bach, Beethoven and Brahms. The only musical casualty of WW II was Puccini's *Madame Butterfly*. The Metropolitan Opera eased it out of the repertory since an American naval officer is the villain and an innocent Japanese woman his victim.

16. See, for example, Harold M. Hyman, *To Try Men's Souls* (Berkeley: University of California Press, 1959), 329.

17. Japanese Buddhist priests in the United States and elsewhere in the Japanese diaspora were subsidized out of Emperor Hirohito's privy purse and thus were considered "agents of a foreign power."

18. The leading cases are *Hirabayashi v. U.S.* 320 US 81 (1943); *Korematsu v. U.S.* 323 US 214 (1944); and *Ex Parte Endo* 323 US 283 (1944). The critical literature is large. Much of it is cited in a work on the so-called coram nobis cases of the 1980s: Peter Irons, ed. *Justice Delayed: The Record of the Japanese American Internment Cases* (Middlebury, Connecticut: Wesleyan University Press, 1989).

19. Knox press conference transcript, December 15, 1941, Knox Collection, Office of Naval History, Washington Navy Yard. Knox knew that this was not the case and orders for the relief of the naval commander in Hawaii, Admiral Husband E. Kimmel, were already being drafted.

20. *Los Angeles Times*, December 8, 1941.

21. A scholar who examined twenty-seven daily newspapers in California, Oregon and Washington reported that "not one of the newspapers editorially opposed mass evacuation and all but two supported either mass evacuation or mass encampment." Lloyd E. Chiasson. "An Editorial Analysis of the Evacuation and Encampment of the Japanese-Americans During World War II" (Ph.D. dissertation, Southern Illinois University, Carbondale, 1983), as reported in *Dissertation Abstracts International*, A-44/07, January 1984, 1959. See also his "Japanese-American Relocation during WW II: A Study of California Editorial Reaction." *Journalism Quarterly* 68:#1-2 (1991), 263-68.

22. Letter, Miller Freeman to L.P. Sieg, President, University of Washington, Freeman mss., University of Washington Archives, January 29, 1942.

23. One of the few who did make this point was Earl Warren, then attorney general of California, soon to be its governor, and then Chief Justice of the United States. In February, 1942, testifying before what is usually called the Tolan Committee of Congress, Warren demonstrated what Richard Hofstadter later called the "paranoid style":

> Unfortunately [many] are of the opinion that because we have had no sabotage and no fifth column activities in this State . . . that means that none have been planned for us. But I take the view that is the most ominous sign in our whole situation. It convinces me more than perhaps any other factor that the sabotage that we are to get, the fifth column activities that we are to get, are timed just like Pearl Harbor was timed and just like the invasion of France, and denmark, and of Norway, and

all of those other countries.

I believe that we are just being lulled into a false sense of security and that the only reason that we haven't had disaster in California is because it has been timed for a different date . . . . Our day of reckoning is bound to come in that regard. When, nobody knows, of course, but we are approaching an invisible deadline.

Earl Warren, testimony, February 21, 1942, *hearings Before the Select Committee Investigating National Defense Migration . . .* , 77th. Cong., 2nd Sess., Part 29 (Washington: GPO, 1942), 11011-12.

24. La Guardia's biographer has documented his wartime anti-Japanese animus. When, in 1944, there was a controversy over the killing of some 200 Japanese prisoners of war in Australia, La Guardia wired his support of Australian actions in a telegram that twice referred to "Jap monkeys." Thomas Kessner, *Fiorello H. La Guardia and the Making of Modern New York* (New York: McGraw-Hill, 1989), 501, 536-8.

25. See Francis Biddle, *In Brief Authority* (New York: Doubleday, 1962), 204-32.

26. This and most other relevant documents may be found, in chronological order, most conveniently in Roger Daniels, ed., *American Concentration Camps: A Documentary History of the Relocation and Incarceration of Japanese Americans, 1941-1945*, 9 volumes (New York: Garland, 1989).

27. For details see Peter S. Sheridan, "The Internment of German and Italian Aliens Compared with the Internment of Japanese Aliens in the United States during World War II: A Brief History and Analysis," *Papers of the U. S. Commission on Wartime Relocation and Internment of Civilians* (Frederick, Maryland: University Publications of America), 1984, (microfilm) reel 24:816-7; Stephen C. Fox. "General John DeWitt and the Proposed Internment of German and Italian Aliens during World War II," *Pacific Historical Review* 57 (1988): 407-38 and *The Unknown Internment: An Oral History of the Relocation of Italian-Americans during World War II* (Boston: Twayne, 1990); and Rose D. Scherini, "Executive Order 9066 and Italian Americans: The San Francisco Story," *California History* 72 (1992): 366-77, 422-4.

28. The story of the wartime resettlement of Japanese Americans in the interior of the United States needs to be told. For a small part of it see Thomas Linehan, "Japanese American Resettlement in Cleveland during and after World War II," *Journal of Urban History* 20 (1993): 54-80.

29. See Dennis M. Ogawa and Evarts C. Fox, Jr, "Japanese Internment and Relocation: The Hawaii Experience," in Daniels et. al. *Japanese Americans*, 135-38 and Gary Y. Okihiro, *Cane Fires: The Anti-Japanese Movement in Hawaii, 1865-1945* (Philadelphia: Temple University Press, 1991).

30. Public Proclamations No. 1 and 2, dated March 2 and 16, divided the American West into six "military zones." Public Proclamation No. 4, March 27, prohibited persons of Japanese ancestry from moving out of the military zone without formal permission (prior to that time

they had been free to seek internal exile to the east and a few thousand Japanese Americans actually did so). These and other proclamations of the period may be consulted in United States. Congress. House of Representatives, *House Report 2124*, 77th Congress, 2nd Session, (Washington: GPO, 1942). (A report of the aforementioned Tolan Committee.)

31. A specimen Civilian Exclusion Order may be consulted conveniently in United States. War Department, *Japanese Evacuation from the West Coast* (Washington: GPO, 1943), 97-100.

32. Franklin Roosevelt had no problem with the term and used it more than once in press conferences and correspondence. But after the liberation of the Nazi death camps American officials went to great lengths to deny that there were American concentration camps. The term is also resisted by some Holocaust survivors who insist that the term can only be used to describe their own experience. See the discussion in Roger Daniels, *Asian America: Chinese and Japanese in the United States since 1850* (Seattle: University of Washington Press, 1988), 227-29.

33. For details see Daniels, "The Bureau of the Census and the Relocation of the Japanese Americans: A Note and a Document," *Amerasia Journal* 8:#2 (1982): 101-6.

34. One assembly center was located in each of the states of Washington, Oregon and Arizona; the rest were in California. The last assembly center (Santa Anita in suburban Los Angeles) closed on October 27, 1942.

35. United States, War Department, *Japanese Evacuation*, gives a detailed account of "Development and Execution of the Evacuation Plan," 77-95.

36. The most famous was Fred Toyosaburo Korematsu, of the *Korematsu* case noted above, who was quickly discovered despite having undergone plastic surgery. While in the local jail he was visited by a civil liberties lawyer, Ernest Besig, who persuaded him to become an appellant to test the constitutionality of the law.

37. The War Relocation Authority was created by Executive Order No. 9102, March 18, 1942.

38. We badly need a balanced study of the War Relocation Authority which neither Richard Drinnon's hostile biography, *Keeper of Concentration Camps: Dillon S. Myer and American Racism* (Berkeley: University od California Press, 1987), nor Dillon S. Myer's self-serving memoir, *Uprooted Americans* (Tucson: University of Arizona Press, 1971), provides. Albert B. Turner's doctoral dissertation, "The Origins and Development of the War Relocation Authority." Duke University, 1967, appropriately remains unpublished. A number of works, some of them outstanding, deal with this or that aspect of the WRA story. One of the best and most recent is Sandra C. Taylor's study of the camp in Utah, *Jewel of the Desert: Japanese American Internment at Topaz* (University of California Press, 1993). See also Douglas W. Nelson, *Heart Mountain: The Story of an American Concentration Camp* (Madison: State Historical Society of Wisconsin, 1976).

39. For details see Donald E. Collins, *Native American Aliens: Disloyalty and Renunciation of Citizenship by Japanese Americans during World War II* (Westport, Connecticut: Greenwood Press, 1985).

40. I comment on the ambiguous nature of American democracy in a forthcoming article "Bad News from the Good War: Democracy at Home during World War II." in Kenneth O'Brien and Lynn H. Parsons, eds., *The Home-Front War* (Westport, Connecticut: Greenwood Press, 1995).

41. Samuel I. Rosenman, comp., *The Public Papers and Addresses of Franklin D. Roosevelt, 1941 volume,* (New York: Harper & Brothers, 1950), 233-37.

42. "Remarks on Presenting a Citation to a Nisei Regiment," *Public Papers of the Presidents of the United States. Harry S. Truman: 1946* (Washington: GPO, 1962), 347.

43. "Special Message to the Congress on Civil Rights," *Public Papers of the Presidents of the United States. Harry S. Truman: 1948* (Washington: GPO, 1964), 125.

44. For a discussion of the passage of the act, see Daniels, *Asian America,* 290-2, 296-99.

45. "Veto ... June 25, 1952," *Public Papers of the Presidents of the United States. Harry S. Truman: 1952-53* (Washington: GPO, 1966), 441.

46. Although Eisenhower made no mention of the multi-racial character of the Hawaiian population during several formal statements in 1959 on statehood, when he addressed the Parliament of India in December, 1959, he said:
> As President of the United States, I welcomed into our Union last year a new sovereign state, Hawaii—4

peopled by all of the races of the earth, men and women of that state
> having their ancestral homes in Asia and Africa and Europe, the two Americas, the islands of the earth. Those peoples are of every creed and color, yet they can live together in neighborly friendliness, in mutual trust, and each can achieve his own good by helping achieve the good of all. Hawaii cries insistently to a divided world that all our differences of race and origin are less than the grand and indestructible unity of our common brotherhood. The world should take time to listen with attentive ear to Hawaii.

"Address ... Parliament of India," *Public Papers of the Presidents of the United States. Dwight D. Eisenhower: 1959* (Washington: GPO, 1960), 831. Cf. Ibid., 109, 243, 286-7, 588-9, 675.

47. For Truman and civil rights generally see Donald R. McCoy and Richard T. Ruetten, *Quest and Response: Minority Rights and the Truman Administration* (Lawrence: University of Kansas Press, 1973) and William C. Berman, *The Politics of Civil Rights in the Truman Administration* (Columbus: Ohio State University Press, 1970).

48. "Special Message to the Congress on Civil Rights," *Public Papers of the Presidents of the United States. Harry S. Truman: 1948* (Washington: GPO, 1964), 126.

49. "Presidential Proclamation 4417," Federal Register, vol. 41, no. 35, (Washington: GPO, Feb. 20, 1976). See also his informal remarks made at the same time in "Remarks Upon Signing a Proclamation Concerning Japanese-American Internment During World War II," *Public Papers of the Presidents of the United States. Gerald R. Ford: 1976-77* (Washington: GPO, 1979), Book I, 366.

50. Commission on Wartime Relocation and Internment of Civilians, *Personal Justice Denied* (Washington: GPO, 1982), 1.

51. Stetson Conn's essay, "The Decision to Relocate the Japanese Americans," in *Command Decisions*, Kent R. Greenfield, ed. (New York: Harcourt, Brace, 1959), was the first authoritative analysis of the military circumstances. He amplified this somewhat in "Japanese Evacuation from the West Coast," in *The United States Army in World War II: The Western Hemisphere: Guarding the United States and its Outposts*, Rose C. Engleman and Byron Fairchild eds., (Washington: GPO, 1964).

52. 64 *U. S. Statutes at Large*, 1019.

53. A rationale for repeal is given in a letter, Deputy Attorney Richard G. Kleindienst to Senator James O. Eastland, December 2, 1969, printed in Daniels, *The Decision to Relocate the Japanese Americans*, 2nd. ed. (Malabar, Florida: Krieger, 1986), 131-32.

Part II

Attitudes and Economic Opportunities in Wyoming

The Heart Mountain Relocation Center under construction during the summer months of 1942. If all of the necessary materials were available, a barrack building could be constructed in fifty-five minutes.

"Temporarily Side-Tracked by Emotionalism": Wyoming Residents Respond to Relocation

Phil Roberts

Wyomingites responded to the issue of Japanese American relocation in the same ways that Americans did elsewhere. In the course of examining those responses from newspaper reports, personal recollections and contemporary letters to congressional officials, it is clear there was no uniform "Wyoming view." In essence, there were no fewer than five categories of response to the relocation.

The most extreme view, perhaps representing a substantial portion of the population in the months immediately after the bombing of Pearl Harbor, was one of xenophobia toward anything Japanese. Maintained by a portion of the population throughout the war years, this view had racist roots in believing that no Japanese could be trusted regardless of the record.

A significant portion of the population, particularly those living in areas potentially benefiting economically from the presence of the camp, saw the economic opportunities that the policy presented and responded according to self-interest. Some recognized the inherent discrimination in the policy, but were either too afraid or too disinterested to speak of it publicly.

Another common view, represented by many Wyomingites, was one of complacency over relocation. The unspoken assumption was the federal government knew best what the wartime conditions required and, if the military said so, the action was necessary for national security.

Many Wyomingites in the 1990s say they are "unaware that the camp existed."[1] A look at contemporary newspapers, particularly those published in small towns outside the Big Horn Basin, suggests this may have been true in the 1940s, too. Except for scattered references, many relating to sports activities in which students at Heart Mountain were involved, small weeklies practically ignored the camp and the surrounding controversies.[2] Typical was an article appearing in the *Jackson's Hole Courier* in April 1943, about four "American-born Japanese, formerly from Seattle, Washington, and now at the Hunt, Idaho, Relocation Center." As the item noted:

> The group came to Jackson under a special permit to enjoy a short vacation before entering the U.S. Army, where the men enlisted. Those in the party are: Franklin Koriyama, Samuel Hokari and Mr. and Mrs. M. Masuda. All were excellent skiers, enjoyed their stay here, and were high in their praise of Jackson Hole hospitality and fine skiing conditions found here. They stayed at the Wort Hotel.[3]

Certainly, the daily newspapers covered news about the camp, but usually, those stories were buried among headlines of wartime actions in Europe and the Pacific.[4]

Only a tiny minority spoke out against the policy. In fact, little evidence exists that more than a mere handful of Wyomingites saw the policy as wrong and spoke out against it. Only one editor, L.L. Newton of the *Wyoming State Journal* in Lander, openly opposed the policy on constitutional grounds.

This paper will explore some of the views Wyomingites took toward relocation by analyzing various editorial comments from some Wyoming newspapers at the time and the congressional mail of Senator Joseph C. O'Mahoney. Various citizens wrote to his office about the issue and, although the individuals who write to congressional representatives concerning any issue are self-selecting, the attitudes expressed in their letters provide an interesting cross-section of Wyoming public opinion at the time.

Even before the federal government announced a site for construction of the Japanese American internment camp between Powell and Cody at Heart Mountain during World War II, Wyoming residents already were expressing opinions about war facilities of various types. A few wrote to the state's congressional delegation, either in response to questions or in unsolicited letters.

Senator Joseph C. O'Mahoney was a senior member of the Democratic majority of the Senate in 1942 when the Heart Mountain camp was established. First appointed to the Senate seat on the death of Senator John B. Kendrick, his former employer, O'Mahoney won reelection in 1934 and 1940. He was a dependable supporter of the New Deal until the Roosevelt administration tried to change the composition of the U.S. Supreme Court in 1937 as a way to keep the high court from striking down what it considered crucial anti-depression legislation. O'Mahoney gained constituent support from what Wyomingites saw as principled opposition to the President.

Before constituent mail is noted, it is important to understand O'Mahoney's position with respect to relocation. No single piece of evidence points to his feelings on wartime relocation. No roll call votes were taken on the various relocation measures in the Senate throughout the duration. O'Mahoney did not speak on the floor either for or against the policy. In fact, nowhere is there a definitive statement on his position. Thus, sections of letters and reactions to correspondence during this period are all there are to go on. Even at that, few hits appear in the correspondence until January 1943 when O'Mahoney was appointed to a special sub-committee of the Senate Military Affairs Committee to investigate the War Relocation Authority.

One of the more explicit explanations of his position was made in two letters to Park County Democratic officials in February 1943. He had written frequently to both men during May 1942 when the senator was seeking sentiment about establishing a relocation camp in Park County.

> I was made a member of the subcommittee which has been going into the matter and I found the testimony both surprising and interesting. It was, for example, clearly brought out by authoritative witnesses, from both the Army

and the Navy, not only that 60 percent of all the evacuees are native-born Americans, but that most of them have been altogether loyal to this country. Some of the most effective work which has been done for the Navy in Hawaii, for instance, has been done by Japanese born in Hawaii.[5]

Later, in the same letter, O'Mahoney quoted former Ambassador Grew who had appeared before his sub-committee and urged that "nothing should be done to alienate the loyalty of the American-born Japanese."

In a letter to the manager of the Holly Sugar Company in Worland during the previous year, O'Mahoney carefully distinguished between residents of prisoner-of-war camps and relocation center internees. ". . . many of them are natives of this country and apparently completely out of harmony with the Japanese militarists, they are not being treated as prisoners of war." Japanese must be "relocated in a manner that will enable them to live as normally as possible," the senator concluded.[6]

In a letter to Heart Mountain Director Guy Robertson in 1943, O'Mahoney wrote: "The treatment that we accord Americans of Japanese ancestry and even alien Japanese has a direct bearing upon the treatment given our own people in the hand of the Japanese."[7]

Because O'Mahoney's position was so publicly ambiguous, his constituents, regardless of what position they personally took on relocation, might have believed, from responses to their letters, that O'Mahoney agreed with them. He favored relocation; he opposed relocation. It depended on how his letters might be read and interpreted. The conclusion could be made, therefore, that his correspondence would contain a broader and more representative sample of opinion than similar constituent mail to someone like Senator E. V. Robertson, an outspoken critic of the War Relocation Authority who was insistent that such camps were necessary.

Before the camp was established on June 5, 1942, several Wyoming constituents wrote to O'Mahoney requesting that prison camps be located in their towns. The economic benefits were of paramount concern.

Elected officials needed to know the sentiments from constituents generally about the location of prison camps or internment centers. O'Mahoney wrote the secretary of the Sheridan Chamber of Commerce, asking about the local feelings of such a facility: "to date, no project in Wyoming is under consideration." The senator then asked if Sheridan residents would welcome such a camp if one were to be located somewhere in the state. The secretary replied in June that most people "did not wish the camp here."[8]

An editorial writer for the Sheridan newspaper, however, left room for more discussion about the camp's location nearby. In an editorial published in March, 1942, titled, "Somebody's Got to Take Them," the writer argued that this would be something Sheridan could do for the war effort:

"We don't want any Japs around here!" That's the first reaction one gets in asking about the possibility of our own region absorbing some of the Japanese who must be evacuated from vital coast regions. We agree. We don't want any Japs. But that doesn't help to solve the question [sic] . . . How would you like to be fighting an invasion of the Japanese from the Pacific, knowing that there was a strip of Japs 2,000 mile long right at your back?[9]

The editorial writer concluded that "it may be possible that Sheridan's greatest contribution to the American cause would be acceptance of some of the Pacific Coast Japanese." The writer quickly added that "we should be given the promise that they will leave as soon as the war is over."[10]

Residents of other towns in Wyoming seemed willing to make such a "contribution." Senator O'Mahoney received letters favorable to establishing a camp in Worland, but because of a controversy involving the availability of water, the site was turned down. The record shows that O'Mahoney pleaded the Worland case with vigor, not only with the War Department and War Relocation Authority, but with the State Engineer's Office in Cheyenne.[11]

The War Relocation Authority officials chose the Heart Mountain site on government land in a relatively remote but agriculturally promising area in the northern Big Horn Basin. O'Mahoney had queried Park County residents about the proposed site in May 1942: Jack Richard, editor of the *Cody Enterprise*, responded that "although we have no great love for the Japanese" the project would be accepted as necessary for the war effort. Paul Stock, Cody mayor, agreed, as long as "they are properly supervised . . . it would be perfectly all right."[12]

Besides concerns about security, two other themes appeared in correspondence from Wyomingites over the next two years: removal of internees after the war (an issue raised in the Sheridan editorial) and use of Japanese labor for agricultural production.

For some letter writers, fears of sabotage seemed extreme by any measure. Park County commissioner Harry Atteberry warned O'Mahoney that the location of the camp at Heart Mountain might cause danger to the Willwood Dam and Corbett Dam, both small irrigation projects near Powell. He wrote that he thought Park County would accept the camp as long as the federal government could guarantee both security and "their removal from the county after the war."[13] The removal theme was to gain added momentum as the war appeared to be winding down.

As soon as the first group of internees began to arrive in August 1942, O'Mahoney started receiving requests from people wanting to obtain the services of the camp residents in fields or businesses. Requests from sugar beet growers were particularly numerous. G. N. Wells, vice president of the Montana-Wyoming Beet Growers Association, wrote to WRA Director Dillon S. Myer in April 1943, asking for labor. He warned that growers would be ruined if labor wasn't furnished from the Japanese ranks. "Too many of our workers are now in the armed forces," he stated.[14]

Even at the beginning of the war before the camp location was established, at least one Wyoming editor foresaw the value of camp internees for agriculture. "The Japanese could take up the loss in farm labor that is growing increasingly serious and they would become a factor in our economic business life," the editor of the *Sheridan Press* wrote in March 1942.[15]

While workers were needed for field work, other industry owners made requests for Japanese American laborers. A Cowley canning company official thanked O'Mahoney for assisting in recruiting labor from the Relocation Center to work in his plant. Labor requests also came from a Casper bowling alley (to alleviate the "war-time pinsetter shortage") and a McFadden rancher wishing for a hired hand.[16] Fremont County farmers felt 'that the crops must be harvested and this is the only solution thus far presented."[17]

In 1944, the Casper Building and Construction Trades Council inquired if internees could be used to help in "tearing up the railroad between Shoshone and Elco"—duplicate tracks of the Chicago and Northwestern, the iron needed for scrap metal. O'Mahoney gave similar replies to such requests. He promised that "a copy of your letter will be forwarded to the WRA."[18]

In the fall of 1943, critics of the center pointed out that school teachers at the Heart Mountain camp were paid "in excess of other teachers in the state." Eugene T. Childers, editor of the *Riverton Review*, editorialized against the "teacher-grabbing policies" of the WRA. "Our Washington delegation should be flooded with protests," he wrote. The Pavillion Grange petitioned the WRA, protesting the high wages paid to camp teachers. The agriculture teacher had been hired away from them before the end of the term, the Grange petition noted, and the community demanded redress. Lander's L.L. Newton pointed out the flaw in such complaints. "The teachers at Heart Mountain are on 11-month contracts," he editorially noted, dismissing the *Review* editor's statements as uninformed.[19]

From the beginning, Wyomingites complained, not about violations of civil liberties, but what they considered as "coddling" of camp residents. The letters to O'Mahoney range from mild complaints to viciously racial diatribes. A former Sheridan resident wrote in February 1943, doubting the need for a large food supply being kept at the Minidoka, Idaho, camp. O'Mahoney answered that an investigation would be held shortly to determine such matters. He added a compliment to the internees at the camp: "The War Department tells us that there has been such a demand among those Japanese [in relocation camps] to serve in our own military forces that the War Department is now raising a Japanese military contingent which is to be sent into the European Theater of War."[20]

O'Mahoney's rather meek response contrasts with the view taken by one Wyoming editor, even early in the war when hysteria and fear were at their greatest. L.L. Newton, editor and publisher of the *Wyoming State Journal* in Lander, stands out among Wyoming journalists for the unequivocal position he took on the camp. Unlike lawyer O'Mahoney, who avoided making legal arguments against the establishment of such camps, Newton flatly declared that the existence of the camps violated the internees' constitutional rights.

A conservative Republican who supported Governor Nels Smith and E. V. Robertson in 1942 general elections, he seemed an unlikely spokesman for constitutional rights of internees. The camp was far from Newton's Lander home. Unlike the publishers of the *Cody Enterprise* and the *Powell Tribune* whose communities were less than 15 miles from the camp, Lander was more than 150 miles and a mountain range beyond.[21] Unlike those respective publishers, however, Newton traveled with his family to the Heart Mountain camp three months after the first evacuees arrived in August 1942. In four consecutive issues of the weekly *State Journal*, Newton described what he had found at the camp in a column he titled "Travel with Your Editor." In the first installment, he stated flatly:

> Let us start out this rather rambling and sketchy story of the project with a few definitions, just to get the story straight. In the first place, they are not Japs . . . . They are American citizens born in this country with the full rights of this country, 'even as you and I.' They do not have any other loyalty than to America and are as much our people as second generation German, Irish, Italian or Scandinavian citizens.[22]

On December 3, Newton's column continued the story by describing the interiors of the buildings and the conditions the evacuees faced. "The rooms are devoid of furniture" and the buildings are cold, he wrote. "You have camped out but you 'had everything' to do it with. These people were dumped down in a new world of sagebrush and desert to be handled by a group of Caucasians who hadn't time to organize themselves, let alone handle such a vast throng of folk."[23]

Newton's columns were widely quoted by other Wyoming newspapers, but not approvingly. Newton responded to the criticisms in his final installment on December 17 by asserting that he wouldn't mind "having any of them care to farm in the Lander Valley" or for physician evacuees to treat him or members of his family. "P.S. (and pardon me)," Newton wrote, "I have had many compliments and words of approval upon these series of 'Travel with Your Editor' articles, but they have all come and only come from those who have visited the Heart Mountain center. In the words of long ago, 'Come and See.'"[24]

In the Christmas Eve issue of the *State Journal*, Newton printed a front-page story about Arapaho Indians packing beans for shipment to Heart Mountain.

> Older tribesmen conjured to their minds the paradox of feeding the Japanese internees at Cody and killing them off in the Solomons where some of their sons are defending their country with their lives. When they learned the Japanese descent people at Cody were really Americans—born in this country and many of them also fought in the Solomons alongside of their war-

riors—they understand they were no different than second generation Germans, Italians and others, also loyal Americans, and gave their approval to the shipment.[25]

Despite the editorial criticisms of his position on the Heart Mountain camp's legality, Newton was elected president of the Wyoming Press Association in January 1943.[26] The new position did not deter him from pointing out the constitutional flaws of keeping American citizens behind barbed wire. In March 1943, the *State Journal* ran a story headlined "Tojo of Heart Mountain Out to Get Tojo of Tokyo, Japan." The story told of Rufus Tojo's vow to avenge the good name of his family by enlisting in the U.S. Army.[27]

In one of the few articles relating to Japanese relocation to appear at any point during the war, the *Jackson' Hole Courier* commented on an enlistment. Under the photograph of a World War I veteran, his wife and son (who enlisted in Hawaii), the *Courier* wrote: "Sends son to fight against homeland."[28]

The editorial writer for the *Sheridan Press* demonstrated an interesting pattern in trying to distinguish his attitude toward Japanese and Japanese American internees from racism. One editorial in January 1942, titled "Let's Salute Joe Louis, An American!", draws one to conclude that the writer wants his readers to understand that he was no racist.[29] An additional editorial later that month makes a similar attempt even though the terminology suggests otherwise. In writing about enlistees from the nearby Crow Reservation in Montana, the editorial notes that they are "making the startling transition from travois-maker to technician."[30]

Judging from the letters sent to Senator O'Mahoney, few Wyomingites shared Newton's concerns for the constitutional rights of the internees while not a few were overtly racist. Most correspondents, however, emphasize either a financial motive for writing or apprehension that internees were receiving "favored treatment."

O'Mahoney received a torrent of mail in April and May 1943, after the *Denver Post* in a series of articles accused the WRA of "pampering the enemy." One of the *Post* headlines read: "Food is Hoarded for Japs in U.S. While Americans in Nippon Are Tortured." The sub-head read: "Openly Disloyal Japs Pampered."[31]

The *Post* article, written by sports writer Jack Carberry, was used by U.S. Senator E. V. Robertson to tell the *New York Times* that he was certain "the Japanese are being pampered." He provided no evidence and he admitted he had not visited the camp to investigate the charges.[32] While his Senate colleague talked to the press about the *Denver Post* story, O'Mahoney did not reply when the managing editor of the Denver paper sent a clipping of the Carberry piece and asked for O'Mahoney's reaction. This was the pattern in his response to inflammatory letters, too. Either he did not answer or he deftly made reference to a single point on common agreement he might have had with the writer.[33]

Angry letters came in from throughout Wyoming. A Buffalo couple suggested that the Japanese Americans be "segregated by sex because we don't need more little Japs." The Brotherhood of Railroad Trainmen in Sheridan wrote that if the Carberry article about "luxuries for the Japanese" were true, why was the rest of the country having to sacrifice? An Arvada man wrote that the *Post* article "is the bitterest pill I've had to swallow yet." A Basin man blamed the defeat of Democrats in the last election on the "information that came out of Heart Mountain project. Now comes the story told by Jack Carberry in the *Denver Post* and once more there is 'hell a poppin.'"[34]

Glenn Neilson, president of Husky Oil Company in Cody, wrote to O'Mahoney that he was "pleased that the *Denver Post* had sufficient nerve to publish the articles about the camp." He claimed that he had tried to recruit labor there and they seemed to be "a lazy and shiftless lot" to him.[35]

O'Mahoney did not respond to Neilson's letter nor to other mail that week. "The senator is ill with the flu and out of the office this week," Mary Mahan , his secretary, wrote. "I will see that he gets your letter when he returns."[36]

The town councils of Powell and Cody met in joint session the same week the *Post* story ran, but it was more than merely "pampering" that concerned both groups. Both issued petitions asking for tighter security and the guarantee that the internees would be moved out after the war.[37]

Others, apparently more as defenders of the War Relocation Authority and its staff than the internees, wrote to protest the "untruths" in the *Post* story. "[They are] ignorant of the facts," a Cody man wrote while a Hiland woman declared, "We know you are opposed to a campaign of retaliation and therefore we feel every confidence in your report. Some of [Senator Robertson's] accusations seem about as ridiculous as a Goebbels fantasy."[38]

Bill Hosokawa, editor for the *Heart Mountain Sentinel*, editorially answered the *Post* charges. He chastised the Cody and Powell councils and stated that the people had been "stampeded by the *Post* articles." He noted that "it is evident that not all of Wyoming's sheep are on the hillsides." Hosokawa pointed to the curious fact that Senator Robertson owned a significant interest in the Cody Trading Company, a firm that supplied the camp. The senator's complaints clearly seem contradictory.[39]

Meanwhile, Senator O'Mahoney quietly consoled camp director Guy Robertson. "You have a difficult job," he wrote. Clearly, the senator accepted Dillon Myer's refutation of the *Post* series.[40]

In a letter to the chairman of the Heart Mountain Volunteers, O'Mahoney made no reference to the *Post* charges, electing instead to salute internees who had enlisted. He wrote: "Let me acknowledge your letter of May 18 enclosing a copy of the credo adopted by the volunteers into the U.S. Armed Services from the relocation centers for Japanese ancestry persons . . . It is indeed gratifying to know that American citizens of Japanese ancestry have thus demonstrated their loyalty and desire to serve in the armed services of the U.S."[41]

A center employee, Scott Taggart of Cody, accused the Post of distorting the facts, but also pointed to Senator Robertson's statements as erroneous.

. . . our security lies in men like you who have grown big enough to be able to approach all problems from the standpoint of right and justice and the public interest without regard to spotted public clamor. The people of Wyoming are both intelligent and honest, and though many may be temporarily side-tracked by emotionalism they will in the long run continue to honor their chosen leaders who have kept their heads in periods of excitement and quiet alike.[42]

Powell attorney Lowell C. Stephens wrote that Senator Robertson "could speak in Philadelphia about the problems of the center although he was too busy to go the 14 miles" out there. Stephens claimed Senator Robertson's source was Cody attorney Milward Simpson, the head of the Park County Civilian Defense. "I think you know the kind of information Milward puts out in anything connected with politics," Stephens wrote. Stephens said he had personally visited the camp and found that the "people in the camp seem to be loyal and law-abiding people and should have fair treatment."[43]

Simpson wrote several times to O'Mahoney commenting on the camp. In one, he pointed out that the court system had been "jammed by Japanese cases." He also questioned the security arrangements at the camp after twenty guards were withdrawn by the WRA:

This [withdrawal] stems from the silly mamby-pamby policy of the WRA to give these people more freedom from restraint. They tell us that these internees will leave the camp and go out into useful occupations over the land. If that is the attitude of the rest, and I am dead sure it is, then by God, we don't want them out away from the enclosure.[44]

Apparently unaware that many of the American citizens in the camp had lost homes and businesses on the West Coast, Simpson continued:

They are a sullen, nasty lot; a good portion of them are not even American born or American citizens. The percentage of native born citizens who have sworn allegiance to the Emperor of Japan is at least 25 percent of the total . . . Having established residence from the standpoint of voting. I know of no member of our delegation who would want their vote.[45]

O'Mahoney answered without specific comment, but tacitly, he disagreed. He promised to check with the army about possible security gaps. Three days later, he wrote Simpson again to report that the Army claimed the "situation was well in hand."[46]

In 1943, O'Mahoney was appointed a member of the Senate's Sub-committee to Investigate the War Relocation Authority, chaired by Senator Albert B.

Chandler (D-Ky.). The committee met during the first part of 1943 and numerous members made inspection visits to the camps. The focal point seemed to be Tule Lake, California, site of various violent incidents during the WRA's short history. O'Mahoney received one memo from the secretary of the committee, asking if he wished to "make an investigation trip West on behalf of the committee." Apparently, he declined.[47] The committee issued its report in June 1943, including testimony from Dillon Myer, J. Edgar Hoover and Assistant Secretary of War John McCloy. Nothing of consequence resulted from the committee's investigations except "junkets" for members.

As U.S. Senator representing a state where an apparent majority of the population was not sympathetic to internees, O'Mahoney demonstrated ambivalence about the camp. O'Mahoney weighed the evidence, agreed that a threat to the nation existed, and therefore, the lock-up was justified. Politically, he defended the administration's War Relocation Authority staff, but he did not become actively involved in the debates over the Heart Mountain Center's "coddling." He stayed above the fray, deferring to his Wyoming colleague E. V. Robertson who, O'Mahoney may have believed, might have a stronger interest in the camp because he was a resident of Park County.

The contrasts are more stark between Newton and Senator E. V. Robertson. In essence, Newton saw relocation as constitutionally flawed while Robertson believed it was a wartime necessity, whether or not it was constitutional.

O'Mahoney, who privately doubted the policy, did not speak out. Unlike editor L. L. Newton, he took no public position opposing relocation on constitutional grounds. While he cannot be charged with actively supporting repressive policies of relocation, O'Mahoney was guilty of doing nothing about the injustices. One can only speculate the result had he publicly questioned relocation on grounds like Newton did in his small weekly newspaper far from the center of federal power.

As for the majority of O'Mahoney's Wyoming constituents, many seemed blissfully unaware that more than ten-thousand people of Japanese descent, seventy percent of who were American citizens, were being held against their will within the borders of Wyoming. The plight of these fellow citizens in their midst seemed drowned out by war news from around the world, letters from loved ones in military service and the daily reminders of war in the form of rationing of food, gasoline and other consumer products.

But even if they had known, it is probable that, like O'Mahoney, they would not have spoken out. Like a letter writer to the *Casper Star-Tribune* wrote fifty years later:

> The sneak attack at Pearl Harbor by the Japanese left the impression that all Japanese were sneaky and dangerous, and many believed the Japanese people in America were here as troops behind the lines for a takeover of America by the Japanese . . . . This hurt many of us as we realized how help-

less we were to help those innocent people caught up in such hatred.[48]

With very few exceptions, none tried to point out the injustice, let alone try to right it.

Notes

1. For examples of all of these views in present times, see the *Casper Star-Tribune* letters to the editor in issues following the Heart Mountain Symposium, particularly those published during the last two weeks of May, 1995.

2. Not all weeklies published in Wyoming were checked for this article but a reasonable sample was consulted. Among the newspapers examined were those published in the following Wyoming towns: Jackson, Lusk, Torrington, Newcastle, Moorcroft, Lander and Riverton. There was no dominant statewide daily at the time, but most residents read local weeklies. The newspapers published in Cody and Powell during the period were not analyzed for this paper because such an analysis has been done, most recently as part of a longer study by Michael Mackey, "Heart Mountain Relocation Center: Both Sides of the Fence" (master's thesis, University of Wyoming, 1993).

3. "Japanese Skiers Spend Weekend in Jackson Hole," *Jackson Hole Courier*, April 8, 1943,

4. The front pages of any Wyoming daily published in this period would demonstrate this fact. One good example is the *Sheridan Press* on which the banner headlines throughout the period featured war reports. Even early in the war, when the U.S. Attorney for Wyoming commented on incidents of Japanese-Americans adhering to federal orders, the item appeared on the second page. See "Enemy Aliens Are Complying with U.S. Order." *Sheridan Press*, January 5, 1942, 2.

5. O'Mahoney to Ed Althoff, Park County Democratic chairman, and Paul Greever, February 6, 1943, Box 85, War Relocation Authority file, O'Mahoney Papers, American Heritage Center, University of Wyoming (henceforth cited as WRA file). Oddly, just ten days after the letter was postmarked, Greever, a former Congressman, died from an accidental shotgun blast in his Cody home. See *Wyoming State Tribune*, February 17, 1943.

6. O'Mahoney to L.E. Laird, June 16, 1942, Box 67, Japanese Evacuation file, O'Mahoney Papers.

7. O'Mahoney to Robertson, February 27, 1943, Box 74, WRA file.

8. O'Mahoney to L.C. Morrison, May 1, 1942; Morrison to O'Mahoney, June 3, 1942, Japanese Evacuation file, O'Mahoney Papers.

9. "Somebody's Got to Take Them," *Sheridan Press*, March 18, 1942, 4.

10. Ibid.

11. O'Mahoney, May 23, 1942; Stock to O'Mahoney, May 12, 1942, Box 74, Japanese Evacuation file, O'Mahoney Papers.

12. Richard to O'Mahoney, May 23, 1942; Stock to O'Mahoney, May 12, 1942, Box 74, Japanese Evacuation file, O'Mahoney Papers.

13. Atteberry to O'Mahoney, May 13, 1942, Box 74, Japanese Evacuation file, O'Mahoney Papers.

14. Wells to O'Mahoney, April 1, 1943, Box 74, WRA file.

15. *Sheridan Press*, March 18, 1942, 4.

16. Big Horn Canning to O'Mahoney, September 22, 1942, Box 74, WRA file.

17. *Riverton Review*, August 5, 1943, 1.

18. Trades Council to O'Mahoney, May 17, 1944, Box 85, WRA file.

19. *Riverton Review*, August 25, 1943, 4; Pavillion Grange resolution, September 21, 143, Box 74, WRA files, O'Mahoney Papers.

20. W. B. Johnson, Mountain Home, Idaho, to O'Mahaney, February 5, 1943; O'Mahoney to Johnson, February 9, 1943, Box 85, WRA file.

21. Actually, the camp was 14 miles from Cody and 10 miles from Powell.

22. "Jap Trap Misnomer for Relocation Center," *Wyoming State Journal*, November 26, 1942, 2.

23. "Evacuees Tell Story of Life at Center," *Wyoming State Journal*, December 3, 1942, 2.

24. Japanese Evacuees Plan to Reclaim Desert," *Wyoming State Journal*, December 17, 1942, 2.

25. "Indian Pack of Canned Beans Go to Feed Japanese," *Wyoming State Journal*, December 24, 1942, 1.

26. "WPA Officers Elected," *Wyoming State Journal*, January 21, 1943, 1.

27. "Tojo . . .," *Wyoming State Journal*, March 11, 1943, 8.

28. *Jackson's Hole Courier*, April 8, 1943, 7.

29. *Sheridan Press*, January 12, 1942, 4.

30. "The First Americans Rise Again to Defend the Homeland," *Sheridan Press*, January 29, 1942, 4.

31. *Denver Post*, April 23, 1943.

32. *New York Times*, May 7, 1943, 5, c. 1.

33. Lawrence Martin to O'Mahoney, April 24, 1943, Box 74, WRA file.

34. Caroll and Mabel Beckwith to O'Mahoney, May 11, 1943; H.E. Fullbright, Secretary-Treasurer, to O'Mahoney, May 12, 1943; G.E. Pollard to O'Mahoney, April 25, 1943; A.W. Coons, Basin, to O'Mahoney, April 29, 1943. Box 74, WRA file.

35. Neilson to O'Mahoney, May 10, 1943, Box 74, WRA file.

36. Mahan to Glenn Neilson, May 10, 1943, Box 74, WRA file.

37. "Resolution of Policy Toward Japanese at Heart Mountain Relocation Center," adopted at joint session of city councils of Cody and Powell, April 24, 1943, Box 74, WRA file, O'Mahoney Papers. The city clerks of each town mailed copies of the resolution to O'Mahoney but, apparently, he did not reply.

38. Fred Butler to O'Mahoney, May 30, 1943; Mrs. Robert Maigh to O'Mahoney, May 1, 1943.

39. *Heart Mountain Sentinel*, May 8, 1943, 2.

40. O'Mahoney to Guy Robertson, February 27, 1943, Box 74, WRA file.

41. O'Mahoney to Abe Cyamanda, May 21, 1943, Box 74, WRA file.

42. Taggart to O'Mahoney, May 12, 1943, Box 74, WRA file.

43. Stephens to O'Mahoney, May 20, 1943, Box 74, WRA file.

44. Simpson to O'Mahoney, April 18, 1944, Box 85, WRA file, O'Mahoney Papers.

45. Ibid.

46. O'Mahoney to Simpson, April 21, 1943. Box 85, WRA file.

47. Letters from the committee, Box 85, Military Affairs file; memo from Walter Mulbry, March 2, 1943, Box 85, Military Affairs file. Committee members were: Senators James E. Murray (D-Mont.); Mon C. Wallgren (D-Wash); Henry Cabot Lodge, Jr. (R-Mass.); Chan Gurney (R-S.D.); Rufus Holman (R- Ore.).

48. Ruby Bolderac, Letter to the Editor, "Sneak attack hit Japanese-Americans," *Casper Star-Tribune*, June 6, 1995, A7.

The Heart Mountain Relocation Center:
Economic Opportunities in Wyoming

Mike Mackey

While Japanese Americans were being rounded up and sent to assembly centers, the decision had been made by the War Relocation Authority (WRA) to go ahead with the construction of permanent relocation camps. A number of communities in Wyoming expressed interest in such projects. The town of Worland, for example, made a concerted effort to bring a relocation center or a prisoner of war camp to that area. Worland had a number projects going for which a great deal of cheap manual labor was required. Early in April 1942, Worland mayor, Ray Bower, contacted Wyoming's senior United States Senator, Joseph C. O'Mahoney, to ask for assistance in getting a camp for his town. The senator informed Bower that sentiment in Wyoming concerning evacuee camps was sharply divided but that he would do what he could. O'Mahoney suggested that the mayor contact WRA Director, Milton Eisenhower, to find out what steps to follow.[1]

Upon hearing from the senator, Bower called a meeting of the Alfalfa Commercial Club (Worland Chamber of Commerce) to present his proposal. The meeting was also attended by members of the Lions Club and a number of area sugar beet growers. W. J. Gorst, President of the Montana-Wyoming Beet Growers Association, had told Governor Nels Smith a month earlier that his organization did not want any Japanese brought into the area to work the beet fields. Gorst apparently did not consult many of his members before coming to that conclusion. Not only did a number of area growers attend the meeting, but L. E. Laird, plant manager of Holly Sugar Corporation's Worland processing plant was also in contact with O'Mahoney on behalf of beet growers who were interested in a war-time labor force.[2]

The consensus at the meeting, which Bower had called, was that Worland should make every effort to get a "Japanese Labor Highway Camp." The labor from such a camp would be used mainly to construct the "Gooseberry Tie-in." The tie-in was a section of highway that would create a shortcut to Yellowstone Park and possibly increase tourism through Worland in the future. Those at the meeting also said such a camp would provide a pool of labor that could be tapped by farmers when it came time for the sugar beet harvest. Bower told those in attendance that the camp would be controlled and financed by the federal government. He believed this would quell any "objection against a white american [sic] community having to eventually absorb an excess of Japanese."[3]

By early May, Governor Smith, who three weeks earlier said that if Japanese were allowed into his state they would "be hanging from every tree,"[4] was contacting the Provost Marshal General's office on Worland's behalf. At that same time, however, Milton Eisenhower of the WRA informed Senator O'Mahoney that the use of CCC camps as relocation centers (which Worland and some other communities pro-

posed) was not practical. Eisenhower said that the WRA had set a minimum population for relocation centers at 5,000. That number was based on calculation as to how
many troops would be necessary to "protect" the evacuees. He pointed out that the
army was not willing to send troops all over the country with evacuees and that the
WRA was looking at a maximum of 15 to 18 camps. Eisenhower did not believe that
any CCC camps in Wyoming were capable of handling 5,000 people and said most
sites for relocation centers had already been chosen.[5]

During the first week of June, 1942, Senator O'Mahoney contacted the
Alfalfa Commercial Club in Worland to inform its members that the WRA had
approved only one site in Wyoming for a relocation center. That site, in Northwest
Wyoming, was located on the forty-two thousand acre Heart Mountain Reclamation
Project between Cody and Powell. Upon receiving this news the Worland group
began to pursue the possibility of acquiring a prisoner-of-war camp, again in an effort
to exploit a possible labor source for their own benefit. Assistant Secretary of War,
John J. McCloy told Senator O'Mahoney that the government had all the prisoner of
war camps that it would need for the time being.[6]

While Worland had been lobbying for its own relocation center or prisoner-
of-war camp, Senator O'Mahoney was taking a survey in the towns of Powell and
Cody. He was trying to get a feeling for the local attitude toward the proposed Heart
Mountain Relocation Center. Cody attorney Paul Greever said the establishment of
a camp at Heart Mountain would not disturb his peace of mind, but he suggested that
there be proper supervision. Mayor Paul Stock of Cody said he would not welcome
the Japanese in the community itself, but if they were kept in the camp and properly
supervised it would be acceptable. Park County Commissioner Harry Attebery said
he found that generally there was opposition to bringing the Japanese into the county. He felt, however, that if the federal government would closely guard these people
and remove them from the county after the war, there would be no problems.
Attebery was concerned that without proper supervision the Japanese could be a menace to nearby irrigation projects. He believed that, "One stick of explosive in the
Corbett Tunnel would destroy the water supply for the irrigation of about 60,000
acres . . . ."[7] Don Jamieson of The Powell Club (Powell Chamber of Commerce)
informed the senator that his group was very interested in the relocation center while
Jack Richard, editor of the *Cody Enterprise*, had no problem with the establishment
of a camp even though he had "no love of the Japanese."[8]

By early June, 1942, the Heart Mountain Relocation Center was becoming
a reality. The camp was to be built on land which was a part of the Heart Mountain
Federal Reclamation Project half way between Powell and Cody, Wyoming. It would
be large enough to house at least 10,000 Japanese. According to R. T. Baird, editor
of the *Powell Tribune*, the new residents were to, "level the land, put in irrigation
ditches, prepare the land for cultivation, . . . [and] they will not be permitted to min-
gle with outsiders."[9]

The effect this camp would have on the two small Wyoming communities was described as a "big boon to business—the biggest thing in the way of industrial and payroll activity that has ever come to Powell."[10] Powell and Cody became busy towns as enough workers were hired to complete construction of the camp in sixty days. Advertisements in local newspapers sought housing for the more than 2,000 workers who were expected to come into the area. A number of local workers quit steady jobs in the hope of earning higher wages paid by the government in connection with the camp's construction.[11]

Within only four weeks of the beginning of construction of the camp, "The payroll from Heart Mountain Relocation Center . . . brought good times and busy times to Powell."[12] The project was described as an answer to prayers that somehow the Big Horn Basin would share in the billions of dollars being spent on the war effort. R. T. Baird said that, "The whole thing was like a dream come true."[13]

With the camp under construction a number of area business men were also looking to profit from the relocation center and the Japanese and Japanese Americans who were to be incarcerated there. Senator O'Mahoney was flooded with requests for help in obtaining government contracts for businessmen from the Big Horn Basin's private sector.

George Reesy, the owner of Reesy Drug Store in Thermopolis, Wyoming told O'Mahoney that he was interested in a drug store concession at the "Jap Camp." Reesy was curious as to whether or not the government was going to be "giving all such concessions, to the Japs . . ."[14] or if any would be given to outsiders. J. A. Morrow of Riverton and Paul Greever of Cody contacted the senator on behalf of George Bonner of Greybull and C. H. Scribner of Riverton. The two men were interested in acquiring a permit which would enable them to open a store within the confines of the camp. It was to be something "along the line of a junior department, [sic] store, . . ."[15]

Stores or concessions at Heart Mountain were not the only possibility of economic benefit in the Powell and Cody area. Dick Jones of Powell Transfer & Storage Company was trying to obtain information on how to put in a bid for the transportation of coal to the camp. (Coal was eventually hauled in by Burlington Northern Railroad Co.) Clyde Gorrell was working through Paul Greever in an attempt to get the camp's garbage disposal contract while Oliver Steadman, secretary of the Cody Club (Cody Chamber of Commerce), was asking Senator O'Mahoney if it were not possible to enlarge the center. Things had been so good for the business community in Cody during the construction phase of the relocation center that Steadman thought the camp should be made bigger.[16]

One of those who received the greatest economic benefit from Heart Mountain after the camp was occupied was T. T. Dodson, owner of the Powell Valley Creamery. Dodson contacted senior administrative official John Nelson at Heart Mountain and after extensive discussions came away believing that he had a good chance at obtaining the milk contract for the camp. Dodson, however, needed to increase his base supply of milk in order to fill current obligations plus those of the camp.[17]

Dodson received the contract in mid August. The intial contract was for thirty days, but after that trial period it would be renewed every three months. The first contract called for the delivery of five hundred gallons of milk four times per week. In order to meet those needs Dodson called on area dairy farmers to increase the size of their herds and he obtained milk from as far away as Bridger, Montana. The Heart Mountain milk contract made the Powell Creamery the third largest in the state of Wyoming. It also contributed $10,000 per month to the income of area dairy farmers.[18]

Dodson was not content to profit from Heart Mountain while it was in operation and then go back to the way things were after the camp closed. In January 1943 he purchased the Rock Creek Cheese Factory in Roberts, Montana and moved it to Powell. Dodson figured that by the time he got the cheese factory into operation the camp would be ready to close.[19]

A number of smaller businesses in Powell and Cody also benefited directly from the relocation center. Tom Scott, the shoe cobbler in Powell had a large increase in business once the camp was occupied and he expressed his thanks to the "soldiers, Japanese and administrative officials and their families."[20] A Powell laundry and dry cleaning service was allowed to set up an office within the confines of the camp in order to meet the needs of internees. The Cody Trading Company established an office in Block 20 where orders were taken for groceries and dry goods with guaranteed delivery in forty-eight hours. Ray Easton, the undertaker in Powell, also saw an increase in business when Heart Mountain, which eventually approached a population of nearly eleven thousand, was located nearby. As the residents of the camp were allowed to apply for passes to shop in Powell or Cody, local merchants also benefited greatly. Al Fryer, a Powell merchant said that by June of 1944 the internees were contributing between $25,000 and $50,000 a year to that town's economy. In addition, internees were required to pay Wyoming sales tax on purchases made within the confines of the camp. In its first year of existence, the residents of Heart Mountain paid $12,260 in Wyoming sales taxes. They also paid $1,166.42 in property taxes. This amount was assessed on unsold goods in the center's canteens. The money collected from property taxes was distributed to the school districts in Park County.[21]

Though many Cody and Powell merchants and businessmen benefited directly from the Heart Mountain Relocation Center, those who received the greatest benefit were area farmers. It can be argued that the Japanese who worked the beet fields were paid the prevailing wage, but had the internees not been willing to go out and participate in the harvest it is more than likely that a substantial part of the 1942 and 1943 sugar beet and bean crops would have rotted in the fields. This is true not only for the Powell and Cody area, but for the states of Montana, Wyoming and Nebraska.

Big Horn Basin area farmers were discussing the farm labor shortage as early as August 1942. As the evacuees began arriving at Heart Mountain during that month, pressure was building on the WRA to allow the Japanese to leave camp and work in the beet fields. Joseph H. Smart, WRA Regional Director in Denver, Colorado, said evacuees would be made available (on a volunteer basis) to area farmers, but that certain qualifications had to be met first. Farmers had to fill out request forms stating what kind of labor was to be done, how many workers would be needed, what the farmer would pay and what type of housing, if necessary, the laborers would be given. Completed forms were first sent to area employment offices to see if requests could be filled by local laborers. The stumbling block came when Smart said that the governor and local law enforcement officials would be responsible for the security of laborers and ensuring that the prevailing wage was paid.[22]

Since state and local authorities were to have the responsibility of protecting internees who were working outside the camp, the governor felt he would require some control over the workers. Smith said he wanted the power to terminate working agreements with the evacuees when "in his judgement, the welfare of the communities, or of the State of Wyoming, can best be served by the return of the Japanese to their relocation centers."[23]

While Smith was standing pat on his requirements for allowing the Japanese to leave Heart Mountain on work passes, he was contacted by: Holly Sugar Company, Great Western Sugar Company, the National Beet Growers Association, the Montana-Wyoming Beet Growers Association, the Wyoming USDA War Board and a number of other groups and individuals, including W. J. Gorst of Worland who had stated earlier that he did not want the Japanese in Wyoming and did not need them to work the beet fields. All of these companies and individuals wanted the governor to make whatever arrangements were necessary in order to get laborers from Heart Mountain to help bring in the crops as soon as possible.[24]

There were delays in getting the volunteers into the fields despite the pleas of the previously mentioned groups. Smith did not feel that as governor he could allow the release of Japanese in Wyoming without restrictions and guarantees as to when they would be returned to the camp. Smith wanted some power over the situation but was informed by WRA Regional Director Joseph Smart that no state official would be allowed to dictate WRA policy. Smart agreed that the volunteer laborers would be returned to the camp if the governor felt it necessary, but he would not allow it to be printed in any labor contracts. Smith's concern was that once these volunteers had been released to work in the fields they would not go back to camp, but would establish permanent residence in Wyoming.[25]

While the governor was concerned with his control over the farm labor situation, Senator O'Mahoney was being flooded with telegrams explaining the farmers' position. The most urgent requests were coming from Sheridan and Johnson counties. The telegrams were all very similar. There were requests for 300 laborers asking that everything possible be done to gain the release of workers from Heart

Mountain. The farmers felt that crops could not be harvested without Japanese labor. Some of them were begging that some kind of arrangement be worked out with the governor because laborers were needed desperately.[26]

The farmers, however, were put on hold by the governor while Senator O'Mahoney tried to work out a deal between Dillon S. Myer, Milton Eisenhower's successor as director of the WRA, and Governor Smith. The governor said that it was his intention to help Wyoming farmers get the labor they needed to harvest the crops. But he added that the people of Wyoming did not want the state, or any section of it, permanently populated with West Coast Japanese. Before he allowed laborers out of Heart Mountain, Smith wanted "some assurance that the Japanese will be reassembled at the relocation center when their services are no longer needed for the emergency."[27]

C. E. Rachford, director of the Heart Mountain Relocation Center, had requests for 2,000 laborers as early as September 1, but an agreement had not been reached between Governor Smith and the WRA until September 21. Smith's attempts to keep some sort of control over the labor situation cost farmers three weeks of valuable time. When he ran for reelection two months later Smith was defeated by Lester Hunt. Smith's insistence on control over laborers from Heart Mountain and the resulting delay in getting those workers into the fields were certainly contributing factors in his political defeat. In the meantime Senator O'Mahoney was contacted by a number of people in farm related industries thanking him for his help in regard to the labor problem. One such individual was P. B. Smith, the plant manager for Great Western Sugar Company in Lovell, Wyoming. Mr. Smith thanked O'Mahoney and added that, "Most of the Japanese appear to be very fine people . . . ."[28]

Despite the profound labor shortage, Heart Mountain internees could not be forced to leave camp to work. Sixty-three percent of Heart Mountain's prospective labor force was made up of American citizens, and federal law prohibited the drafting of Americans for labor projects against their will. Furthermore, under the Geneva Convention, Japanese aliens could not be forced to work either, so all labor was voluntary. In spite of objections by some local farmers who felt they should be able to hire all the laborers they could afford, workers from the camp were distributed to farming areas according to the number of acres planted. The worker distribution formula and Governor Smith's holdout for a satisfactory agreement, which resulted in laborers being held in camp until late in the season, led to many complaints from farming communities.[29]

The Sheridan County Beet Growers Association felt that it was extremely unfair that Japanese laborers from Heart Mountain had to be shared with the state of Nebraska.[30] W. E. Pearson, president of the First National Bank in Lovell, said the beet harvest was being impaired by a continuing labor shortage. He said that businessmen and high school students were all working in the beet fields and claimed that out of 12,000 Japanese at Heart Mountain only 1050 were working. "In this emergency they are being mollycoddled by relocation authorities. If they are American citizens they should accept the same responsibilities as the rest of us . . . , "[31] he said.

Regional Director Joseph Smart told Senator O'Mahoney to have Pearson visit the center where he could get the correct figures which would answer his criticisms. Smart said that as of October 14, 1942, there were 510 evacuees working in Wyoming and 653 working in Montana and a few in Nebraska. Director Myer added that that number of laborers came from a population at Heart Mountain, as of October 21, of 9,757, not 12,000.[32] Neither man was very receptive to Pearson's ill informed accusations.

Despite a number of problems and complaints the 1942 beet crop was brought in without much trouble. S. B. Smith, of Great Western Sugar Company in Lovell, reported that by mid December 112,000 tons of beets had been refined. He added that 400 volunteers from Heart Mountain helped with the crop at various stages and that while for the most part they were inexperienced in the sugar beet business, they learned quickly and made excellent workers.[33]

During the three year and three month existence of the Heart Mountain Relocation Center, its residents made significant contributions to the local and state economies, not to mention the agricultural economies of Montana and Nebraska. Some of those who employed internees from Heart Mountain, the mayor of Lovell for example, expounded on the obligation of the Japanese as American citizens to leave the camp to work. However, no consideration was given by these individuals to the issue of how America was treating its citizens of Japanese ancestry. Economic self benefit was the only concern of the majority of those employing the residents of Heart Mountain.

Notes

1. Joseph C. O'Mahoney to Ray Bower, April 9, 1942, Joseph C. O'Mahoney collection, American Heritage Center, University of Wyoming.

2. A. B. Chapman to Joseph O'Mahoney, April 11, 1942, L. E. Laird to O'Mahoney, April 28, 1942, O'Mahoney collection.

3. A. B. Chapman to Joseph O'Mahoney, April 11, 1942, O'Mahoney collection.

4. Roger Daniels, *Prisoners Without Trial: Japanese Americans in World War II* (New York: Hill and Wang, 1993), 57.

4. B. M. Bryan to Nels Smith, May 2, 1942, Smith collection, American Heritage Center, University of Wyoming; Milton Eisenhower to Joseph O'Mahoney, May 4, 1942, O'Mahoney collection.

5. Joseph O'Mahoney to A. B. Chapman, June 3, 1942; A. B. Chapman to Joseph O'Mahoney May 27, 1942; John J. McCloy to Joseph O'Mahoney, July 25, 1942;

O'Mahoney collection.

6. Harry Attebery to Joseph O'Mahoney, May 13, 1942, O'Mahoney collection.

7. Paul Greever to Joseph O'Mahoney, May 11, 1942; Paul Stock to Joseph O'Mahoney, May 12, 1942; Harry Attebery to Joseph O'Mahoney, May 13, 1942; Don Jamieson to Joseph O'Mahoney, May 26, 1942; Jack Richard to Joseph O'Mahoney, May 23, 1942, O'Mahoney collection.

8. *Powell Tribune*, June 4, 1942.

9. Ibid.

10. *Powell Tribune*, June 11, 1942. *Powell Tribune*, June 18, 1942. *Cody Enterprise*, June 3, 1942.

11. *Powell Tribune*, July 9, 1942.

12. Ibid.

13. George Reesy to Joseph O'Mahoney, June 20, 1942, O'Mahoney collection.

14. Paul Greever,to Joseph O'Mahoney, June 29, 1942; J. A. Morrow to Joseph O'Mahoney, June 30, 1942, O'Mahoney collection.

15. Richard Jones to Joseph O'Mahoney, July 2, 1942; Paul Greever to Joseph O'Mahoney, August 11, 1942; Oliver Steadman to Joseph O'Mahoney, August 12, 1942, O'Mahoney collection.

16. *Powell Tribune*, July 30, 1942.

17. *Powell Tribune*, August 20, 1942. *Powell Tribune*, October 1, 1942.

18. *Powell Tribune*, January 18, 1943.

19. *Powell Tribune*, September 24, 1942.

20. *Heart Mountain Sentinel*, October 31, 1942. *Heart Mountain Sentinel*, November 21, 1942. *Powell Tribune*, January 7, 1943. Al Fryer to Lester Hunt, June 21, 1944, Lester Hunt collection, American Heritage Center, University of Wyoming. *Powell Tribune*, September 2, 1944.

21. *Powell Tribune*, August 13, 1942. Powell Tribune, September 3, 1942.

22. Nels Smith to Joseph O'Mahoney, September 14, 1942, O'Mahoney collection.

23. Ibid.

24. Ibid.

25. G. W. Hardy to Joseph O'Mahoney, September 15, 1942; John Fowler to Joseph O'Mahoney, September 15, 1942; Phil Schuman to Joseph O'Mahoney, September 15, 1942; Paul Pabst to Joseph O'Mahoney, September 15, 1942; Harry Kaiser to Joseph O'Mahoney, September 15, 1942, O'Mahoney collection.

26. Nels Smith to Joseph O'Mahoney, September 17, 1942, O'Mahoney collection.

27. P. B. Smith to Joseph O'Mahoney, September 21, 1942, O'Mahoney collection. *Cody Enterprise*, September 2, 1942.

28. *Powell Tribune*, September 24, 1942. *Powell Tribune*, October 8, 1942. John McElroy to
Joseph O'Mahoney, September 28, 1942, O'Mahoney collection.

29. Alex Kaufmann to Joseph O'Mahoney, September 25, 1942, O'Mahoney collection.

30. W. E. Pearson to Joseph O'Mahoney, October 13, 1942, O'Mahoney collection.

31. Joseph Smart to Joseph O'Mahoney, October 14, 1942; Dillon S. Myer to Joseph O'Mahoney, October 21, 1942, O'Mahoney collection.

32. *Powell Tribune*, December 24, 1942.

Part III

Important Institutions in Community Life at Heart Mountain

The Fujiwara family arriving at Heart Mountain in August of 1942. After seeing what was to be their home for the next three years, a number of the female internees sat down and cried.

The Sentinel Story

Bill Hosokawa

The *Heart Mountain Sentinel*, a newspaper. Born October 14, 1942, under extraordinary circumstances. Died July 28, 1945 after 145 issues, its duty done. May it rest in peace.

But it has not enjoyed a peaceful rest. Its fate has been to be exhumed time and again, to be read and studied and frequently criticized by latter-day experts for what it did or did not do in its brief lifetime. Their interest does the *Sentinel* honor for it is recognition of the impact this little eight-page tabloid newspaper had on its times.

I was privileged to be present at the *Sentinel's* birth. In fact, I had a hand in naming it. I was its editor for the first fifty-two issues. Then, in October of 1943, I, like many other residents of Heart Mountain, left the camp for life on the outside, leaving the *Sentinel* in other hands. While I no longer had any responsibility for the *Sentinel* after that date, the new editor, Haruo Imura, invited me to write a column which appropriately was called "From the Outside." This I continued until the *Sentinel* was laid to rest as a dwindling camp population made publication impractical.

Now I would like to tell you about the *Sentinel*—how it was conceived, its purpose, how it functioned, what it tried to accomplish, what it did accomplish, what it was and what it was not.

A newspaper within a detention camp—concentration camp, if you will—written, edited and published freely by the inmates themselves, would seem to be an anomaly, a paradox, but that is what the *Sentinel* was.

The *Sentinel* was the brainchild of Vaughn Mechau, better known as Bonnie Mechau, a blithe spirit and former newspaperman whose title on the War Relocation Authority payroll was reports officer. I met him within a few hours after I arrived at the camp on a hot August day in 1942.

At this point it is necessary to tell you something about myself, and how I happened to reach Heart Mountain. I had grown up in Seattle, Washington, studied journalism at the University of Washington and, unable to find a job after graduation 1937, had gone to Singapore to work on an English language newspaper. You should be aware that any kind of job was difficult to find in 1937 when the nation was still in a deep economic depression, and it was unheard of for a newspaper of general circulation to hire anyone other than a certified white Caucasian. Several of my professors had warned me of this probability and urged me to switch to some field other than journalism. I decided I would take my chances.

After a year and a half in Singapore, I moved to another job in Shanghai, worked there a year, and returned to the U.S. just five weeks before the outbreak of war on December 7, 1941. This fortunate bit of timing caused some U.S. authorities to wonder whether I was some secret agent planted by the Japanese in anticipation of doing dirty work on their behalf when war broke out. I can understand their suspicion and I mention it because it has some bearing on what I will say later.

Like other Japanese Americans in Seattle, I was evacuated to the temporary assembly center in Puyallup, Washington. The Puyallup evacuees were scheduled to be sent to the Minidoka War Relocation Authority camp in Idaho. For some still unexplained reason my wife and I and our eighteen-month-old son were separated from our friends and shipped to Heart Mountain on three hours' notice.

Heart Mountain's evacuee population when I arrived was 292, the advance contingent from Pomona which had been sent to Wyoming to prepare the way for the thousands who soon would be coming. I didn't know a single one of that first group, nor did I know many of the nearly eleven-thousand who were to populate the camp. The people I knew were in Idaho.

One recent critic of the *Sentinel* has suggested that I was named to edit the camp newspaper because I was an "accomodationist" who presumably could be manipulated by the WRA and who somehow would influence the readership in favor of our jail keepers. This critic gives the WRA much more credit than it was entitled to have. The struggling WRA did not even have a policy regarding camp newspapers at the time except that it was okay to have them—just as it did not have a policy for a lot of other matters. In the decades since hustling Indians into reservations, the United States government had acquired little experience in running concentration camps. Bonnie Mechau knew that the Heart Mountain camp would have to have a newspaper, but he had no idea what it would look like or how it would be written, edited and published, but only a few hours after we met, and learning of my professional background, he offered me the editorship of a non-existing newspaper for a non-existing community.

The camp filled up rapidly with a trainload of five or six hundred evacuees arriving every few days. There was a need to get information out to these people. Bonnie solved that problem by putting together a mimeographed—this was before computers—bulletin which told the newcomers something about the Heart Mountain camp, its area and anticipated population, what to expect of the weather, where to go to get cots, medical aid and food, who was in charge of what, that the water was safe to drink despite its taste and smell, and a lot of other basic information. Only after the camp had reached capacity and was beginning to function as a city did we get back to the idea of a newspaper.

Well, how do you go about establishing a newspaper for the residents of a totally untypical community? You study its needs and produce a product to serve them.

Let me give you a quick overview of what Heart Mountain was like. It was Wyoming's third largest city, its population trailing only Cheyenne and Casper. It was peopled by many bewildered, unhappy and angry individuals. Until very recently they had been free, self-respecting, industrious, law-abiding citizens and legal resident aliens. Overnight, for reasons beyond their control and understanding, they were transformed in the government's eyes and the public's view into such dangerous security risks that they had to be herded into concentration camps in violation of their constitutional rights. It was an extremely volatile situation and it easily could erupt once the shock of being thus mistreated wore off.

In retrospect, it would seem the federal government added insult to injury by telling Japanese Americans it was their patriotic duty to cooperate with their government in its hour of peril and we could demonstrate our loyalty by accepting whatever injustice the United States asked of us. What Washington was ordering, not asking, was that we cooperate in the suspension of our rights. And like good soldiers the great majority of Japanese Americans honored this order. Other participants at this conference no doubt will tell us why we did so, although it is pertinent to note the foolhardiness of defying orders backed by soldiers with loaded guns and very nervous trigger fingers. For the purposes of my paper, it is sufficient that I note only the mood and temper of the residents and their relationship to founding a newspaper.

The great majority of the evacuees, for a variety of reasons, decided to make the best of their lot. Some said "shikata ga nai"—it can't be helped. Others said the evacuation was a damned dirty deal but if my country is asking this of me as my contribution to the war effort, I'll accept it. And in a few, anger surfaced after they had been in the camps for a while, the shock had worn off, and they had little to do and much time to brood.

Bonnie Mechau and I agreed that people of a community like ours deserved more than a bland bulletin board type of publication that listed only vital statistics, club notices and official handouts. We saw the need for a strong community newspaper which, as in any normal American community, would print the news, provide editorial leadership, and offer a forum for commentary from both readers and editors. As with any strong newspaper, the editors would voice opinions which might not necessarily reflect all segments of community opinion. Equally important, the newspaper would open its pages to dissenting views.

There was considerable discussion about a name for the paper. I must confess I suggested not quite seriously that, since the Heart Mountain camp was in the Big Horn Basin, it should be called Big Horn Echo. We settled on *Sentinel* because the mountain stood like a sentinel over the camp, and we wanted a guardian role for the newspaper. Neil Fujita, who after military service became a prominent New York art designer, designed the masthead which featured the mountain and the word "Sentinel."

Page one would carry the week's most important news, local and national, including items about WRA policies that affected the residents. Pages two and three were devoted to local news of secondary importance, news of club meetings, weddings, births, church service schedules, lists of visitors to the camp, etc. Page four was the editorial page and page five was devoted to a variety of columns, letters from readers, essays, and general commentary from anyone who wanted to get something off his chest. In thus dedicating pages four and five, one-fourth of the available space was being reserved for opinion. Pages six and eight carried more community news and page seven was for sports.

Once the philosophy was established, we started on the mechanical detail. Jack Richard, editor and general manager of the weekly *Cody Enterprise*, assured us that his allocation of government-restricted newsprint was sufficient to take care of our needs, that his plant could set the type, make up eight tabloid pages and print up to six-thousand copies a week. The headlines had to be hand-set, that is type had to be picked out by hand from a tray as in the more primitive days of printing.

Earlier, I told you that most residents of Heart Mountain were strangers to me, but I knew a few by reputation from my experience with Japanese Americans who had worked on the Nisei press. Haruo Imura of San Francisco was one. I invited him to become the *Sentinel's* managing editor. Louise Suski, who had worked on the *Rafu Shimpo* in Los Angeles was another. She became city editor, supervising the reporters. Michi Onuma, who had experience on the business side of newspapers as well as newspaper production, was named business manager. With the help of these individuals we selected younger men and women who had picked up a little writing experience or were anxious to learn. Eventually we developed an excellent and dedicated staff, many of whom went on to newspaper, editing or advertising jobs when they left the camp. I wish I could name them all, but there is time only to mention Miwako Oana who wrote a delightful column titled "Mo's Scratchpad." She became assistant dean of Columbia University's prestigious school of journalism. Keeping up the *Sentinel's* standards was difficult because of more able, more ambitious members of the staff were among the first to leave Heart Mountain for jobs in the midwest and east as soon as the WRA implemented its relocation policy.

The *Sentinel's* copy would be written and edited in our offices in one end of a barracks building, and dropped off at the *Enterprise* by WRA employees who commuted to homes in Cody. On Friday afternoon several members of the staff, escorted by Bonnie Mechau, would be allowed to go to Cody and read proof and supervise the makeup. Then, while the ancient press was running—going clunk, clunk, clunk while it printed one sheet at a time, four pages on each side of the sheet—the staff would enjoy the luxury of dinner at the Mayflower Cafe, a great treat after the routine of mess hall food, and see a movie. We paid for our own meals and movie tickets. By the time the movie ended the printing would be nearly completed. The staff would fold the printed sheets into an eight-page paper, load the newspapers into the car trunk, and head back for camp.

Incidentally, the founding of the *Sentinel* led to two paying jobs for Heart Mountain residents at the *Cody Enterprise*. Leroy Takaichi, who with his brother had operated a printing shop in San Jose, California, and John Yamamoto, a former Los Angeles linotype operator, were hired as full-time employees to handle the *Sentinel* as well as other work being done at the *Enterprise*. Leroy and John were professionals and their skills added much to the quality of work turned out at the *Enterprise*.

The Sentinel Story

As noted earlier, the first issue was published October 24, 1942. The business details were handled by Community Enterprises, the camp co-operative that ran two canteen type dry goods stores where Heart Mountaineers could go to buy toothpaste, candy bars, canned soup, laundry soap or whatever. The paper sold for three cents a copy at the stores—the price was reduced to two cents by the fifth week—and the first edition of thirty-five hundred copies quickly sold out. Another one-thousand copies were printed and they, too, sold out. Thereafter, the press run was set at six-thousand copies.

The top story in the first issue had to do with an election being called to name delegates who would draw up a charter for self-government in the camps. The second top story reported that two railroad carloads of heavy clothing, which was to have been distributed at the Santa Anita assembly center in California, were en route to Heart Mountain. It also featured a front-page editorial announcing the birth of the paper and its goals. Looking back on it now, it is evident that my enthusiasm as a newspaperman overwhelmed more important considerations.

> The *Sentinel*, the editorial said, would try in its humble way to maintain and further the tradition of a free and watchful press. "The editors," the editorial continued, "have no illusions as to the magnitude of this task. These are not normal times nor is this an ordinary community. There is confusion, doubt and fear mingled together with hope and courage as the community goes about the task of rebuilding many dear things that were crumbled as if by a giant hand. The need for a newspaper in which the residents of this community might find expression has been urgent . . . . The *Sentinel's* shortcomings are apparent to the editors. It is their ultimate aim to distribute it without charge to every family unit. In time the editors hope to be able to publish a newspaper superior in content and format more often—twice weekly, three times weekly, and perhaps in some distant happy time, daily.

Today I blush at the expression "some distant happy time." It should be noted that at that time the WRA had no long range policy. So far as we knew, we would be kept imprisoned for "the duration," whatever that might mean. There was talk of setting up semi-permanent industrial operations in the camp and there were no provisions for release of the residents. I'm afraid we were carried away by the idea of a semi-permanent newspaper serving a semi-permanent community.

The *Sentinel* was warmly received and before long we discovered that while we were limited to printing only six-thousand copies a week, some forty-five hundred of them were being mailed out regularly from the camp post office to be shared with friends back home and in other camps.

But we did have trouble, and it came from elsewhere. I cannot remember exactly what the problem was, but my recollection is that someone in the WRA's Washington office was alarmed by the idea of a real live newspaper being published by people who were considered national security risks for readers also considered to be national security risks. The WRA understood that newspapers were necessary in the camps, but apparently had not thought the issue through. Whatever the case, the staff was told to prepare for the second issue but to be aware that it might never be printed.

Volume 1, No. 1 had been published on a Saturday. There was an explanation of sorts in Volume 1, No. 2. It said:

> The full story isn't known yet, but the *Heart Mountain Sentinel* almost died a'borning. Just a few hours after the first issue hit the street it looked as if the Sentinel were finished for the time being due to some unforeseen technicalities. Monday night it appeared as if the newspaper were definitely doomed, and the gloom was as thick as a project dust storm. Then on Tuesday morning the congratulatory wire from regional director Joseph H. Smart (published on page one) came along and there was a moment of wild elation. Since the telegram was addressed to the editor, and therefore unofficial, and because of the ominous note which could be read into the next to the last sentence, the elation was short-lived. Only after Project Director Chris Rachford called Denver for confirmation were we sure that "The Sentinel" had been reprieved. Just what had been going on in higher circles during that time is somewhat of a mystery, but it is understood that the issue went to the very top for a decision.

The telegram had said: "Heartiest congratulations to you and staff on inauguration of *Sentinel*. Delighted with organization and contents of material," etc. The next to last sentence mentioned above was: "Regardless of any barriers or disappointments, keep up the good work."

I have no recollection that the issue ever came up again, nor any memory about what had caused the fuss. Nor do I have any recollection that Bonnie Mechau put any sort of restrictions on me, or that he indicated he had been given authority to censor the publication.

How well did the *Sentinel* perform? About three years ago an organizer of this conference, Mike Mackey, asked me as part of his research for his master's thesis, to respond to some comments about Heart Mountain by historian Douglas Nelson. I would like to quote some portions of my response to Mackey relating to the *Sentinel*.

Dr. Nelson is in the audience today and I have warned him that some of my comments about his views are not complimentary. In the interest of fairness I would be happy to yield some of my time later for a rebuttal. I wrote:

> I'm not sure that Mr. Nelson understands the function of a community newspaper, which the *Sentinel* was. Such a newspaper prints the news. It pro-

vides editorial leadership. It also offers a forum for a variety of opinions, including those of the people who run the paper. If the editors don't have opinions, if they aren't ready and willing to articulate them, they shouldn't be editors. The newspaper's opinion doesn't necessarily reflect the thinking of every one of its readers. The newspaper, in its commentary sections, tries to lead community opinion which the *Sentinel* did, and not necessarily reflect the thinking of every one of its readers. Nelson notes that the *Sentinel's* position was not 'representative.' I'm not sure what he means, but no newspaper worth reading can or should strive to satisfy the demands of all its readers . . . . In addition to taking editorial stands, newspapers have an obligation to make space available to a diversity of opinion which the *Sentinel* did regularly and liberally. At no time did the *Sentinel* try to suppress or ignore opinions contrary to its own. If you will check some of the early issues, you will find a feature called 'I'd Like to See.' It was introduced as space open to residents in which 'they may think out loud, or air their pet peeves, or present theories of plans that they have been working on to improve our position . . . . We want every resident of Heart Mountain to feel that this is his newspaper, and be free to write in and express his views.' There was also an extensive letters to the editor department.

My letter to Mike Mackey continued:

If you will read the news columns, you will find prominently displayed stories about community protests against the government's decision to fence the camp, complaints about food and fuel shortages, and reports of violence in other camps. Such news coverage is in the best tradition of reporting the news. I also urge you to read our coverage of community council meetings. I think you will find the coverage balanced. Such coverage was hardly servile pandering to the authorities which Nelson seems to feel was the case. I am also puzzled by Nelson's implied criticism of the *Sentinel* for 'energetically attacking' those who 'refused to abandon the old racist stereotypes' of Japanese Americans while sparing from 'direct criticism' those 'who show any flexibility or open-mindedness.' I find nothing strange about assailing our tormentors and recognizing our friends. When Senator E.V. Robertson of Wyoming, without ever visiting the camp, sounded off about how we were being pampered, his remarks were widely published as gospel without further confirmation. Could we expect the *Casper Star Tribune* or the *Billings Gazette* or the *Laramie Boomerang* or the Cheyenne and Denver papers to investigate and refute his charges? No. The *Sentinel* was the only media voice to challenge Robertson and other critics to seek out the truth and our readers knew it and appreciated it.

Specifically, the *Sentinel* sent Senator Robertson a telegram inviting him to visit Heart Mountain and published the text on page one. The Senator did not respond but he kept sounding off.

Back in 1988 a scholarly journal called *Journalism History*, published by the Department of Journalism at California State University at Northridge, printed an article titled "Fettered Freedoms: The Journalism of World War II Japanese Internment Camps." I saw a copy of the article late in 1989. The author was Associate Professor Lauren Kessler of the University of Oregon's school of journalism. Although she had never communicated with me or had been in contact with anyone else on the *Sentinel* staff, she commented in detail on the paper. She praised the *Sentinel* as by far "the most professionally produced and edited paper" in the ten WRA camps. She said it had "the clean, competent look of a good small-town newspaper" and that the stories were "succinct and well-edited." But she also wrote some things and drew some conclusions that caused me to send her a letter running five and one half pages, single-spaced, in which I pointed out what I perceived as errors of fact or interpretation. I accused her of either carelessness or having approached the subject with preconceptions and choosing to ignore facts that did not support them. Why else would she fail to consult a primary source of information, namely me? Mine was a snotty letter and her reply, when it arrived was similarly snotty although she protested innocence. Except for one paragraph her three-page letter managed to avoid addressing my concerns.

It was obvious Professor Kessler was not about to straighten the record or give me any satisfaction. So I wrote to Professor Susan Henry, editor of *Journalism History*, which had published Professor Kessler's article, asking that my letter to the author be printed. I said I wished to provide another viewpoint in rebuttal to her flawed paper which had become a part of the literature on WRA camps available for future research.

Professor Henry's response was disappointing. Because of lack of space, she said, and because virtually everything published in *Journalism History* could be disagreed with by someone, she held "to the policy of not printing responses to anything that appears in the journal." While space limitations are real and understandable, it seemed peculiar to me that a journal dedicated to publishing scholarly research had an inflexible policy against acknowledging other viewpoints in its pages.

Why did I react the way I did to Professor Kessler's treatise? Her finding was that WRA appointed its newspaper editors because they were "accomodationists" who were in position to get preferential treatment if they toed the line. This led, she indicated, to compliant editors who, in words that I am supplying, saw no evil, heard no evil and spoke no evil where WRA was concerned in hopes of being rewarded.

The following is quoted from Professor Kessler's article:

When the newspaper" that is, the *Sentinel* "did recognize controversial issues, it invariably took the side of the administration. In the fall of 1942 when the camp first opened, inmates staged a series of unsuccessful protests and demonstrations over the erection of barbed wire around the camp perimeter. The *Sentinel* didn't cover the protests, but after the enclosure was completed, Hosokawa praised the camp administration for its 'reasonableness' and 'understanding.'

Now, if this were true, it would be an outrageous misuse of editorial responsibility. What really happened?

Let's look at copies of the *Sentinel* during that period. The issue of November 21, 1942, carried a bannerline across the top of the front page saying "Protest Petition Sent to WRA Director." The smaller headline under it said "Removal of barbed wire fence asked." The story reported that more than three-thousand adults in the camp had signed the petition whose text was included in the story. There had been much public discussion and unhappiness about the fence, but I can recall no "demonstrations." The decision of Camp leaders was to petition the WRA and this was duly reported. If this isn't coverage of an issue that affected every resident, I don't know what to call it. The fence episode took place at a time when riots in the Poston camp resulted in twenty-thousand inmates being placed under direct military guard. It would have been dangerously irresponsible to handle the Heart Mountain situation other than objectively, which the *Sentinel* did.

Checking the November 21 editorial, I found the words "reasonableness" and "understanding," but Professor Kessler had taken them out of context. Those words were in unmistakable reference to the attitude of the Heart Mountain WRA staff in listening to inmate concerns. They were not used, as Professor Kessler implied, to praise the decision to build the fence. Let me cite several other instances in which the *Sentinel* criticized what it perceived as wrong or unfair in WRA policy.

On November 14, 1942, an editorial challenged a WRA directive banning Issei—the older, non-citizen generation—from serving on the self-governing charter commission. Said the editorial: "We are opposed to the view that non-citizens must play an inconsequential role in the self-government scheme for they are indeed valuable members of the community."

On December 19, 1942, the *Sentinel* protested a Wyoming Department of Education ruling, which WRA had accepted, discriminating against Japanese Americans teaching in camp schools.

On January 9, 1943, the *Sentinel* challenged WRA regulations restricting the operation of community co-op stores on which inmates depended for everyday needs and to supplement mess hall rations.

There are many other examples to refute the charge that "accomodationist" editors at the *Sentinel* failed to exhibit zeal for criticizing the WRA when things went wrong. It must be remembered that while our civil rights were of greatest concern, most camp inmates spent more time worrying about meeting creature needs—coping with cold, dust, heat, mud, boredom, indifferent food, lack of hot water in the laundry and shower rooms, crying babies and quarrel some neighbors on the other side of flimsy barracks partitions. In the prison camp environment these were volatile issues. When the *Sentinel* scolded mess hall strikers as irresponsible instead of siding with them, it was not toadying to the WRA but expressing concern for residents who could not walk down to the supermarket and buy groceries for their families. If the *Sentinel* fretted editorially about coal supplies being disrupted by unhappy delivery crews, it had in mind the health and comfort of the residents of drafty barracks with no fuel for their stoves in sub-freezing weather. The welfare of residents was paramount where food and heat were concerned, and any responsible editor would contend that issues so vital to the public should be resolved by negotiation rather than strikes and riots. I see those positions as responsible rather than "accomodationist."

Editorial integrity was a very important element in the abnormal atmosphere of the WRA camps where there was strong and growing resentment against the injustice of evacuation and imprisonment. The reality was that the *Sentinel* could not have served its constituency for long if it bowed to the demands of every vocal minority element, and here let me identify some that we knew to be possible targets for violence: WRA employees, internal police officers, members of the Japanese American Citizens League, strongly pro-American leaders, strongly pro-Japanese leaders, members of certain clubs with roots back in pre-evacuation communities, etcetera, etcetera, etcetera.

Professor Kessler makes quite a point of the *Sentinel's* failure to cover what she calls "the biggest, and probably the strangest, story of the season: the mass arrest of thirty-two inmates for violating security. Those arrested and taken into custody by the U.S. Army were children found sledding on a hill just outside camp boundaries. None was older than 11."

Was it a legitimate news story that thirty-two little kids had sneaked under a three-strand wire fence to go sledding in a prohibited area and had been rounded up and turned over to their parents? If that was the "biggest" story of the winter, and the *Sentinel* had not published it, the rest of the stuff in the paper must have been dull indeed.

I would like to conclude by touching briefly on the *Sentinel's* treatment of the Fair Play Committee and the trial and conviction of sixty-three or sixty-five Heart Mountain residents for violation of the Selective Service Law. Other seminar speakers who were directly involved in that historic episode will tell you what the issue was all about. Since I had left Heart Mountain for a job in Iowa many months before the draft resistance movement came to a head, my comments will be based on the reading of *Sentinel* files. It is indeed true that the *Sentinel* used some rather intemperate language in criticizing the draft resisters, language that I probably would have avoided had I been on the scene. But as a newspaperman I must defend the *Sentinel's* right to publish what it believed to be right, and I also defend the way the *Sentinel* provided space for response from those it criticized.

The *Sentinel's* criticism was published in two forms. First were signed articles whose authors were identified by what are called by-lines which identify the person expressing his opinions. Second were editorials, unidentified as to authorship and published on the editorial page as the opinion of the newspaper speaking as an institution. Publication of both forms of commentary is a legitimate newspaper function. Editorials do not have the obligation to be objective or even fair. Their function is to express an opinion, to condemn or praise or propose or point with pride or alarm as the case may be. The limiting factor is that a newspaper that is excessively strident or outrageous defeats its own purpose by alienating its readers and losing its influence and subscribers.

In good newspaper practice it is obligatory to give targets of editorial attack access to its columns for rebuttal. This the *Sentinel* did, and in so doing it performed the important democratic function of stimulating thought and debate through presenting views opposed to its own. In its issue of March 11, 1944, the *Sentinel* published an editorial highly critical of the Fair Play Committee's position which urged Nisei to protest suspension of their rights by refusing to undergo the Army's pre-induction physical examination. The following week the *Sentinel* published a rebuttal from Paul Nakadate, a member of the Fair Play Committee, which began with this sentence: "Last week's editorial, 'Our Cards on the Table,' was the weakest and cheapest editorial I've seen." His letter expanding on this theme ran nearly two full columns.

The following week, March 25, the *Sentinel* published the first part of a letter from Frank Emi, a founder of the Fair Play Committee, which began: "In defense of the FPC against the intimidations and slanderous editorials of the *Heart Mountain Sentinel*, the center's newspaper, I am writing this article." It was so long that the letter was continued in the April 1 issue, taking up a total of nearly four columns of type which was somewhat longer than the original editorial. Parenthetically I might add that the record for lengthy writing in the *Sentinel* may belong to a person who originally was scheduled to speak at this symposium, Dr. Frank Inouye, whose philosophizing about democracy, life and courage ran in three consecutive 1944 issues for a total of more than seven columns of space.

The *Sentinel* led an exciting and useful life. It provided information, stimulated debate, enhanced morale during a very difficult time. It recorded events that now are fading into history. In a more direct way, the *Sentinel* shared in the sacrifice demanded by war. Two of its promising young reporters, Fred Yamamoto and Ted Fujioka, volunteered for military service and died in action. Another *Sentinel* associate, Lt. Moe Yonemura, also was killed in battle. Despite all that it accomplished, the *Sentinel* should never have been born. The circumstances that made the *Heart Mountain Sentinel* important should never have occurred.

Heart Mountain High School, 1942-1945

Mamoru Inouye

This Chronology of Heart Mountain High School is part of a larger story following the ethnic cleansing of 110,000 persons of Japanese ancestry, two-thirds of them American citizens, from the West Coast during World War II. That mass evacuation was the beginning of tens of thousands of traumatic experiences that brought one evacuee in ten to the sagebrush-covered desert of northwest Wyoming. The evacuees generally believed that after initially being herded into temporary internment camps, called assembly centers, the relocation centers would be their "permanent" homes for the duration of the war. Not fully conveyed to the internees was the War Relocation Authority's policy that the relocation centers were also temporary internment camps from which internees could be resettled in areas outside the prohibited West Coast zone. Construction of the high school at the Heart Mountain Relocation Center reinforced the internee's notion of permanency, but more significantly, was an important factor in the education of 1,700 junior and senior high school students.

BEGINNINGS, 1942-1943

Two months after the arrival of the first evacuees in August, 1942, Heart Mountain High School, comprising the seventh through twelfth grades, opened on October 12, in Block 7, which was completed as half a block. Classes were held in six barracks, each 20 feet wide and 120 feet long, partitioned into six units similar to the barracks used for living quarters. The thirty-six units included an office, store room, and thirty-four classrooms. Furnishings were sparse, with a blackboard and table for the teacher, and benches and tables for students. Desks did not arrive until January 1943.[1] The elementary schools that were constructed and furnished similarly, were described as inadequate for educational purposes.[2] No laboratories were installed and the absence of ceilings allowed disturbances from adjoining rooms to disrupt classes. A Wyoming State high school accrediting committee which visited the Block 7 school later in the school year "did not feel that the physical facilities were on a par with other schools of the state."[3] A former Civilian Conservation Corps camp in Powell was a source of equipment, but lack of space precluded its use until completion of the new school building.

The Superintendent of Education (the WRA version of Superintendent of Schools), Clifford D. Carter, who served previously in the same capacity at Torrington, Wyoming for eight years, was hired by the WRA on August 6, 1942, followed by Principal Corbett on August 12 and Assistant Principal Forsythe on August 26. Superintendent Carter contacted Civil Service officials in Denver and teachers' institutions to recruit teachers, while Principal Corbett set up a program of studies and interviewed local applicants. In accordance with a July 1942 agreement between the

Wyoming State Department of Education and the WRA, only persons qualified for certification in Wyoming could teach in the Heart Mountain Relocation Center schools. The majority of the original Caucasian teachers came from Wyoming and Nebraska. They received War Service appointments for the duration of the war and six months thereafter but could be dismissed for unsatisfactory performance at any time during the first year. Base Civil Service salaries were $2,000 per annum for instructors and $2,600 per annum for senior teachers. With the work week set at eight hours per day, Monday through Saturday, overtime was paid at time and a half for the additional eight hours on Saturday. The seemingly higher pay drew adverse criticism in Wyoming. A faculty of thirty-seven teachers was approved for the high school, but the actual number of Caucasian teachers on opening day was twenty-six.[4] Also on the administrative staff were Bernadene Schunk, Supervisor of Student Teachers, and Virginia Lynn, Student Counselor.[5] Robert W. Farmer, Robert Graham and Ray Thompson joined the faculty in December 1942,[6] but Farmer left for the army five months later.

The Caucasian teachers had had little contact, if any, with Japanese Americans prior to coming to Heart Mountain. Principal John (Jack) Corbett and his wife, Clarissa, who taught home economics, also had some doubts initially. In an interview many years later, Clarissa Corbett would admit, "Well, at first I had a little prejudice, but I will never have that prejudice now."[7] John Corbett, whose father was a teacher, was born in Cambridge, Massachusetts[8] and moved to Wyoming as a youth. He graduated in 1925 from the University of Wyoming, earning a Master's degree. He also spent a summer studying at Stanford University.[9] In 1942 Corbett was Superintendent of Schools for Lingle in Southeast Wyoming and Principal of Lingle High School, a six-year school with barely over a hundred students.[10] According to Clarissa Corbett, "When the war relocation center set up, they advertised and Jack thought it would be a good experience, so that's where we went."[11] Heart Mountain High School was fortunate to gain a capable and experienced administrator as principal.

As evacuees arrived at the Center, they signed up for work. One in ten had attended college and more than 350 internees had completed four years.[12] Only a few possessed teaching credentials because Japanese Americans were discouraged from becoming teachers in California where public schools rarely hired non-whites. Some internees with college degrees volunteered to teach and were hired following an interview with Superintendent Carter. Four regular teachers: Takayoshi Kawahara, Masami Kuwahara, Riyo Sato and Florence Tsuneishi, and thirteen assistant teachers: Kaoru Inouye, Takeo Ishikawa, Mary Ishimoto, Mitsuye Kakuuchi, Kikuye Kimura, Misako Maruyama, Eddie Matsumoto, Mary Nakagawa, Frances Bukie Nakamoto, Beatrice Otera, Martha Tomita, Sachiko Yasumi and Eiko Yokota, joined the high school faculty[13]

Among the regular teachers, Sato earned her bachelor of arts degree in art education at the California College of Arts and Crafts in June 1940 after completing the applied arts course at the same institution in May 1935.[14] Tsuneishi received her special secondary school credential in music in June 1939 after earning a bachelor of education degree at UCLA.[15] Kawahara received his general secondary school credential with a major in biological science and a minor in social science at Santa Anita Assembly Center on June 6, 1942, after earning bachelor and Master's degrees at the University of Southern California in 1941 and 1942, respectively. On September 1, 1942, Kawahara was issued a War Emergency Certificate to teach high school in Wyoming but with the proviso, "Valid at Heart Mountain Only," handwritten on the back.[16] Caucasian teachers with similar qualifications received War Emergency Certificates without such a restriction. This bias by the Wyoming State Board of Education caused discontent among the internee teachers and was the subject of a *Sentinel* editorial that urged the internee teachers to accept this discrimination for the sake of the school children.[17] After some training, other internee teachers were granted similar certificates. Their compensation was $228 per annum. Kawahara complained about his status and compensation to the U.S. Commissioner of Education only to receive a reply from the WRA Education Consultant, Lester K. Ade, who wrote, "We are treating evacuees who are working on the educational program on the same basis as all evacuees are being treated in other activities in the center other than education."[18] Medical doctors, for example, were paid the maximum rate of $228 per annum, which was set by the WRA to be less than an Army private's pay. In contrast, prisoners of war were compensated, in accordance with the Geneva Convention of 1929, commensurate with a soldier performing identical work.[19]

Some of the assistant teachers served as regular teachers and others took charge of classes for Caucasian teachers in cases of illness, emergencies or resignations. Inouye earned a bachelor of arts degree in chemistry from the University of California at Berkeley, and although classified as a science laboratory assistant, taught high school chemistry and physics. Matsumoto earned a bachelor of science degree from the Radio Institute of California and taught high school electricity and electronics.[20] Yasumi was a sophomore at UCLA before the evacuation and assisted Clarissa Corbett in high school home economics.[21] Yokota had completed a year and a half of the pre- education courses at Los Angeles City College and taught junior high English, arithmetic, spelling, and art.[22] The assistant teachers earned the praise of the administrators for being "very helpful in organizing and operating a large school smoothly and efficiently. . . [performed] many small jobs . . . many times done outside of assigned hours without thought of compensation."[23]

The original student body of 1,500 from a Center population of 10,700 was comprised of evacuees from Southern California, Santa Clara County, San Francisco and Central Washington. With immigration from Japan halted in 1924, over ninety-nine percent were American citizens.[24] The majority were evacuated prior to completion of the previous school term and spent the spring and summer of 1942 in temporary internment camps located at the Santa Anita Race Track in Arcadia and Los Angeles County Fairgrounds in Pomona, both in Southern California, and the Pacific

International Livestock Exhibition Center in Portland, Oregon. All students faced the transition from a predominantly Caucasian and integrated school to a segregated school.

The high school curriculum and class schedules were established during the two months when teachers were being hired and evacuees continued to arrive from the temporary internment camps. The results of a Stanford University graduate seminar on curriculum held in the summer of 1942 were used.[25] The educational philosophy followed the WRA's objective to resettle internees; the schools would serve as temporary institutions to prepare students for return to life outside. The curriculum reflected this objective as well as the need for accreditation by the Wyoming State Department of Education. During the first year, senior high school students were offered fifty-seven courses under ten departments: art, commercial, English, language, industrial arts, mathematics, music, science, social studies and vocational. Just two foreign languages, Latin and Spanish, were offered. Seventh and eighth graders were required to take classes in English, arithmetic, history, art and physical education. Eighth graders were also required to take science. Boys were required to take shop while girls took home economics.[26]

Class placement and selection of courses were major problems during the first year. After being set back by evacuation in mid-term, some students were further impacted by transfer to the Wyoming school system from California where large school districts enrolled students both in the fall and at mid year. Junior high school students who had completed half a year either skipped to the next grade or were forced to repeat the first semester. Senior high school students were hampered more by the limited selection of courses and the lack of chemistry and physics laboratories. Students who had studied French or German previously had to choose between Spanish and Latin. Graduation was determined by the number of credits completed, and seventy-one seniors earned sufficient credits to graduate at the end of the first semester.[27] Graduation requirements, curricula for different tracks and courses offered were described in the twenty-five-page *Students Handbook* distributed on April 30, 1943, to all senior high school students.[28] An extensive testing program was carried out to determine placement in grades and to aid in making changes in the curriculum to meet student requirements. The Stanford Terman-McNemar Test of Mental Ability, Form C, was given to all junior and senior high school students on December 15, 1942.[29]

Student activities were limited, but the journalism class under faculty advisor Sidney Melby and editor Hisako Takehara, later assisted by co-editor Alice Tanouye, began publication of a bi-weekly, four-page, mimeographed newspaper, *Echoes*, on November 12, 1942. Albert Saijo took over the editorship during the spring semester. A student government was formed, and a constitution governing the seventh through twelfth grades was ratified on December 17, 1942.[30]

Through the efforts of Ted Fujioka and the Senior Hi-Y Club, arrangements were made to move a flag pole from the former CCC camp in Powell, and the Stars and Stripes were hoisted outside the principal's office on December 22, with the Boy Scout Drum and Bugle Corps playing *To the Colors*.[31] Principal Corbett had doubts about conducting the ceremony, "I told Ted (Fujioka) that maybe students wouldn't want to salute the flag after all they've been through," but he was reassured by Fujioka that there was nothing to worry about.[32] In January 1943, *Life* magazine photographers, Hansel Mieth and her husband, Otto Hagel, visited Heart Mountain on assignment.[33] Mieth photographed a geometry class, March of Dimes benefit dance, and flag raising ceremony where Fujioka and Principal Corbett led an assembly of students and faculty in a pledge of allegiance, probably a reenactment of the ceremony held a month earlier.[34] None of the photographs were published during the war, but the flag raising ceremony was published nearly forty years later in *Time* magazine.[35] The other photographs were discovered recently and published in an exhibition catalog.[36]

Fujioka was elected the first Student Body President on February 4, 1943. Plans to publish an annual were voted down by the Student Council in concert with other Wyoming schools to conserve essential materials, such as paper, film, and copper engraving plates, for the war effort.[37] The student body chose the eagle as the school symbol over pioneers, and blue and white as the school colors over blue and gold.[38] In April 1943, the *Echoes* received a letter from Superintendent R.G. Crook of Lyman High School in Southwest Wyoming, which used the same symbol and colors. Crook wrote, "May we share with you the joy that comes when our colors wave in victory in champion for right. We send our hearty congratulations to you with a bond of friendship across the state."[39]

The eighty-member Wyoming High School Athletic Association voted to admit Heart Mountain as a member in November 1942. Principal Corbett had been a member of the Association for a number of years, and the athletic director, Ray Thompson, was a graduate of the University of Wyoming and had coached at Cody High School and other schools in the vicinity. Together they were able to schedule contests with outside schools, including several in Montana, which had a reciprocity agreement with Wyoming.[40] The first interscholastic competition was participation in the free-throw league sponsored by the *Billings Gazette* and conducted by mail. The Heart Mountain Eagles coached by internee Art Kaihatsu finished second in the ten-team league with a 19-2 record.[41] The first face-to-face interscholastic competition was a basketball game with the Lovell Bulldogs on February 27, 1943, followed by games with the Byron Eagles and Cowley Jaguars. With only outside courts at the Center, Heart Mountain played (and lost) all these games in the neighboring towns. Scores are shown in Table I. Babe Nomura led the team in scoring for the season with 28 points. The first high school team to visit the Center was the Lovell softball team on April 23, 1943. Scoring twelve runs in the first two innings, the Eagles won 18-7 before an estimated crowd of 5,000.[42] A return engagement on the Lovell diamond was canceled due to transportation difficulties.

The opening event in the auditorium of the newly completed high school on June 4, 1943, was the Senior Class Play, "Mumbo Jumbo," written by Jack Barnard and set in the living room of the summer home of the Reynolds family in Wyoming. Frank Mouri and Shogo Iwasaki took leading roles in the three-act play, which was directed by art instructor Joy Krueger with the assistance of Nobuko Okano.[43] The second event in the auditorium was the Junior-Senior Prom on June 5 where Fumiye Ishimoto was crowned queen.[44]

The first year of school at Heart Mountain was capped with commencement exercises on June 10, 1943. Music was provided by pianists and the high school sextette directed by Opal M. Carter. The invocation was given by the Reverend Father Harold Felsecker and the benediction by internee the Rev. Donald Toriumi. A total of 249 graduates received their diplomas from Project Director Guy Robertson with faculty representative Kaoru Inouye as presenter. Student speakers were valedictorian Frances Kako and salutatorian Masako Kamei. The commencement speaker was Ernest J. Goppert, Cody attorney and Wyoming State Commander of the American Legion, who gave the graduates three choices: resettle into freedom, relocate temporarily to help with the war effort or remain in the Center. Goppert added, "To all of you who are good loyal American citizens, there is given the job of so living and conducting yourselves—that your fellow citizens who are hoping to see restored to you your privileges and rights of American citizenship, are not embarrassed by your failure, be it ever so slight, of your duties and obligations as Americans." Valedictorian Kako exhorted her classmates with the closing words: "We must pledge ourselves and all the energy of our youthful enthusiasm to the future. We must take the lead, not only of other nisei but also for our parents who led our way in the past."[45]

The first year at Heart Mountain High School was difficult for the 1,500 students with different backgrounds from widely scattered communities. The normal school system in an integrated American community, which was funded by the residents and overseen by an elected school board that hired the superintendent and principal, was replaced by an autocratic segregated system operated by the WRA. Neither the Center nor the school administration had any experience in such an endeavor, and the two months between August and October 1942 were too short a time to provide adequate facilities, faculty, and supplies. The students were accustomed to considerably better educational conditions than those at the Center, and after accepting and enduring the evacuation, were disappointed with what the WRA had to offer. The Caucasian faculty, on the other hand, believed as most Americans did, that the evacuation was justified, and their attitudes and expectations reflected that view.

Little can be said about the quality of education during the first year of Heart Mountain High School. However, given the short time frame and limited resources, credit is due Superintendent Carter, Principal Corbett, and the teachers, (who left secure positions to face the unknown challenges at Heart Mountain), that classes were even held during the first year. The most significant accomplishment was that the faculty and students became acquainted with each other and adjusted to the unique circumstance of studying democracy inside a relocation center. The press and official WRA reports emphasized the accomplishments of the educational system and did not dwell on the shortcomings. Simple arithmetic would have shown that Heart Mountain High School, in the first year, had one certificated teacher for nearly fifty students and classroom space of less than ten square feet per student, without allowing any room for the teacher, stove, aisles and entry way. Not surprisingly, the Wyoming State Board of Education did not assign a rating to the school.

The WRA was interested in the social conditions, including education, at Heart Mountain, and hired Community Analyst, Dr. Forrest LaViolette, in May 1943. Dr. LaViolette came from McGill University in Montreal, Canada, where he was an assistant professor of sociology. He had also worked at the University of Washington in Seattle, where he had had contact with Japanese Americans.[46] Although registration, segregation, and labor disputes at the motor pool and hospital were major concerns of the WRA, Dr. LaViolette focused on the welfare of the students, interviewing nine Caucasian teachers, six women and three men, who were mostly members of the high school faculty, during the summer of 1943. His purpose was not an appraisal of the school system but to study how the physical conditions and equipment affected the adjustment of the students and teachers to the system, the discipline problems and the changing attitudes of the students and teachers.

Dr. LaViolette's report provides some insight into the conditions at Heart Mountain High School during 1942-1943.[47] The students were crowded into classrooms set up in barracks that were sparsely furnished with benches and a coal stove, which did not always function properly. Absences were common as the students from warmer climates were unprepared for a cold Wyoming winter. The number of textbooks for a given subject was sufficient for just one class, forcing several students to share them during the day. Books could be checked out overnight but were not always returned, further reducing the available number. The teachers generally agreed that nearly three months elapsed before the students responded to the teachers' efforts; the simplistic reason given by the teachers was that the students did not know each other. The teachers had orders to avoid mentioning the evacuation but the topic inevitably came up in civics and history classes, leading to confrontations. Seventh graders suffered through the largest classes with many changes of teachers during the year, which led to discipline problems and lack of attention to studies. Discipline problems were few, in general, but some teachers lost control of classes. Internee teachers were especially prone to this problem , but Inouye and Kawahara were singled out as being qualified teachers who did not have discipline trouble. In addition to several children of Caucasian employees, who enrolled after the first year, the high school had a minority group of kibei students—nisei who had been sent to Japan for education. Many kibei were handicapped by being set back in learning English. They were also older than their nisei classmates, who tended to resent them. The Caucasian teachers had differences with the internee teachers, other Caucasian employees in the Center's administration, internee leaders in the Center, and among themselves. Teachers who lived at the Center and participated in after-hours activities resented those who left by bus in the late afternoon to return to their homes in Powell or Cody. All groups suffered from preconceived ideas about the others and were prone to believe rumors circulated within the Center and allegations printed in the outside press. Two months before the end of the school year, the traditional teacher-student relationship appeared to have been established, and despite all the problems, twenty-one of the twenty-six Caucasian teachers who taught that first year at Heart Mountain, returned for the fall semester. The undergraduate students had very little choice.

SETTLED YEAR, 1943-1944

During construction of the Heart Mountain Relocation Center, Blocks 13 and 16 were purposely left vacant and reserved for a high school. Original plans from WRA headquarters for the new school were modified to accommodate the actual enrollment, which registered more junior and senior high school students and fewer elementary school students than predicted. Construction on the $140,000 project, carried out by Bennett & Lewis contractors of Billings, Montana, began in November 1942, with Ben B. Lummis as WRA project engineer. The exterior of the single-story E-shaped frame structure, was sheathed in gray granulated wallboard with white trim, and the interior finished with plywood and celotex. In addition to thirty-nine classrooms, the structure included a 4,320 square foot home economics room, a 5,400 square foot wood and machine workshop, a library with capacity for 12,000 volumes, a study hall, offices, and an 80 by 156 foot combination auditorium-gymnasium seating 1,100 for stage productions and 700 for basketball games.[48] Attendance figures reported subsequently in the *Sentinel* were 2,000 and 1,500 for the auditorium and gymnasium, respectively. The library had seating for fifty-two students and a collection of 3,115 gift books, 486 books purchased by the WRA, copies of fifty magazines and five daily newspapers.[49] The high school was certified as complete on May 27, 1943, by project engineer Leon C. Goodrich,[50] who had succeeded Lummis in March.

A total of 1,300 students enrolled for the fall semester, which opened on September 7, 1943. The seventh and eighth grade students were grouped according to results from the Terman-McNemar tests administered the previous year rather than alphabetically by surname as in the first year. Seventh grade students were divided into four groups, 7-1 to 7-4, and eighth grade students were divided into five groups, 8-1 to 8-5, each group consisting of the same classmates throughout the day.

Heart Mountain High School was always beset by high turnover of faculty members. Some classes were disrupted with reassignment of teachers during the middle of the semester. Superintendent Carter was called to active duty in the army from June to December of 1943, with Principal Corbett becoming acting superintendent, and Assistant Principal Forsythe becoming acting principal for six months. A number of teachers, including a few women, joined the armed forces, and the vocational agriculture instructor, Fay Thompson, resigned to join the Powell High School faculty in September 1943.[51] The total number of faculty members in the fall of 1943 was reported by the *Sentinel* to be sixty-six, including thirty-four Caucasian teachers and thirty-two internee teachers—two regular and thirty assistants. Fourteen of the Caucasian teachers were new from the spring semester. (Names of the faculty members are listed in Appendix I.)[52] The names and numbers show some slight discrepancies with the final report,[53] but not as large as those of the Annual School Report,[54] which showed the number of teachers as forty-seven appointed (Caucasian), one certified (regular) evacuee, and twenty-three non-certified (assistant) evacuees.[55]

The turnover of internee assistant teachers was even higher than that for Caucasian teachers. Internees who joined the faculty were among the first to relocate either to complete their education or obtain employment. Including the pre-school and elementary school staff, the turnover was 42 percent for the period from October 1942 through December 1943, and 203 percent for the period from January 1944 through June 1945. Despite the high turnover rate, the internees contributed substantially to the organization and operation of the high school by taking over classes until replacements were hired for Caucasian teachers who had resigned. And they worked outside assigned hours without overtime pay, which was not recognized under WRA work rules. The athletic programs were directed by Caucasian teachers, but most of the coaching responsibilities were delegated to internees. Contributions of a technical nature were especially significant. Eddie Matsumoto and Kaoru Inouye were responsible for the use of the public address system for all school functions, an area where the Caucasian staff had no training. They provided a valuable service by repairing and building equipment for the science department, recording students' voices for the language department, and repairing instruments for the music department. Inouye also rescued the athletic department from having to cancel the first basketball game with an outside school in the new gymnasium. The newly painted lines on the floor did not dry in time until he solved the problem with the application of lampblack. Inouye was especially valuable at commencement time. "Acting as class sponsor he worked many hours on the senior line-up and in perfecting the mechanics of the program. He read the names on the diplomas as they were presented. This was valuable inasmuch as the pronunciation of names was difficult for many Caucasians and because he knew nearly all the graduates personally."[56] Inouye was recognized by the *Sentinel* as one of "This Week's Heroes."[57]

The new building with regular classrooms and desks, laboratories, shops, and an auditorium-gymnasium was a major step toward normalizing life at Heart Mountain High School. The environment for learning improved considerably. The curriculum expanded to seventy-two courses offered under the ten departments, with half of the increase occurring in music.[58] On December 10, 1943, Heart Mountain High School was rated Class One by the Wyoming State Department of Education and the University of Wyoming, which allowed graduates to enter the university without examination.[59] Athletic facilities included a football field without any turf. The auditorium-gymnasium was the major facility and used extensively for school and community events.

After a year of incarceration, students adjusted to living in the Center and reconciled themselves to remaining there for the war's duration—an indeterminable length of time. School activities proliferated with the formation of clubs and organizations. Notable was the absence of an honor society. On October 19, 1943, the first printed issue of the school newspaper made its debut without a name, then was called *Re-Echoes* for one issue until the student body voted to rename it the *Eagle*. Printing was done by the *Powell Tribune*. Yoshiaki Ito was the editor with Claire Sudderth serving as faculty advisor.[60] Plans were made to publish an annual. Students with musical talents could join the orchestra, band or girls' glee club. Fred Oda served as Student Body President during the fall semester and was succeeded by Kunio Yamamoto in the spring.

The auditorium was the center of activity. The drama class under Lois Runden presented two one-act plays for the Thanksgiving assembly on November 24, 1943. George Yoshinaga starred in "A Night in the Inn," directed by Katsumi Hirooka, and Gladys Shimasaki and Susie Nakada starred in "The Calf That Laid the Golden Egg," directed by June Zaiman. Although handicapped by poor acoustics, both plays received favorable comments.[61] The drama class also participated in the Center Christmas program on December 24 with a play, "Why the Chimes Rang."[62] The Senior Class Play, "'Young April," a three-act comedy starring Stella Nitahara and Shig Otani and directed by Runden, was presented on March 31, 1944.[63] The "Coronation Ball," where Hisako Takehara was crowned queen, and the Junior-Senior Prom were among dances held in the gymnasium while smaller class parties were held in the study hall.

One of the highlights of the school year was the visit by Army Air Force hero, Sergeant Ben Kuroki, on April 26, 1944. Kuroki said, "I don't want to be acclaimed as a hero. I only did my duty."[64]

Interscholastic athletic events served as the principal means of contact with outside schools. All football games were played at the Center, and Heart Mountain teams never visited communities where anti-Japanese sentiment was high. Travel considerations were probably a factor as well. The football team, coached by Ray Thompson and internee Jack Kawasaki, won three games during the fall of 1943. (See Table II for scores.) The first interscholastic football game took place against the visiting Worland Warriors on October 1 before 4,000 fans. Both teams had opportunities to score but the game was scoreless until four minutes remained in the fourth quarter when quarterback Babe Nomura passed four yards to fullback Mas Yoshiyama for a touchdown. The standout for Worland was quarterback Ray Saito, who averaged 40 yards on five punts to keep the home team at bay. Saito was of Japanese ancestry but not interned because Wyoming was outside the prohibited West Coast zone. He would return later as captain and guard on the Worland basketball team and shortstop on the baseball team. In the second game, the Eagles routed the

Carbon County Coyotes from Red Lodge, Montana. Nomura took a hand-off from Keiichi Ikeda on the opening kick-off and raced for a touchdown on a play covering 90 yards. After sitting out the second quarter, Nomura returned in the second half to score on a 47-yard run from scrimmage. For the final game with the Lovell Bulldogs, Nomura was declared "ineligible on technicalities." The game was scoreless until Yoshiyama crossed the goal line from five yards out in the final minutes. Surprisingly, Lovell's starting line-up averaging 146 pounds was outweighed four pounds by the Eagles.[65]

Basketball was the most popular sport, and the intimacy of the gymnasium gave students their closest contact with students from the Bighorn Basin and beyond. New schools on the schedule included the Burlington Greyhounds, Cody Broncs, Deaver Trojans, Powell Panthers, Thermopolis Bobcats, and Rapelje Jackrabbits from Montana. Coached by internees Jim Uyeda and Hank Sakauye, the Eagles opened the season at home on December 15, 1943, against Thermopolis, reigning Wyoming state champions and the first high school basketball team to visit the Center. The Bobcats, averaging just an inch under six feet, had a three-inch height advantage over the speedier Eagles. Trailing 9-8 at the intermission, the Bobcats picked up the action in the second half and went on to win 29-21.[66] Behind Ikeda's 15 points, the Eagles finally won their first game on January 5, 1944, defeating Cowley.[67] The Eagles ended the season with ten wins and nine losses against taller opponents. Five-foot, seven-inch Ikeda led the team in scoring with 174 points. (Scores are shown in Table I.)

Interscholastic competition at the junior high school level occurred between Powell and Heart Mountain eighth graders in basketball. On March 1, 1944, the Eaglets visited Powell. After trailing by a score of 6 to 4 at the end of three quarters, the Eaglets soared to a 14 to 7 win. Jackie Ishikawa, Kazuo Morimoto, and John Murata scored four points each to share high point honors. In the return encounter on March 8 at the Center, the Eaglets won again by the score of 29 to 6. Chiaki Kumano and Morimoto took high point honors with six points each.[68] The trip to Powell was a rare outing, and Morimoto fondly recalled, "Coach Thompson treated everyone (for winning) to a malt and hamburger."[69]

Powell High School also competed with Heart Mountain in girls' sports. The volleyball teams met on October 30, 1943, in the Center gymnasium. The Eagle-ettes, captained by Yoshiko Hata, won two games played on a time basis. In the return match at Powell on December 4, 1943, the Eagle-ettes won two of three games. (Results are shown in Table IV.)[70] The basketball teams met in the Center gymnasium on March 11, 1944. The Eagle-ettes, led by Hata's 13 points, defeated the taller Powell team with Anna Pond scoring 12 points in a losing effort. In the return game at Powell on April 1, the Eagle-ettes were victorious again. The scoring was led by Agnes Akizuki, with nine points, followed closely by Florence Nakamoto and Norrie Yamagiwa with eight points each. (Scores are shown in Table I.)[71]

The baseball team, coached by Jack Kawasaki, split a pair of games with

Worland, losing at home and winning on the road by the scores shown in Table III. The first was a five-inning game shortened by rain. In the return engagement, a three-run homer by Tosh Umemoto was the margin of victory. George Iseri allowed seven hits, including three by shortstop Saito, who had a perfect day at the plate.[72]

The second year of Heart Mountain High School is recorded for posterity in the slick paper, clothbound, 104-page annual, titled *Tempo*, co-edited by Hannah Hayano and Fred Oda and guided by faculty advisors Kaoru Inouye, Joy Krueger and Claire Sudderth. The volume is not unlike other high school annuals except for the unique make-up of the student body, which existed at the other nine relocation high schools on the U.S. mainland. With "Ballad of Americans" as the theme, the faculty, graduating seniors and students from juniors down to seventh graders are shown together as classmates and in various school activities. In addition to the numerous photographs taken by Center photographers Bud Aoyama and Hikaru Iwasaki, drawings by Stanley Hayami and cartoons by Hideo Magara illustrate the annual.

The end of the second year was marked by commencement exercises on May 11, 1944. The 302 graduates, wearing traditional caps and gowns, marched into the auditorium to the music of the high school orchestra, directed by Phyllis Cowger. The Reverend Donald Toriumi gave the invocation, and the Reverend Father Francis T. Penny gave the benediction. Project Director Guy Robertson handed out the diplomas with the assistance of Kaoru Inouye. Paul Mayekawa and Katsumi Hirooka were valedictorian and salutatorian, respectively. The commencement speaker was Frank H. Brown, Mayor of Lovell, who spoke on "What Is Our Goal?" Mayor Brown told the graduates that academic subjects are only a means to the end of developing clear thinking. He compared the hardships faced by the evacuees at Heart Mountain to those of the Israelites'. "Like the children of Israel, who were led by Moses, the evacuees will come through with flying colors." Valedictorian Mayekawa quoted from President Roosevelt's "Four Freedoms" message and declared that "although each of us has his own aspirations and hopes for the future, there is one ideal which we all have in common—that out of the chaos and disillusionment of this war will come a new way of life, that which was described by President Roosevelt."[73]

THE END, 1944-1945

What turned out to be the last year of Heart Mountain High School opened on September 4, 1944, with enrollment still numbering 1,300, bolstered by sixty-five transfers from the Jerome Relocation Center in Arkansas. A two-week vacation was proclaimed on September 25 to harvest the Center's crops.[74] The students picked over 800,000 pounds of potatoes, harvested daikon, carrots, cabbage, and other produce, stacked thirty acres of grain, and assisted in baling seventy-two tons of straw to support the Center's livestock projects.[75] According to Superintendent Carter, the faculty was staffed better than in the previous two years with thirty-nine regular teachers, including Eddie Matsumoto, who was the only internee to teach all three years. Both

Kaoru Inouye and Takayoshi Kawahara had been drafted into the U.S. Army. The turnover of Caucasian staff continued and twelve new teachers were hired since the spring semester (See Appendix I for complete list.)[76] The Annual School Report showed forty appointed (Caucasian), two certified evacuee (one man and one woman) and eighteen non-certified evacuee teachers.[77]

The school paper, *Eagle*, reverted to a mimeographed publication with May Kakebe as editor and Janette O'Brien as faculty advisor. Evan Oyakawa served as Student Body President until he graduated at the end of first semester and was succeeded by vice-president Edith Ritchie. O'Brien also served as senior class advisor, and Mary Pagano served as advisor to the Student Council.[78]

Interscholastic athletics began with the football season. The Eagles were coached by Yosai Sakamoto until his relocation; whereupon he was succeeded by Babe Nomura with assistants Yukio Kimura and Tak Nomura. In the opening game against Worland, with less than a minute remaining, Babe Fujioka passed 14 yards to George Yahiro in the end zone for the only score. Led by co-captains, 130-pound center Yoichi Hosozawa and fullback Mas Ogimachi, the Eagles defeated Carbon County, Montana and Lovell, to remain undefeated and unscored upon (See Table II). Both streaks ended on November 4, 1944, against the Casper Mustangs, whose linemen, averaging 180 pounds, enjoyed a 30-pound weight advantage. The Eagles employed the T-formation to exploit their speed, but the Mustangs, led by 210-pound, all-State fullback Leroy Pearce, who rushed for two touchdowns, emerged victorious, 19-13. Starting at halfback for the Mustangs was Suyematsu, another Wyoming resident of Japanese ancestry who was not interned. Halfback Yahiro led the Eagles in scoring for the season with 33 points on five touchdowns and three conversions. A six-man team coached by Talbot Rudolph went undefeated through a four-game schedule and allowed only one touchdown (See Table II for scores). Earning a letter on the team was Bob Rudolph,[79] son of the coach and one of several offspring of Caucasian employees who attended Heart Mountain High School. The other Caucasian students included Rudolph's younger sister Shirley; Morris Church, son of Chief Engineer Maury A. Church; and Tom Main, son of Supply Officer Lundgren T. Main and who attended for two years. Basketball was again the most popular sport, and the Eagles, coached by internee Fuzzy Shimada, finished with six wins and four losses (See Table I for complete record).[80] New schools on the schedule included the Basin Bobcats, Rawlins Outlaws, Riverton Wolverines, Shoshoni Warriors, and Hardin Indians from Montana. Completion of eligibility at the semester break deprived Ikeda from repeating as scoring leader, and Mas Hamamoto led the team with 71 points.

No baseball team was fielded, so players participated in the Center community activities leagues.

A series of announcements in December made it clear that Heart Mountain High School would close following completion of the 1944-45 academic year. First, the War Department's Western Defense Command issued a proclamation on

December 17, 1944, stating that military considerations no longer required the exclusion of Japanese Americans from the West Coast, effective January 2, 1945.[81] On the following day, the WRA announced, "All relocation centers will be closed within six months to one year . . . . Schools will be maintained at the centers through the end of the present school year."[82] Personnel reductions were instituted with the elimination of two head teacher positions and a limit of thirty-one classroom teachers, effective February 15, 1945.[83]

The Senior Class play, "Cyclone Sally," a three-act comedy, was presented in the auditorium on April 20, 1945, with Gladys Shimasaki in the lead role. Directors were Dixie Lee Boller and James Elmore.[84] The cast was privileged to visit Powell High School on April 24 to attend a performance of their Senior Class play, "You Can't Take It With You." The group was invited to Principal Corbett's home afterwards and later had a get together with Powell's cast at the home of Margaret Rinnan, Heart Mountain home economics teacher.[85] The Junior-Senior Prom was held on May 5, 1945, in the gymnasium.

The 1945 *Tempo* was edited by Kiyoto Imai with Janette O'Brien as faculty advisor. This annual was scaled down considerably from the previous year, omitting the seventh and eighth graders but still documenting the final year's activities.

The last commencement exercise was held on May 24, 1945, with 262 graduates. Music was provided by the high school orchestra under the direction of Phyllis Cowger, a violin sextette, and the girls' chorus, directed by Mona Rudolph. The Reverend J. Clyde Keegan of the Cody Methodist Church gave the invocation and benediction. Diplomas were handed out by Project Director Guy Robertson, who was assisted by Keen Yanagi. Student speakers were valedictorian Kikuye Inouye and salutatorian Mitsuko Mutaguchi. The commencement speaker was Dr. L. R. Kilzer, Director of Secondary Education at the University of Wyoming, whose presentation was titled, "When Tomorrow Comes."[86]

As Heart Mountain High School prepared to close, the Caucasian teachers either left or transferred to other positions in the Center.[87] Superintendent Carter accepted a position as Chief of the Education and Training Subdivision with the Veterans Administration in Cheyenne.[88] Principal Corbett's abilities were recognized by the city of Laramie, which appointed him Principal of the Senior and Junior High School, effective July 1, 1945.[89] The experience and feelings of one Caucasian teacher are documented in a personal report by Irene Damme appended to Carter's final report on the Education Section.[90] Damme was hired to teach commercial subjects, but upon reporting for duty on July 1, 1943, was detailed for the summer as a part-time secretary to the Community Analyst, Dr. LaViolette. She described her work as "especially interesting and helpful because I had never known Japanese people before." Damme taught typing, shorthand, and bookkeeping until November 15, 1944, when she was promoted to guidance counselor, while also serving as the junior class advisor. She concluded her personal report with the following observations:

As I look back over my two years of work here, I feel that I might have gained the confidence of the students more quickly had I been a bit more friendly from the start. The students seemed to be afraid at first and it took quite a while to break down the barrier that seemed to exist between the students and me. . . . My experience here has proven to be extremely valuable and I am grateful that I came. When Mr. Carter contacted me for the position, I was very reluctant to accept—in fact, I allowed myself to be talked into coming. I had never been around Japanese Americans before and was afraid that I was letting myself in for a lot of trouble. On the contrary, everything has run very smoothly for me here and I have enjoyed it more than I did public school work. I encountered no discipline problems whatever and all of the students I had contact with were courteous and well-behaved.[91]

A former teacher able to offer current recollections of Heart Mountain High School is Barbara (Miller) Nyden, who joined the faculty in March 1945, fresh out of the University of Colorado at Boulder, with a major in home economics with a nutrition specialty and minors in Spanish and chemistry. Nyden remembers the physical environment at Heart Mountain as "bleakness, cold wind and very little beauty anywhere except toward the mountain." During the three months that Nyden taught seventh grade arithmetic and junior high home economics, she adapted the classwork to the students' abilities and interests and met several of the mothers, one of whom she asked to give a lecture and demonstration on flower arranging. Nyden faced a few discipline problems, mostly from kibei boys. She considers her experience at Heart Mountain as "successful and somewhat satisfying, and I liked my students, but, in truth, I did not enjoy it."[92]

The student body and internee faculty at Heart Mountain High School were in a constant state of change. In September 1943, 865 internees were banished to the Tule Lake Segregation Center with 1339 transferred in return to Heart Mountain.[93] In June 1944, the Jerome Relocation Center in Arkansas was closed and 500 internees were transferred to Heart Mountain. As early as 1943, families resettled in the Rocky Mountain states, the Midwest, or on the East Coast. High school graduates worked in the Center or outside, attended college or served in the Army. The National Japanese American Student Relocation Council, which was created in December 1942 and located in Philadelphia, worked on behalf of students, colleges and the government in making arrangements for application and admission to colleges willing to accept Japanese American students.[94] Both Ted Fujioka, who volunteered for service, and Stanley Hayami, who was drafted following graduation, were killed in action in Europe. Former teacher, Sergeant Robert Farmer, was killed in action in Italy. Although internees were allowed to return to the Pacific Coast in January of 1945, the vast majority with children waited until the end of the school year to avoid another disruption in their education. On May 25, 1945, Heart Mountain High School closed its doors permanently.

EPILOGUE

The serene beauty of Heart Mountain, overlooking what was a World War II internment camp, stands as a silent reminder of experiences that are difficult to forget despite the passage of half a century. Nearly forty years elapsed before former internees gathered for a reunion in Los Angeles in April 1982. A concrete block that was part of the boiler room and is now surrounded by plowed fields, marks the site of Heart Mountain High School.

Relocation, resettlement, or return to a so-called, "normal society," was another traumatic experience which compounded the economic, social and educational problems induced by the evacuation and internment. In spite of the crowded living conditions in the Heart Mountain Relocation Center, internees faced few threats from other internees, who were in the same situation. The outside world could be more threatening. The return from a segregated society to an integrated one dominated by Caucasians was not an easy transition and caused severe anxieties.

Our issei forebears struggled to rebuild lives interrupted by the evacuation. Some did not survive the internment, and the majority did not live to receive an apology and redress for the wartime injustices. The older nisei began to assume more responsibility in the internment camps. A number of them remained in the Heart Mountain Relocation Center during the war, rather than resettling, in order to teach and carry out other functions required to operate a community of eleven thousand people. The vast majority of Heart Mountain High School alumni persevered despite this setback in their lives and strove to establish successful careers.

The lessons of half a century ago must not be forgotten, however, as recognized in 1945 by the Assistant Project Director at the Heart Mountain Relocation Center, Douglas M. Todd, who wrote, "Little can be said on the human side of the question, however, to justify evacuation. It is an experience Americans must absorb their lessons from but resolve that it never again will occur on the grounds which gave birth to this episode in American history."[95]

TABLE I

Basketball Games*

1942-1943

Mar. 1, 1943	Heart Mtn	21	Lovell	50
Mar. 12, 1943	Heart Mtn	20	Byron	42
Apr. 7, 1943	Hcart Mtn	32	Cowley	37

1943-1944

Dec. 15, 1943	Thermopolis	29	Heart Mtn	21
Dec. 18, 1943	Lovell	21	Heart Mtn	19
Dec. 23, 1943	Heart Mtn	28	Lovell	29
Dec. 29, 1943	Cody	31	Heart Mtn	10
Jan. 5, 1944	Cowley	22	Heart Mtn	39
Jan. 12, 1944	Heart Mtn	24	Cowley	22
Jan. 14, 1944	Worland	33	Heart Mtn	17
Jan. 19, 1944	Burlington	23	Heart Mtn	38
Jan. 21, 1944	Heart Mtn	30	Deaver	21
Jan. 22, 1944	Powell	31	Heart Mtn	24
Jan. 28, 1944	Deaver	14	Heart Mtn	28
Jan. 29, 1944	Byron	24	Heart Mtn	32
Feb. 1, 1944	Carbon Co.	29	Heart Mtn	31
Feb. 5, 1944	Cody	37	Heart Mtn	34
Feb. 8, 1944	Heart Mtn	26	Worland	37
Feb. 11, 1944	Rapelje	11	Heart Mtn	42
Feb. 15, 1944	Heart Mtn	35	Byron	22
Feb. 19, 1944	Cowley	28	Heart Mtn	25
Feb. 25, 1944	Heart Mtn	42	Burlington	32

Girls Games

Mar. 11, 1944	Powell	20	Heart Mtn	28
Apr. 1, 1944	Heart Mtn	27	Powell	18

1944-1945

Dec. 15, 1944	Cowley	11	Heart Mtn	45
Dec. 21, 1944	Thermopolis	38	Heart Mtn	33
Dec. 28, 1944	Rawlins	21	Heart Mtn	19
Jan. 5, 1945	Basin	30	Heart Mtn	26
Jan. 19, 1945	Shoshoni	19	Heart Mtn	45
Jan. 24, 1945	Lovell	25	Heart Mtn	22
Jan. 29, 1945	Carbon Co.	27	Heart Mtn	37
Feb. 2, 1945	Riverton	19	Heart Mtn	41
Feb. 9, 1945	Hardin	25	Heart Mtn	38
Feb. 13, 1945	Cody	20	Heart Mtn	44

Visiting team listed first.

TABLE II

Football Games

1943-1944

Oct. 1, 1943	Worland	0	Heart Mtn	7
Oct. 9, 1943	Carbon Co.	0	Heart Mtn	25
Oct. 23, 1943	Lovell	0	Heart Mtn	6

1944-1945

Sept. 22, 1944	Worland	0	Heart Mtn	7
Oct. 7, 1944	Carbon Co.	0	Heart Mtn	60
Oct. 21, 1944	Lovell	0	Heart Mtn	32
Nov. 4, 1944	Casper	19	Heart Mtn	13

Six-man Team, 1944-1945

Oct. 6, 1944	Byron	0	Heart Mtn	31
Oct. 28, 1944	Burlington	0	Heart Mtn	44
Nov. 3, 1944	Cowley	6	Heart Mtn	46
Nov. 11, 1944	Byron	0	Heart Mtn	46

TABLE III

Baseball Games

Softball, 1942-1943

Apr. 23, 1943	Lovell	7	Heart Mtn	18

Hardball, 1943-1944

Apr. 28, 1944	Worland	3	Heart Mtn	2
May 8, 1944	Heart Mtn	7	Worland	5

TABLE IV

Girls Volleyball Games

1943-1944

Oct. 30, 1943	Powell	10	Heart Mtn	61
	Powell	24	Heart Mtn	46
Dec. 4, 1943	Heart Mtn	14	Powell	31
	Heart Mtn	31	Powell	23
	Heart Mtn	17	Powell	15

Heart Mountain High School

Appendix I

Heart Mountain High School Faculty

E.O.D.	1942-1943		E.O.D.	1943-1944		E.O.D.	1944-1945	Term.
8/42	Corbett, John			Corbett, John			Corbett, John	(6/45)
8/42	Forsythe, Ralph			Forsythe, Ralph			Forsythe, Ralph	
8/42	Schunk, Bernadene			Schunk, Bernadene			Schunk, Bernadene	(6/45)
10/42	Lynn, Virginia			Lynn, Virginia			Lynn, Virginia	(10/44)
						3/45	*Anderson, Glenice*	
9/42	**Baimonte, John**			Baimonte, John			Baimonte, John	(11/44)
			6/43	**Ballinger, Dan**	(6/44)			
10/42	**Bell, Frances**	(6/43)						
						8/44	**Boyer-Boller, Dixie Lee**	
						8/44	**Broska, Bonnie**	
9/42	**Bugbee, Howard**			Bugbee, Howard	(1/44)			
9/42	**Bugbee, Thelma**			Bugbee, Thelma			Bugbee, Thelma	
8/42	**Carter, Opal**			Carter, Opal			Carter, Opal	
3/43	*Chambers, Russell*			Chambers, Russell			Chambers, Russell	
9/42	**Chase, Clarice**	(4/43)						
	Christie, Cameron	(4/43)						
	Christie, Phyllis	(4/43)						
			6/43	**Clark, Ernest**			Clark, Ernest	
4/43	*Clausen, Clyde*			Clausen, Clyde	(2/44)			
4/43	*Clausen, Wilmetta*			Clausen, Wilmetta	(2/44)			
						8/44	**Clayton, Betty**	(2/45)
			6/43	**Colleran, Martha**	(1/44)			
						7/44	**Cooper, Jean**	
9/42	**Corbett, Clarissa**			Corbett, Clarissa			Corbett, Clarissa	(6/45)
			6/43	**Cowger, Clifford**			Cowger, Clifford	
			6/43	**Cowger, Phyllis**			Cowger, Phyllis	(5/45)
			7/43	**Damme, Irene**			Damme, Irene	(5/45)
9/42	**Davis, James**	(12/42)						
						7/44	**Domenico, Lillian**	
			6/43	Dougherty, Frances	(8/43)			
						12/44	*Elmore, James*	
			6/43	Evans, Wesley	(6/43)			
12/42	*Farmer, Robert*	(5/43)						
			1/44	*Givens, Edna*	(2/44)			
9/42	**Feemster, Elizabeth**			Gladden, Elizabeth			Gladden, Elizabeth	
			9/43	**Gladden, James**			Gladden, James	

93

Appendix I (cont.)

Heart Mountain High School Faculty

E.O.D.	1942-1943		1943-1944		1944-1945	Term.
12/42	*Graham, Robert*		Graham, Robert		Graham, Robert	(10/44)
				8/44	**Greene, Bernis**	
				9/44	**Hill-Wyrough, Lorna**	
9/42	**Hillers, Sally**	(12/42)				
		6/43	**Hittinger, Ruth**	(7/44)		
10/42	**Hunt, Lee**	(3/43)				
10/42	**Hunt, Mary**	(3/43)				
		3/44	*Johnson, Marilynn*		Johnson, Marilynn	(11/44)
		1/44	*Jones, James*		Jones, James	(3/45)
		2/44	*Kassing, Alberta*		Kassing, Alberta	
		3/44	*Kautzman, Betty*		Kautzman, Betty	
9/42	**Kawahara, Takayoshi**		Kawahara, Takayoshi	(4/44)		
9/42	**Kribbs, Urban**	(12/42)				
9/42	**Krueger, Joy**		Krueger, Joy		Krueger, Joy	
9/42	**Kurtz, Lois**		Kurtz, Lois		Kurtz, Lois	
9/42	**Kuwahara, Masami**					
				7/44	Lee, Dorothy	(8/44)
8/42	**Lewis, Marjorie E.**		Lewis, Marjorie E.	(6/44)		
11/42	*Lewis, Marjery R.*		Lewis, Marjery R.	(11/43)		
		7/43	**Manley, Betty**	(11/43)		
			Matsumoto, Eddie		Matsumoto, Eddie	
		11/43	*McCartney, David*		McCartney, David	(10/44)
9/42	**Melby, Sidney**		Melby, Sidney	(10/43)		
				3/45	*Miller, Barbara*	
		10/43	**Morton, Jean**		Morton, Jean	
9/42	**Myers, Ruth**		Myers, Ruth		Myers-Irwin, Ruth	(1/45)
				7/44	**Neikirk, Carl**	(3/45)
				11/44	*Nelson, Robert*	
9/42	**Niland, Mary**	(8/43)				
		3/44	*O'Brien, Janette*		O'Brien, Janette	
		7/43	**Pagano, Mary**		Pagano, Mary	
				7/44	**Rinnan, Margaret**	(5/45)
				9/44	**Rudolph, Mona**	
				9/44	**Rudolph, Talbot**	
3/43	*Runden, Lois*		Runden, Lois	(8/44)		

Appendix I (concl.)

Heart Mountain High School Faculty

E.O.D.	1942-1943		1943-1944		1944-1945	Term.
		6/43	Samuelson, Alfred	(8/43)		
				1/45	*Sanzenbacher, Dorothea*	
		6/43	**Sanderson, Lynn**		Sanderson, Lynn	
9/42	**Sato, Riyo**					
		1/44	*Satorius, Richard*		Satorius, Richard	
1/43	*Sparlin, Alberta*	(6/43)				
9/42	**Steinheider, Juliana**		Steinheider, Juliana	(1/44)		
8/42	**Story, Adeline**	(6/43)				
		7/43	**Sudderth, Claire**	(8/44)		
1/43	*Sudin, Samuel*	(7/43)				
		9/43	**Sutherland, Eva**	(9/44)		
		2/44	*Swisher, Lula*		Swisher, Lula	
8/42	**Thompson, Fay**		Thompson, Fay	(10/43)		
		1/44	*Thompson, Geneva*	(7/44)		
12/42	*Thompson, Ray*		Thompson, Ray	(9/44)		
9/42	**Tsuneishi, Florence**					
		3/44	*Underwood, Verne*	(8/44)		
9/42	**Valley, Aurelia**		Valley, Aurelia	(8/44)		
		8/43	**Vonburg, Lois**		Vonburg, Lois	
		3/44	*Wilkins, Marie*		Wilkins, Marie	
				9/44	**Wolman, Bernice**	
8/42	**Wood, Earl**	(10/42)				

Notes: Compiled from Corbett & Forsythe, Heart Mountain Eagle, Echoes, Sentinel, & Tempo
New teachers at fall opening in bold type
Hires after fall opening italicized
Dates are entered on duty dates
(Dates) are termination dates as of July 1945

Notes

1. John K. Corbett and Ralph Forsythe, *Final Report*, 1945, Education Section, Heart Mountain Relocation Center, Record Group 210, War Relocation Authority records, National Archives and Records Administration, Washington, DC (hereafter cited as RG 210 WRANA).

2. Paul L. Christensen, "An Evaluation of Certain Phases of Heart Mountain Elementary Schools" (master's thesis, University of Wyoming, 1943), 91.

3. Corbett and Forsythe, *Final Report*.

4. Names are shown in bold type in Appendix I

5. Corbett and Forsythe, *Final Report*.

6. *Heart Mountain Sentinel*, December 12, 1942.

7. Clarissa Corbett interview, November 13, 1979, Biographical file, American Heritage Center, University of Wyoming.

8. *Heart Mountian Echoes,* November 25, 1942

9. EmmaJo Spiegelberg to author, March 24, 1996.

10. *Wyoming Education Directory*, 1941-1942.

11. Clarissa Corbett interview.

12. *Heart Mountain Sentinel*, November 14, 1942.

13. Ibid., October 31, 1942.

14. Riyo Sato to author, January 25, 1996.

15. Paul Tsuneishi to author, December 1995.

16. Takayoshi Kawahara to author, March 24, 1995.

17. *Heart Mountain Sentinel*, December 19, 1942.

18. Lester K. Ade to Takayoshi Kawahara, January 5, 1943, RG 210 WRANA.

19. Louis Fiset, *Imprisoned Apart: The World War II Correspondence of an Issei Couple* (Seattle: University of Washington Press, 1997), 42-43.

20. Heart Mountain High School Annual, *Tempo*, 1944.

21. Sachiko (Yasumi) Koto to author, June 4, 1996.

22. Eiko (Yokota) Koto to author, February 20, 1996.

23. Corbett and Forsythe, *Final Report*.

24. Christensen, "Heart Mountain Elementary Schools," 13.

25. Thomas James, *Exile Within: The Schooling of Japanese Americans 1942-1945* (Cambridge: Harvard University Press, 1987), 38-39.

26. Clifford D. Carter, *Summary Report of the School Program*, April 1945, RG 210 WRANA.

27. *Heart Mountain Echoes*, March 10, 1943.

28. Heart Mountain High School, *Students Handbook*, April 1943.

29. Corbett and Forsythe, *Final Report*.

30. *Heart Mountain Echoes,* December 22, 1942.

31. *Heart Mountain Sentinel,* December 24, 1942.

32. Ibid., August 12, 1944.

33. Ibid., January 23, 1943.

34. *Echoes*, January 27, 1943.

35. Jane O'Reilly, "The Burden of Shame," *Time* (August 17, 1981): 32.

36. Mamoru Inouye and Grace Schaub, *The Heart Mountain Story: Photographs by Hansel Mieth and Otto Hagel of the World War II Internment of Japanese Americans* (Los Gatos, California: published privately, 1997).

37. *Heart Mountain Echoes*, April 16, 1943.

38. Ibid., March 17, 1943.

39. Ibid., April 23, 1943.

40. Corbett and Forsythe, *Final Report.*

41. *Heart Mountain Sentinel*, March 20, 1943.

42. *Heart Mountain Echoes*, April 30, 1943.

43. Program from Heart Mountain High School Play, *Mumbo Jumbo*, June 4, 1943.

44. *Heart Mountain Sentinel*, June 12, 1943.

45. Ibid., June 5 and 12, 1943.

46. Ibid., May 15, 1943.

47. Forrest LaViolette, *Interviews with School Teachers*, Heart Mountain Community Analysis Report, September 1, 1943, M1342, Roll 16, National Archives Microfilm, 1986.

48. *Heart Mountain Sentinel*, October 24, 1942.

49. Corbett and Forsythe, *Final Report*.

50. Leon C. Goodrich, Memorandum to D. M. Todd, May 27, 1943, RG 210 WRANA.

51. *Heart Mountain Sentinel*, September 18, 1943.

52. Ibid., September 4 and 11, 1943.

53. Corbett and Forsythe, *Final Report*.

54. Clifford D. Carter, *Annual School Report*, August 9, 1944, RG 210 WRANA.

55. The total of forty-seven Caucasian teachers is too high and erroneously includes teachers hired during the year to replace those who had resigned. Such cases should have never been reported as one position.

56. Corbett and Forsythe, *Final Report*.

57. *Heart Mountain Sentinel*, June 17, 1944.

58. Carter, *Summary Report*, April 1945.

59. *Heart Mountain Eagle*, December 14, 1943.

60. Ibid., November 2, 1943.

61. *Heart Mountain Sentinel*, November 20 and 27, 1943.

62. Ibid., December 31, 1943.

63. Ibid., April 8, 1944.

64. Ibid., April 29, 1944.

65. Ibid., October 2 , 16, 23 and 30, 1943.

66. Ibid., December 11 and 18, 1943.

67. Ibid., January 9, 1944.

68. *Heart Mountain Eagle*, March 7 and 14, 1944.

69. Raymond Uno, "Tracking the Class of 1948 of Heart Mountain, Wyoming" (paper presented at *After 50 Years—Japanese American History: The Heart Mountain Experience*, Northwest College, Powell, Wyoming, May 21, 1995).

70. *Tempo*, 1944.

71. *Heart Mountain Eagle*, March 14, April 3, 1944.

72. *Heart Mountain Sentinel*, April 29 and May 13, 1944.

73. Ibid., May 13, 1944.

74. *Heart Mountain Eagle*, September 22, 1944.

75. Alden S. Ingraham, Memorandum to Clifford D. Carter, October 19, 1944, in Corbett and Forsythe, *Final Report*.

76. Heart *Mountain Sentinel*, September 2, 1944.

77. Ralph A. Forsythe, *Annual School Report*, July 19, 1945, RG 210 WRANA.

78. *Tempo*, 1945.

79. *Heart Mountain Sentinel*, September 23, October 14 and 28, November 4 and 11, 1944.

80. *Tempo*, 1945.

81. *Heart Mountain Sentinel*, December 23, 1944.

82. Dillon S. Myer, *Uprooted Americans* (Tucson: University of Arizona Press, 1971), 188-89.

83. Guy Robertson, Memorandum to Dillon Myer, January 5, 1945, RG 210 WRANA.

84. *Heart Mountain Eagle*, March 9, April 6, 1945.

85. Ibid., May 4, 1945.

86. Heart Mountain High School Commencement Program, May 24, 1945.

87. *Heart Mountain Sentinel,* May 26, 1945.

88. Ibid., May 19, 1945.

89. Ibid., Dec. 23, 1944.

90. Carter, *Summary Report of the School Program,* April 1945.

91. Irene H. Damme, personal report attached to, Clifford D. Carter, *Summary Report of the School Program*, April 1945.

92. Barbara (Miller) Nyden to author, December 15, 1995.

93. *Heart Mountain Sentinel*, October 9, 1943.

94. Corbett and Forsythe, *Final Report.*

95. Douglas M. Todd, *Cover Report*, 1945, Operations Division, RG 210 WRANA. The author wishes to acknowledge the assistance, documents and photographs received from Rick Ewig and Jennifer King of the University of Wyoming's, American Heritage Center, Michael Mackey, Hansel Mieth, Jennifer Mikami of JANM, Barbara Nyden, Seizo Oka of JAHA, Aloha South of NARA, EmmaJo Spiegelberg of Laramie Senior High School and former internees Jimmie Akiya, Ed Chikasuye, Ernest Hanada, Yoichi Hosozawa, Kaoru Inouye, Takayoshi Kawahara, Grace Kawakami, Dr. Wright Kawakami, Eiko Koto, Sachiko Koto, Katsumi Kunitsugu, Richard Kushino, Eiichi Sakauye, Riyo Sato, Paul Tsuneishi, Haruo Yamaji and Alice Yamane.

The Heart Mountain Hospital Strike of June 24, 1943

Louis Fiset

INTRODUCTION

On October 31, 1942 the *Heart Mountain Sentinel* published a brief but laudatory article on the project's hospital under the headline, "Camp Hospital Expands, Among State's Best." With five wards and three operating suites for major and minor surgeries and emergencies, the writer cited it as one of the largest and best equipped hospitals in Wyoming. The seventeen-wing facility was staffed by 150 employees, including nine physicians, ten registered nurses, three graduate nurses, and forty-nine nurses aides. Others included ten licensed pharmacists, eleven dentists, and three optometrists, as well as additional employees to staff the public health department and conduct sanitary inspections in the community.[1] Interestingly, the reporter's optimism concerned Army officials who feared a backlash from an angry public who might interpret the new hospital as coddling.[2]

The *Sentinel*, however, painted an inaccurate picture of actual conditions at the project hospital. Lack of equipment and an acute shortage of supplies hampered operations, forcing the physicians to transport patients to the nearby towns of Cody and Powell, or as far away as Billings, Montana, for surgeries or therapies not yet available at the center. Back-ordered supplies failed to arrive, causing the chief medical officer, Dr. Charles E. Irwin, to scramble for basic supplies such as swabs, needles, and drugs, on the local economy.

More importantly, because of the War Relocation Authority's (WRA) delay in recruiting a suitable chief nurse for the hospital, the non-professional staff, which would grow to more than three hundred, was poorly organized, developed little professional discipline, and became unmanageable. The chief medical officer and his appointed staff lacked cultural awareness and exerted poor judgment when handling escalating problems with the Japanese medical staff. The physicians themselves, having suffered loss of prestige after being forced to abandon their prewar medical practices and accept demeaning salaries and spartan living conditions in the relocation centers, escalated prewar professional jealousies and rivalries during their confinement, and turned on each other, affecting the whole hospital. As a result, resentments built up against the Caucasian authority and resulted in two hospital walkouts in 1943.

An examination of the events leading up to these strikes may provide clues to the causes of other inter-group conflicts at both Heart Mountain and the other nine relocation centers administered by the WRA.

EARLY DAYS OF HEART MOUNTAIN HOSPITAL

The hospital first opened as a clinic on August 12, 1942, following the arrival of one evacuee doctor, a senior medical student, a registered nurse, and an evacuee student nurse. They were among an advance group of 292 men and women from the Pomona Assembly Center sent to help prepare the center for the later arrival of ten thousand residents from Pomona and the Santa Anita Assembly Centers.[3] With a Public Health officer present on loan from the Wyoming State Health Department as an overseer, the clinic saw its first patients in a converted recreation hall in Block 1. It was a crude beginning, with sheetless army cots, water unfit for use, equipment borrowed from physicians' own personal kits, and sterilization of instruments provided from the heat of steno cans. One of the two appointed (Caucasian) nurses on duty at the time explained:

> We were giving baths in fire buckets. We had no towels, wash cloths, or soap. We did have blankets, mattresses, and pillows. For a long time it was quite a common sight to see patients lying without pillow cases on their pillows; maybe they would be covered with towels and maybe they wouldn't.[4]

On August 13th a worried Dr. G.D. Carlyle Thompson, the WRA's chief regional medical officer wrote of his concerns that the Army Corps of Engineers might not complete construction on the seventeen-wing hospital by their August 20, deadline.

> The foundation of the power house has just been poured and the chimney is still in the process of building. None of the wards is completed. Only the foundation of the mess hall has been laid. There has been absolutely no work done on the steam lines and there are major gaps in the plumbing. None of the floors is down.[5]

Although two carloads of medical equipment had arrived by August 13, equipment for the one hundred bed hospital unit and fifty and twenty-five bed expansion units were still "in transit," as was diagnostic x-ray equipment. Because of the unavailability of necessary surgical equipment, the first surgical case, a Cesarean operation, had to be sent out to a surgeon in nearby Cody, on September 4, 1942. By November 24, nearly seven months after the evacuation from the West Coast began, less than seventy-five percent of the 175 bed units were on hand, and instrument sterilizers for each ward, as well as sterilizers for the obstetrical delivery room, and a disinfector, were still missing.[6] Medical students provided their personal microscopes to enable minimal blood work in the reagent-poor medical laboratory.

Despite these handicaps, the resourceful staff had treated 178 inpatients, with fifty-four still on the wards by October 1, less than two months after its opening.

The average hospital stay was eight and one-half days. The hospital's success included the arrival of two new-borns.[7]

APPOINTED PERSONNEL

Heart Mountain's chief medical officer, Dr. Charles E. Irwin, arrived at the project on August 17. He assumed overall responsibility for hospital operations with instructions from his superior, Dr. Thompson, to run the facility autonomously. His orders were to develop and maintain the medical staff, run the public health program, whose mission was to check communicable diseases and prevent epidemics, procure all necessary equipment and supplies, and oversee the steam laundry for the entire center. Because of his clinical background in radiology and surgery,[8] he was expected to provide care for the center residents, as well. In addition to Thompson, Irwin was accountable to the project director.

United States Public Health Service advisors to the WRA recommended in June 1942 that one nurse be made available for every two hundred residents and one physician for each one thousand residents.[9] These optimistic projections proved unattainable because of the increasing drain on medical manpower caused by the war and because too few Japanese physicians and nurses were available to meet this need.[10] The goal, which would have provided one nurse for every five patients on the wards far exceeded Dr. Irwin's more modest plan to provide eighteen to twenty Caucasian nurses to supplement what the Japanese could contribute. This would have placed one nurse for each 350 residents. In fact, his staff never included more than ten total nurses at any one time. Recruitment of civil service nurses was difficult because the WRA had to compete with hospitals and clinics throughout the country begging for help to replace staff going off to war, and were offering higher salaries and more comfortable working conditions. Turnover in Caucasian staff at WRA hospitals was high due to both spartan and difficult living conditions, and difficulties of getting along with the Japanese staff. Recruitment of a chief nurse for the project hospital proved the most difficult task of all, and the delay in finding someone to accept long term appointment led to serious consequences for the hospital.

The first chief nurse, Mrs. Martha Partridge, arrived with Dr. Irwin on August 17, to relieve Miss Gertrude Wetzel who had been on hand as a temporary coordinator to greet the first arrivals. Partridge soon demonstrated she was unequipped to handle the daunting task of setting up a hospital from scratch, and her inability to get along with Irwin quickly led to a loss of confidence. The evacuee physicians, who had no say in her hiring and were bristling at the idea of taking orders from a woman, cooperated with Dr. Irwin in communicating the medical staff's dissatisfaction to Dr. Thompson, hoping that with her departure they themselves might take over the organization and running of the hospital. Partridge left the project after only six weeks on the job.[11]

At the time of Mrs. Partridge's departure in October, the physicians' ranks swelled to nine, providing one physician for every eleven hundred residents, more favorable than the 1 to 1,500 ratio considered by public health officials as the minimum acceptable standard during wartime. (See Table). This physician-to-population ratio exceeded that for seventeen states in 1940.[12] Although no board certified specialists were among the group, at least three competent, general surgeons (Kimura, Nakaya, and Hanaoka) were represented, as well as an obstetrician [Kimura], and a pediatrician [Ito].

The nursing staff was also at its peak, with ten Japanese registered nurses (RN) and graduate nurses, and five appointed nurses. Although at full capacity this number could provide only one nurse for every thirteen ward patients, it nevertheless compared favorably with the nurse-to-patient ratios at other centers.

Unfortunately, a decline in professional staff soon followed, beginning in November, from which the hospital would never recover.

LACK OF ORGANIZATION

Mrs. Partridge's departure left a void in the office of chief nurse that would last for three months. During this time the hospital enjoyed little, if any, organizational leadership. Irwin had no administrative assistant on whom to delegate tasks that would free up time to take over the chief nurse's official duties. This would have provided an opportunity for the Japanese physicians to step forward and model the hospital after their own perceived needs. It is unclear the extent to which they possessed the necessary skills to organize the ever growing institution. In addition, the doctors were becoming very busy, especially now that some physicians were relocating in search of medical opportunities elsewhere.[13] Many residents, having come from farm areas in Southern California where rural medicine was more primitive and less available than in urban areas, were taking advantage of the opportunities for free medical care. Also, because of spartan living conditions in the center's barracks, with their lack of running water and lavatory facilities, home care and post-illness recoveries with family members in attendance were difficult, making hospital patients out of individuals with otherwise minor illnesses. This took away nursing staff from the outpatient clinic areas, making the doctors' time less efficient.

More important, the doctors were themselves unorganized as a group. As a result of developing factions, jealousies, and professional rivalries that preceded their movement to Heart Mountain, which increased with their demeaning circumstances, the physicians expended much energy attacking each other, uniting only against a common opponent, the administration, that obligated them to toil under oppressive conditions. A disorganized and resentful hospital staff greeted Margaret Graham, the new chief nurse, on her arrival at the project in January 1943.

THE MARGARET GRAHAM INCIDENT

The hospital employed more than six hundred workers, most of whom had little or no previous experience in hospitals and were non-professionals drawn from the Heart Mountain population and trained on the job. Workers were hired for the dietary kitchen and mess hall, as clerks, secretaries and other front office workers, clinic section aides and orderlies, ambulance drivers, nurses aides, laundry workers, janitors and maintenance workers. The majority of hospital employees were under twenty-five years of age, ranging in age from fifteen to seventy-one.[14] All came from the imprisoned population whose pro-rated salaries of $12 to $16 per month provided them with little more than pin money. For many the resentment of incarceration spilled over to a general resentment of all authority, including that of the hospital administration. As a fringe benefit of hospital employment many of the workers, especially the more youthful ones, felt fun should be part of the job. As a result the hospital, over time, gradually became a meeting place for off-hours recreation. The mess hall became a gathering area away from the drab and unexciting barrack life, and activity went on late into the night, at the expense of patients recovering in the surrounding wards. Parties became commonplace occurrences. Cheers followed lunch hour home runs on the makeshift diamond between the nurses' quarters and the obstetrics ward. From a hospital administrator's point of view, the hospital staff was amok.

In addition, the hospital mess hall workers were on the Transportation and Supply Department payroll, as were all mess hall workers. But because the hospital mess hall was an integral part of the hospital complex, the workers fell under the natural authority of the chief medical officer. But the invisible Dr. Irwin exerted little control over the workers, who preferred to answer to their own, more permissive steward, Mr. Haller.

Expectations of the non-professional staff toward how the hospital should be run was building for five months, and a collision between the new, no-nonsense chief nurse and the youthful workers and seething professional staff seemed inevitable.

On January 13, 1943, Margaret Graham arrived at the project, having been dispatched from the Minidoka Relocation Center by Dr. Thompson. This new assignment would mark her third as a chief nurse in WRA hospitals. She brought a reputation of competency and an ability to perform her assigned duties in a prison hospital environment. Soon, however, she revealed herself to be brusque in demeanor, with little patience for the gross inefficiencies and lack of organization that confronted her.[15] Without regard for the etiology of the "pathological" conditions facing her, she set forth to clean up the mess. The evacuee registered nurses, the student nurses, and the majority of the nurses aides, all of whom were trained by the nursing staff, reluctantly saw the need for her presence and supported her efforts. The non-professional staff, however, saw trouble ahead with the potential loss of their "fringe benefit" and immediately began circulating a petition designed to rid the community of this

individual they described as "dictatorial, snoopy, brusque, uncooperative and prejudiced." It was to be a single incident involving Miss Graham and the doctors, however, that resulted in a walkout to protest her authority.

With reorganization of the hospital came reshuffling of office space and
office furniture from temporary into permanent quarters. On February 11, less than
one month after her arrival, and under Irwin's instruction, but without his first advis-
ing the doctors, Miss Graham removed desks from the doctors' quarters, and in so
doing piled the contents of the drawers and desktops on the floor. This enraged three
of the doctors (Suski, Ito, and Hanaoka), who may have been looking for an excuse
to react. The three immediately signed a circulating petition demanding her removal,
and further, requested an audience with Project Director Guy Robertson later in that
same day. The petition, dated February 13, 1943, specifically omitted the office of
the chief nurse as the source of their protest, directing their demands squarely at Miss
Graham who was seen as "antagonistic, abusive and dictatorial beyond reason" and a
detriment to the morale of the hospital. The petition carried three hundred signatures.[16]

In the meantime the on-duty medical staff refused to open the clinic; the
entire outpatient clinic, with the exception of the evacuee RN in charge, walked out
in sympathy with the doctors. As patients left the hospital the pharmacy put up a sign
"ON VACATION."[17]

Following the hearing with the doctors, in which Robertson sided with the
physicians, the project director sent a memorandum to his subordinate, Dr. Irwin, outlining his reasons for supporting them. He cited the employee staff as a loosely knit
organization unaccustomed to discipline, organization, and hard work, and who
would resent anyone who attempted to establish hospital discipline and organization.
This resulted from the project's failure to successfully recruit a long term chief nurse
to train and guide the employees and who could develop the hospital into an efficient
organization, having to rely instead on staff unfamiliar with hospital protocol and
unaccustomed to the strict discipline required in most hospitals. Although those tasks
might naturally have shifted onto Irwin's shoulders, his staff "have had too much
work to do to be able to give time and attention to this office which is outside their
responsibility as to details of performance."

More important, to Robertson's eyes, was the general opinion among the
hospital workers that Miss Graham appeared to exhibit a racially superior attitude and
demonstrated bad manners in her general conduct and attitude. He dismissed the
racial feeling as a mutual antagonism based upon her strict discipline and her failure
to gain cooperation in the conduct of her office. But at the same time he confided to
Irwin that he believed Graham too gruff and with too high expectations of inexperienced help. He also placed responsibility on the evacuee medical and nursing staff
for having too little understanding of the difficulties of the tasks burdening the chief
nurse, as well as demonstrating too little cooperation from the outset. Robertson
encouraged both sides to work out "an amicable and satisfactory conclusion for the

peaceful and efficient operation of the hospital."[18]

Miss Graham, upon receiving a copy of the memorandum, became enraged and wired her resignation to Dr. Thompson. In a personal letter to Miss Stuart, Thompson's chief nurse assistant, Graham blamed both Irwin and Robertson for failing to back her.[19] Thompson, in turn, now faced with the difficulty of recruiting a new head nurse, was furious with Irwin whom he held responsible for the whole affair and thought should have taken the heat rather than the chief nurse. In his mind the "books on the floor" incident was used by the physicians to gain their point, which was to run the hospital, including the nursing service details.[20] But there was little Thompson could do in light of the resignation but attempt to recruit another chief nurse from the dwindling employee pool.

The walkout ended quickly, with the employees returning to work for the sake of the residents, and knowing the administration was on the side of the evacuees. The hospital continued to provide much needed service to the community. By spring the last of the delayed equipment had arrived, making Heart Mountain a fully operational hospital. The need to farm out surgeries to outside hospitals dwindled to only the most difficult medical situations. In March, the camp population stood at 10,691.[21] But now there were six evacuee physicians, a net loss of two from the previous month, dropping the physician-to-population ratio to 1 to 1,781, below the minimum acceptable wartime standard.

The month long interim period between Graham's departure and the arrival of her replacement, Miss Anna Van Kirk, offered yet a second opportunity for the evacuee physicians to take control of the hospital. That they failed to take advantage of the opportunity resulted from their own internal dissension.

PHYSICIAN DISCONTENT

Dr. Wilfred Hanaoka arrived at Heart mountain with the advance group from the Pomona Assembly Center the previous August. While at Pomona he had become the hospital's chief physician, which served a population of 5,681, mostly from the Los Angeles area.[22] Because of his experience organizing that medical unit, he volunteered to help set up the Heart Mountain facility and thus stepped into the position of assistant to the chief medical officer, Dr. Charles Irwin. A month later six physicians were on duty. Four, including Hanaoka, left behind prewar practices in Los Angeles; three of the group practiced at the Pomona Assembly Center. Only Dr. Robert Kinoshita, from Medford, Oregon, was an unknown outside the greater Los Angeles area.

Although Hanaoka's colleagues accepted his role as Irwin's assistant, it nevertheless rankled the others that he should have that status while being the youngest physician in the group, at thirty-four. He had received his medical license in 1935, ranking him only fourth in professional seniority. Asian culture places strong emphasis on age and experience, and certainly the older Dr. Ito, at fifty-four and with twenty years of medical experience, would have been a more likely candidate to serve as Irwin's assistant.

Hanoaka's duties as Irwin's assistant encompassed the recruitment of hospital workers, authorization of recommended surgeries, and in the absence of a chief nurse, responsibilities related to housekeeping and operations of the hospital. Soon grumbling from the residents about favoritism in hiring practices reached Irwin's ears, and by Christmas, alliances were forming among the physicians whose ranks had now reached eight.

The rivalries among the LA physicians likely began prior to the war, and they intensified during their incarceration at Heart Mountain. Three of the younger physicians took sides against Hanoaka and two older physicians for popularity among the center residents, a feud that spilled over into the surgery room. During one routine operation Dr. Kimura (licensed in 1941) began to lecture Dr. Nakaya (1918) on the fundamentals of surgery, including basic suturing technique, creating a tense and humiliating experience for the older, Japan-born physician. Later, Kimura began to horde his personal surgical instruments, transporting them home with him and thus denying his colleagues, especially the older physicians use of an important set of scarce gynecology instruments. He later came to near blows with Dr. Hanoaka during an operation in which Kimura administered anesthesia.[23]

Dr. Hanoaka, Hawaii-born, was raised in a more racially tolerant environment than what he experienced following his move to the mainland. Soon after arriving at Heart Mountain, before the hospital was adequately equipped to perform major surgeries, it became necessary to transport a pregnant woman to the hospital in the nearby town of Cody to stop vaginal bleeding from *placenta previa*[24]. Hanoaka, in the presence of Dr. Irwin and Mrs. Jackson, the acting chief nurse, was subjected to verbal abuse by the surgeon, who opposed the presence of the growing Japanese compound in the area and apparently upset with having a member of the "enemy race"as a colleague. According to Irwin, Hanoaka was visibly shaken by the experience, and the memory of it may have influenced a growing resentment against Caucasian authority.

He was not alone in this building resentment. At one point Dr. Ito (1922) accused acting chief nurse Jackson of lying to him and his colleagues and attempting to dominate the doctors. Since Miss Jackson was present at the center hospital only for the first three months of its history, resentment toward the Caucasian staff appears to have gained momentum quickly.[25]

ARRIVAL OF ANNA VAN KIRK

Following Margaret Graham's departure, Gertrude Wetzel returned to the project on February 26th, on loan from Manzanar as interim chief nurse. Dr. Thompson detailed her from the Manzanar Relocation Center with instructions to remain until the difficult task of finding a permanent replacement could be completed. She remained until March 16, ten days beyond the arrival of Miss Anna S. Van Kirk. Thompson's original intention had been to send Van Kirk to the Gila River Relocation Center, which had been without a chief nurse for six months. But Heart Mountain, he decided, was in greater need, having never enjoyed the long term presence of a chief nurse, resulting in a project hospital in great disarray. He therefore diverted her to Irwin's hospital. It must have felt to Thompson like a continuous wartime juggling act in attempting to meet the employment needs of the ten project hospitals for which he had overall responsibility.

Van Kirk's history was unusual in that she had sailed for Japan in 1921 to serve as a missionary nurse and stayed for nineteen years. She became director of a staff of eighty-five nurses at the St. Barnabas hospital in Osaka, a position she held for the last ten years of missionary life. There she learned to speak Japanese. Returning to the U.S. in 1941, on one of the last returning ships prior to the outbreak of the Pacific war, she took a position at a hospital in her home town near Philadelphia, turning down Public Health Service employment with the WRA to be near her family. In early 1943, however, she changed her mind, and sought out the WRA. Dr. Thompson greeted her application enthusiastically.[26]

At the time of Van Kirk's arrival in March eight other appointed nurses were on staff, complementing an evacuee staff of two RNs, two graduate nurses, and six student nurses. Six Japanese doctors staffed the wards and clinics, and eighty-three resident nurses aides, clinic aides, and dental aides were on hand. Among the non-professional hospital staff were many new faces, as a result of a high turn-over rate among the predominantly youthful work force.[27]

Trouble began almost immediately. Van Kirk withheld her knowledge of Japanese from the employees for more than two weeks while she sized up what was being talked about on the wards. Finally, her fluency was made public in the *Sentinel* on March 27, 1943. Now, in the minds of many hospital workers, there was a spy in their midst. Like her predecessor, Van Kirk set out to bring order and discipline to the hospital, and in doing so rekindled the resentment of the employees. Little apparently had changed in the attitudes of the employees or the appointed personnel in the interim period. One difference between Graham and Van Kirk, however, was that the latter vowed to stay on.

With little resolution to the growing resentment, on May 15, 1943 Dr. Hanaoka requested a meeting with the chief medical officer regarding his concerns about the relationship between the Caucasian and Japanese medical staffs. Van Kirk, he argued, worked in Japan for twenty years where the Japanese were accustomed to accepting orders. But here in the United States, he explained, Japanese are accustomed to democracy and refuse to accept such orders. He demanded that the powers of the chief nurse be rescinded and warned of an increase in sentiment against both Van Kirk and the chief medical officer if she continued to administer. He then handed Irwin a petition signed by the five physicians on hand, dated May 10, 1943. Its demands included the medical staff be put in charge of the medical lab, x-ray department, pharmacy, surgery, and the ambulance department. The petition further demanded the medical staff be consulted before any new announcements or changes of ruling by the chief nurse were made. Current working conditions, the petition concluded, were oppressive.[28]

Although the language of this petition was strong, it carried no threat of a walkout which an earlier petition contained. Further, the consensus of the doctors soon appeared to weaken in the days that followed. Drs. Ito and Kimura reported to Irwin their reluctance in having signed the petition, expressing the desire to rescind their signatures, as they did not agree with all its points. This "act of sabotage" increased disharmony within the physicians' ranks.

The factions appeared so deep seated that Irwin called off further staff meetings until matters could cool down. On June 15, 1943, with Van Kirk still at the project, Dr. Hanaoka further complained to Irwin that Dr. Ito, a pediatrician, was not qualified to consult or assist surgical cases and gynecology. He further admitted to Dr. Irwin that he was "out to get" Dr. Kimura for disparaging him professionally.

With Drs. Ito and Kimura opposed to the petition's demands, Dr. Nakaya now on short term leave from the hospital, and with little hope that his rivals would offer support, Dr. Hanaoka was alone among the physicians in his outrage toward the administration as the hospital staff began its walkout on June 24. Further, Dr. Ito turned in the names of boys threatening to harm members of the hospital staff if they did not strike. The physicians, with the possible exception of Hanaoka, took no part in the walkout.[29]

THE JUNE 24TH HOSPITAL WALKOUT

The walkout began at approximately 9:45 a.m. on Thursday, June 24, 1943. The first workers to leave the hospital were the thirty-three mess hall workers who went out in unison. They were followed by the pharmacy, ambulance drivers, clinic section workers and aides, the sanitation department, the x-ray department, and the telephone operators. All told, 102 workers participated in the strike among the 346 employees working directly in the hospital complex. Notably absent from the group, however, was the front office staff, which contributed only three of its twenty workers, and the nurses aides, whose eighty-nine members contributed only one strike participant. None of the laundry crew walked out, and the physician and nursing staff continued to work. Rumors circulating that the nurses aides and laundry workers would soon join the protesters failed to materialize.

In order to continue hospital operations a skeleton crew of appointed personnel operated the diet kitchen, the warehouse, and the pharmacy, while others drove ambulances at midnight and early morning to pick up nurses aides about to go on duty. The police department handled emergency calls, and Boy Scouts patrolled the hospital corridors at night to control admission to the hospital. These arrangements remained in force until the walkout ended on June 28.

The Hospital Strike

Although fewer than a third of the hospital workers participated in the strike, and despite the non-participation of the doctors and nurses, the walkout created a serious situation for the administration, as well as for the ten thousand residents who relied on the medical and surgical services. No one could predict the extent to which anti-administration reaction might spread, nor could anyone foretell the amount of violence which might break out. The issues were not yet clear and the potential for future trouble was great. Moreover, Heart Mountain had established an earlier precedent for strikes. Earlier, workers had demanded the removal of the Project Steward, the Police and Fire Protection Officer, and the head of the motor pool. Other strikes were threatened by sawmill workers and the carpenters. Thus, the hospital was only one of numerous conflicts between workers and their overseers.

Within two days, however, it became clear that the hospital walkout would not generate excitement within the community. This may partly be explained by the *Sentinel* editor's decision not to cover the story, leaving rumor and exaggerated truths to explain the drama. Informants for the Internal Security Department, which became an active participant in the investigation of the strikers, soon revealed the community to be negative toward the strikers, but who also showed little initial sentiment in forcing the workers back to their jobs.

The residents had little accurate information of their own because the strikers apparently had no leaders and the walkout was poorly planned. No open meetings were held beforehand or after the strike began to discuss the issues, nor were issues ever publicly presented. Neither the administration nor the hospital committee of the Japanese Community Council, an ad hoc group formed as a go-between between the workers and the administration, could locate people to present the case of the workers or take responsibility for their actions.

Thus, the administration waited out the strike until June 28, at which time it terminated all workers involved in the walkout. Project Director Robertson then instructed the Chief of Internal Security to interrogate twenty-nine strike participants to determine who the troublemakers had been. Dr. Irwin and Miss Van Kirk followed with an additional eighty-seven interviews to determine the employees to be reinstated.[30]

The interviews produced transcripts revealing a poorly organized strike; many of the workers appear to have been uninformed in advance of the strike and could not point to certain individuals as leaders. In the end, the interviews, informants' testimony, and conversations overheard by Van Kirk, herself, revealed that no other issue except the removal of the chief nurse was involved. Van Kirk was painted with the same colors as her predecessor, Margaret Graham. A general grudge against the administration pointed directly at the chief nurse.

The interrogations by the Internal Security investigators produced the names of two young Nisei as being the organizers of the resentment, although neither had previous experience as organizers nor had much knowledge of how walkouts should be conducted. In addition to the two young agitators, a third individual, Dr. Hanaoka, himself, was implicated. Although it appears he did not participate directly in the walkout, his anti-administration and anti-Caucasian bitterness was well known. The loss of his practice in Los Angeles just at the time it began to flourish may have added to the difficulty of rationalizing his evacuation experience. It was no surprise to Dr. Irwin that investigators pointed their fingers toward him as a sympathizer and potential agitator. The ad hoc hospital committee also suspected Hanaoka as a player. But if Hanaoka directly participated in the strike he acted alone, for he had no allies among his peers, even though the other physicians demonstrated little respect for the office of the chief nurse.

In the end the walkout failed for a lack of specific issues and demands, weak leadership among the strikers, and a failure of the physicians to provide leadership for the strikers directly or behind the scenes.

The workers, in the meantime, were in a quandary because they had been terminated, and most wanted their jobs reinstated. On June 30, after all interviews had been completed, a significant number of the former workers presented their apologies to the chief medical officer as a group.

The two young Nisei instigators were banished to the WRA's camp for dissenters, located at Leupp, Arizona. Although a similar fate for Dr. Hanaoka must have been discussed by Director Robertson and his subordinates, this would have resulted in loss of yet another physician in the already dwindling corps of evacuee doctors. Nevertheless, relations with his professional peers had become so strained and his bitterness against Caucasian authority so strong that his presence at Heart Mountain could not continue. Hanaoka's opponents threatened Dr. Irwin with their resignations if their colleague was not transferred.

Irwin provided Hanaoka with the courtesy of requesting his own transfer, and he soon left the project for the Manzanar Relocation Center. Ironically, this move came just months after the surgeon at Manzanar, Dr. James Goto, transferred to the Central Utah Relocation Center in the wake of fallout from the Manzanar riot that occurred in December 1942.[31] Goto, in addition to professional rivalries with other physicians on the staff, had refused to cooperate with authorities in altering autopsy reports on two Japanese American men who had died in the incident, thus branding himself a "troublemaker" in the eyes of the administration.[32]

CONCLUSIONS

The Margaret Graham incident of February 11-13 and the unsuccessful hospital walkout of June 24-28 ultimately imposed little interruption of health care services for Heart Mountain residents. Few patients were inconvenienced, and those turned away soon returned as order was restored. Emergency units were manned with temporary help from the appointed personnel. Although these incidents proved to be minor episodes in the life of a small city hospital that oversaw 84,587 out-patient visits, 5,486 hospital admissions, 391 major surgeries, and 548 live births, they reveal a complex of factors that help explain the negative interactions between the evacuees and their Caucasian overseers in terms other than pure racism. To be sure, the origins of the incarceration following on the heels of Executive Order 9066 proved to be racist rather than "military necessity."[33] However, the inter-group conflicts at the Heart Mountain hospital have much to do with a wartime bureaucracy unprepared to oversee ten hospitals for 120,000 people in unprecedented prison like settings, with cultural ignorance and insensitivity on the part of its administration, and with professional rivalries and jealousies by the incarcerated physicians. Could the walkouts at the Heart Mountain center's hospital have been avoided?

Recruitment of doctors became a chronic problem that only increased over time as physicians relocated to new practices in the Midwest and East, or took advantage of residencies and other openings resulting from the continuing drain of physicians to the war effort. The nineteen dollars per month professional salary was demeaning and provided little incentive in keeping the physicians on the projects. One early solution proposed to stop the relocation was to offer the doctors commissions in the U.S. Public Health Service, thereby providing them with both prestige and meaningful salaries. This proposal would likely have kept many evacuee physicians at project hospitals, and would certainly have improved morale at Heart Mountain. Although this proposal received consideration as late as November 1943, The WRA ultimately abandoned the plan because of a threat to WRA autonomy, which wanted no interference from outside agencies.[34]

Similarly lacking were recruitment incentives for civil service nurses that might outweigh the spartan living conditions imposed upon otherwise willing registered nurses. That they were never provided contributed to a paucity of chief nurses, too few to adequately staff all ten centers. Heart Mountain suffered because the chief nurse's office was empty at a critical time in the hospital's infancy. The government's bureaucracy was simply too unwieldy to make the necessary accommodations under these unprecedented conditions.

At the project level, Dr. Irwin and his appointed staff, including the nurses, revealed themselves to be ignorant of or insensitive to the cultural needs of the evacuee physicians. Forced upon them was a female in a position of authority, hired to bring organization and discipline to a group of people for whom taking orders from a woman was anathema. Irwin could have tempered growing resentments by making his chief nurses, Partridge, Graham, and Van Kirk less visible. For example, he might have facilitated the chief nurse functions by having her orders written over his signature (i.e., a male colleague).

One of the most difficult aspects of medical practice for the evacuee physicians during incarceration was their perceived lack of voice in policy making matters. They felt powerless. Prior to the war the Japanese constituted a small minority of physicians in hospital settings. They worked in hospitals already well organized and with professionally disciplined staffs. At Heart Mountain, on the other hand, they found themselves to be the majority of physicians, if not the sole providers of care to the community, and yet found themselves subordinate in all aspects of life. They lived in barracks and ate in mess halls similar to all the evacuees at the center, and received demeaning salaries. They were not free to come and go as they wished. Moreover, their practices were clinical, for which they received little direct compensation from their patients, unlike the private practices in California which they were forced to abandon. Irwin apparently failed to recognize this. Had he done so he might have drawn them into discussions in an advisory capacity. The appearance of power, authority, or control is often as important as having it in reality. Irwin could have consulted them on the hiring of new Caucasian personnel and on the acquisition of new equipment and supplies. The physicians could have been problem solvers rather than part of the problem.

Dr. Irwin additionally seemed unaware of the importance of age and experience in positions of authority. Dr. Hanaoka's position as chief assistant despite his youthful age and lesser experience infuriated his colleagues. The problem was further compounded when Irwin dismissed him unceremoniously, causing him to lose face in front of the entire residential community, as well as his peers. Irwin also seemed unaware of the importance of the trappings of professionalism among the Japanese. The doctors' quarters could easily have been outfitted with furniture comparable to that of offices of the appointed personnel, especially Irwin's own office.

The physicians themselves, however, participated in their own misfortunes. Their professional jealousies and internal quarreling diverted attention from their larger purpose, to organize the hospital after their own vision. Had they taken advantage of the WRA's inability to staff the chief nurse's office at a time when Dr. Hanaoka was in good stead with Dr. Irwin, the hospital might have become a more harmonious place for all the workers. At the least, the non-professional employees who made up the vast bulk of workers, would have had role models to guide them in their professional behaviors.

The conflicted relationship between the Japanese medical staff and the WRA's hospital administration persisted throughout much of the life of the Heart Mountain Relocation Center. Whether or not the walkouts were avoidable may never be known. However, good relations between the groups hinged upon a bureaucracy that was malleable, a local administration with cultural awareness, and an evacuee professional staff capable of transcending its own pettiness.

Table: Licensed Japanese physicians who practiced at the Heart Mountain Relocation Center hospital during part or all of August 1942 - June 1943[35]

Name	Prewar Calif. Address	Assembly Center	Year Born	Medical License
HANAOKA, Wilfred Yoichi*	Los Angeles	Pomona	1908	1935
IKI, George Shigeki*	Sacramento	Sacramento	1892	1921
ITO, Paul Kiuji	Pomona	Pomona	1888	1922
KIMURA, Motonori Morton*	Los Angeles	Pomona	1906	1941
KINOSHITA, Robert Shizuo	Medford, OR	Portland	1906	1936
NAKAKI, Kiyohide*	Los Angeles	Santa Anita (?)	1874	1915
NAKAYA, Fusataro	Los Angeles	Santa Anita	1887	1918
SUSKI, Peter Marie*	Los Angeles	Santa Anita (?)	1875	1917
SUENAGA, Howard Japmes	Guadalupe	Fresno	1909	1938
USHIRO, California Seiki	Palo Alto (?)	Tanforan	1916	1942

*On staff at time of June 24, 1943 hospital strike

Notes

1. Health services provided at Heart Mountain also included dentistry, sanitation, public health, and social welfare activities. Although the workers in these departments had significant impact on the lives of the residents, none participated in the walkouts, likely because most worked outside the actual confines of the hospital and did not come into daily contact with the central administration. Therefore, these departments and their employees will not be considered further.

2. John Baker to Col. E.M. Wilson, November 19, 1942. Records of the War Relocation authority (RG210), Entry 4(b), Box 50, File Health. National Archives, Washington DC (hereafter cited as, RG210).

3. United States, *Final Report: Japanese Evacuation from the West Coast 1942* (Washington
DC.: Government Printing Office, 1943), Table 33, 282-84.

4. "The Hospital Walkout," 5.

5. "The Heart Mountain Hospital Walkout June 24,1943," Community Analysis Section Report 38a, Microfilm M1342, Reel 16, frames 546ff, 2. Hereafter cited as "Hospital Walkout."

6. United States. *Final Report: Japanese Evacuation from the West Coast 1942,* (Washington
DC: Government Printing Office, 1943), 563-66.

7. "Hospital Walkout," Appendix A.

8. *Heart Mountain Sentinel*, February 27, 1943.

9. "War Relocation Authority Manual for Medical Service in Relocation Centers," RG210, Entry 16, Box 374.

10. During World War II one-third of the physicians and nurses in the United States were drawn off to the war effort. Frederick D. Mott and Milton I. Roemer, *Rural Health and Medical Care* (New York: McGraw-Hill, 1948), 206.

11. "Hospital Walkout," Chapter 3, 4-5.

12. Mott, *Rural Health and Medical Care*, 206-07.

13. Although the WRA would like to have kept evacuee physicians on the projects, they did not force them to stay, enabling individuals to seek residencies or other employment opportunities that were arising as a result of the wartime drain of physicians.

14. "Hospital Walkout," 26.

15. Guy Robertson to Dillon Myer, February 18, 1943, RG210, Entry 16, Box 369, File 62.010#2.

16. "Hospital Walkout," Appendix X.

17. Margaret Graham to Miss Stuart, February 18, 1943, RG210, Entry 16, Box 369, File 62.010#2.

18. Guy Robertson to Dr. C. E. Irwin, February 16, 1943, RG210, Entry 16, Box 369, File 62.010#2.

19. Graham to Stuart, February 18, 1942.

20. Thompson's handwritten notes on Robertson to Myer letter, February 18, 1943.

21. U.S. Department of the Interior, *The Evacuated People: A Quantitative Description* (Washington DC: Government Printing Office, 1946), Table 7, 19.

22. *Final Report*, Table 50, 373.

23. Dictation by Dr. C.E. Irwin, June 27, 1943, "Hospital Walkout," Appendix E.

24. A condition during pregnancy when the placenta implants in the lower part of the uterus and obstructs the cervical opening to the vagina.

25. Dr. C.E. Irwin Report, May 3, 1943, "Hospital Walkout," Appendix E.

26. *Heart Mountain Sentinel*, March 27, 1943.

27. "Hospital Walkout," Charts I, II and III, and Table III.

28. Petition, May 10, 1943, "Hospital Walkout," Appendix E.

29. Dictation by Dr. C.E. Irwin, June 27, 1943, "Hospital Walkout," Appendix E.

30. Transcripts of these interviews may be found in "Hospital Walkout," Appendix F.

31. For details of the Manzanar riot see Michi Weglyn, *Years of Infamy: The Untold Story of America's Concentration Camps* (New York: Morrow Quill Paperbacks, 1976), 121-25, 132-33.

32. Louis Fiset, "Health Care at the Central Utah (Topaz) Relocation Center," *Journal of the West,* in press.

33. Commission on the Wartime Relocation and Internment of Civilians, *Personal Justice Denied* (Seattle: University of Washington Press, 1997), xi.

34. Dillon Myer and John Provine to G.D. Carlyle Thompson, November 13, 1943, RG210, Entry 16, Box 68, File 62.010#1.

35. American Medical Association, *American Medical Association Directory* (Chicago: American Medical Association Press, 1942, 1950).

Part IV

To Serve or Not to Serve, the Military Question

The Yamano family posing on the porch of their barrack apartment. One son
serves in the army while the rest of the family remains behind the barbed wire
confines of the camp.

Immediate Origins of the Heart Mountain Draft Resistance Movement

Frank T. Inouye

INTRODUCTION

One of the most dramatic incidents in the history of the relocation centers housing Japanese and Japanese Americans during World War II was the draft resistance movement at Heart Mountain, Wyoming. There were many elements of high drama in this episode. A group of Nisei (second generation) youths defied the demands of a universal wartime draft. A legal battle ensued over the issues of American citizenship and the mutual obligations of government during wartime. The battle was conducted in what was then a heartland of anti-Japanese sentiment and against a background of world war against Nazi tyranny and Japanese aggression. And watching all these wrenching conflicts was a silent majority of internees whose loyalty to America had been shaken by their sudden and forceful evacuation from their West Coast homes. The story of the draft resistance movement is today little known even among Japanese Americans. For fifty years Nisei writers have avoided this story of wartime civil disobedience. What purpose, they might have asked themselves, would be served by highlighting the resistance of ninety-two Nisei to the Selective Service Act during a conflict in which the all-Nisei 100th Battalion and 442nd Regimental Combat Team distinguished themselves on the battlefields of Europe?

The passage of fifty years and the redress of the great wrongs done to over one-hundred thousand Japanese aliens and Japanese American citizens by the U.S. Government during World War II now provide us with some historical perspective with which to view this problem. Why, for example, did the draft resistance movement originate and peak at Heart Mountain? What conditions existed in the camp that led to confrontation with the armed might of a country at war? Why did the Nisei draft resisters remain defiant in the face of certain imprisonment and the opprobrium of their peers and the white community? This paper will attempt to address some of these issues.

BACKGROUND OF THE DRAFT RESISTANCE MOVEMENT

An important clue to the origin of the draft resistance movement at Heart Mountain may be found in the discrepancy between official War Relocation Authority (WRA) evaluations of the camp as a "model" community and the realities of the camp experiences for the internees. WRA camp director Guy Robertson emphasized in his reports to his superiors in Washington, D.C. that the Heart Mountain camp was an efficient but humane settlement. A WRA Community Analysis entitled "The Heart

Mountain Community" contrasted the peaceful atmosphere at that camp with the disruptive violence that had occurred at Manzanar.[1] The analysis concluded that Heart Mountain lacked the militant leadership of other camps and that its administration was less prone to turnover.[2]

On the surface Heart Mountain indeed appeared to be a calm and orderly settlement. There was, of course, dissatisfaction with the quality of the food, the confinement within barbed wire fences, the occasional lack of coal during frigid winter months, the "whites only" policy of segregation between administrators and internees, and the lack of adequate privacy in the female shower rooms. However, these complaints did not lead to organized resistance or violent confrontation. Indeed, the de facto prisoners who came from several geographic areas of the West Coast were able to organize themselves into a functioning community with a minimum of friction. This may have been due to their ingrained Japanese sense of community, order and acceptance of authority. Life for most of the residents became a well-organized routine: morning ablutions in the block washrooms followed by community meals in the mess hall, then dispersal to various work stations where workers were paid according to their skills and/or professional status. Within a short time the evacuees had become "institutionalized."

But beneath the surface calm at Heart Mountain there were significant conflicts and stresses, dormant-like geographic faults but susceptible to violent movement if sufficient pressure was generated. The very fact of Heart Mountain's existence, that it was a community of ten thousand people forcibly removed from their homes without explanation or due process, was an anomaly fraught with potential hazard. The camp, like any prison, held numbers of residents whose frustration, bitterness and anger were compounded by their situation and held in check only by the threat of authority and the community's apathy and fatalism. Given the proper provocation, the calm and order of camp life could be torn asunder.

On September 6, 1942, an evacuee cook suddenly attacked his white superior's assistant steward with a meat cleaver and butcher knife. Only the intervention of some Japanese women in the kitchen prevented him from killing or maiming his victim.[3] Ostensibly the cook was frustrated by late food deliveries, a lack of menus, stolen food and a number of other culinary misfortunes. The Army's director of Internal Security at Heart Mountain filed a confidential report on the incident that stated, "the . . . evacuee chief . . . would have killed the white employees' Japanese assistant." It went on to say, "all [of the camp] cooks appear to be banded together in some type of union . . . ." A spokesman for the cooks was reported to have said, "if [the] soldiers try to prevent [a] strike someon[e] [sic] would be killed and he would also kill someone."[4]

In October, 1942, thirty-two children ranging in ages from seven to eleven were caught riding homemade sleds on a hill just outside of a proposed Army fence line. The Military Police "arrested" the children, confiscated their sleds, and took them to the center's police station. The children were later released to their parents, but news of the incident action spread through the camp. The cruel and arbitrary act visited on helpless children fanned the inmates' antagonism toward their supposed protectors.[5]

Later in October the Army began to erect a barbed wire enclosure around the camp, presumably to keep the cattle out. The internees knew better. The Army had planned to use them as volunteer workers, but most of the eligible men went on strike. Those who assisted the Army were ridiculed and even physically threatened. Nevertheless, the MP commander vowed that "he would get the fence built whether or not the evacuees worked on it."[6] On November 13 the camp administrators faced a mass meeting of angry evacuees who charged that the fence was an unnecessary and immoral violation of their rights.[7] A petition signed by three-thousand internees was sent to WRA Director Dillon Myer charging that the fence proved that Heart Mountain was a "concentration camp" and that the evacuees were "prisoners of war."[8]

The completion of the fence, with its elevated sentry posts manned by armed soldiers, and the presence of MPs at the front gate seemed to verify this contention. On several occasions Nisei men found near the fence or gate were pushed or shoved by guards, and they retaliated with angry cries of "Go ahead, shoot me!" The MPs, in fact, came to embody everything that the Nisei hated about the evacuation and relocation: militarism, imprisonment and humiliation.

In early 1943, the WRA announced a plan to convert the government-owned and operated Community Enterprises stores in the camps into cooperatives owned and operated by the internees. The purpose was to give the evacuees direct responsibility for owning and operating the largest commercial operation in the camp. The WRA thought the plan would be received with gratitude and acceptance. Instead, the internees almost overwhelmingly rejected the plan. One of the spokesmen for the opposition was Kiyoshi Okamoto.

Okamoto was a forty-eight year-old, Hawaii-born Nisei. He had previously been a sharp critic of the Japanese American Citizens League, which he considered a Quisling organization because of its earlier cooperation and collaboration with the federal authorities during the 1942 evacuation. He now led the open opposition to the WRA cooperative plan. He argued in block meetings and in letters to the camp newspaper that the cooperative plan was an attempt by the government to legitimize the relocation; that is, if the internees accepted direct responsibility for operating the cooperatives, they would also be accepting the relocation as a valid and necessary move.[9] Okamoto asserted that because the relocation was illegal, the government and only the government was fully responsible for the welfare of the camp residents. His view held sway in the camp, and the WRA abandoned its plan. This marked the first in a series of "victories" by the Heart Mountain evacuees over the WRA. It gave them a sense of limited control over their circumstances and encouraged later and more far-reaching dissident movements.

This seemingly unrelated series of confrontations leading from one of the camp's kitchens to the defeat of the Community Services cooperative plan signified that there were irreconcilable differences in attitude between the detainees and the white administrators. For the former the WRA and military were daily reminders of the humiliation and deprivation suffered during the relocation. Each instance of camp mismanagement and inefficiency, whether related to feeding, housing, clothing or security, reinforced their sense of outrage. Each incident added to the cumulative store of anger and frustration.

The WRA administrators typified by men such as Guy Robertson at Heart Mountain, viewed the evacuees as charges for whose welfare they were responsible. They believed they were serving the evacuees' best interest by providing a "safe" environment protected from the hostility of the rest of the country. The irony of safeguarding their charges by imprisoning them behind barbed wire probably escaped them; prisoners after all were better off in jail than among a lynch mob. Robertson had the sensitivity to realize that the Nisei "came to the center feeling persecuted and that anything offered by the Government must be looked at with wariness."[10] However, his sensitivity did not extend to taking measures to alleviate the sense of persecution and intimidation which the internees felt. In fact, the creation of the concentration camp atmosphere had just the opposite effect. The administration's shortsightedness, bungling, lack of empathy and pig-headedness go far in explaining the turmoil that developed in the ensuing months.

The Military Police who guarded the camp borders considered the evacuees to be prisoners of war. They were "Japs," no different from the ones their kinsmen and friends were fighting in the Pacific Theater. They were constrained only by the Geneva Convention and the civilian authority of the WRA. It is little wonder then that the one attitude that bound the Nisei was their hatred and contempt for the U.S. Army.

The stage was now set for the Army's first defeat at the hands of an unarmed but by no means passive Heart Mountain population.

THE REGISTRATION CRISIS

In June, 1942, the troopship *Maui* brought fourteen-hundred Nisei volunteers from Hawaii to Oakland. This group would become the 100th Infantry Battalion. In February, 1943, encouraged by the success of the 100th Battalion, the government changed the Selective Service Act barring Nisei enlistees, in order to create an all-Nisei 442nd Infantry Regimental Combat Team.[11] The military expected fifteen-hundred volunteers from the Island but was inundated by over ten-thousand. Surely, the Army reasoned, the ten camps on the Mainland could provide an equal number. But the jubilant, festive atmosphere in Hawaii was not matched in the gloomy camps. Even some of the WRA administrators expressed serious doubts that the volunteer plan would succeed.[12] Nevertheless, the Cabinet officer most supportive of the evacuation of Japanese and Japanese Americans, Secretary of War Henry Stimson, now became a leading advocate of volunteerism in the camps. Canny enough to perceive the inconsistency of allowing former "security risks" to become American soldiers, Stimson decided to initiate a screening system to separate what he called the "traitors" or "rotten apples" from the "patriots." He asserted, "it is only by mutual confidence and cooperation that the loyal Japanese Americans can be restored to their civil rights."[13] The irony of this statement did not escape the Nisei in the relocation camps. The "mutual confidence" Stimson mentioned would be manifested on their part by their being allowed to die for their country. America's confidence had already been demonstrated by indicting, judging, convicting, sentencing, imprisoning and dispossessing one-hundred thousand people without evidence or legal formalities.

The WRA in the meantime had been searching for a more efficient way of determining which internees would be permitted to work outside the camps. When they learned that a questionnaire had been prepared by the War Department (Form 126) for the purpose of recruiting, they decided to use some of their questions for their leave questionnaire (Form 304A).[14] The documents that resulted triggered the first in another series of confrontations between the internees and the government.

Two questions in particular aroused resentment:

| No. 27. | Are you willing to serve in the Armed Forces of the United States on combat duty whenever ordered? |
| No. 28. | Will you swear unqualified allegiance to the United States of America? |

The WRA required every adult male and female to complete the form. The Issei, first generation immigrants, were not citizens of the United States, and for them to swear allegiance to this country meant termination of their Japanese citizenship. They would become people without countries.

The Nisei were infuriated by question 28, asking for their "unqualified allegiance." This implied that they were foreign immigrants aspiring to American citizenship. They also saw in both questions a clever trap: by signing the questionnaire "yes/yes," they could be immediately drafted into the Armed Services as volunteers without further processing or exemptions. They would then be forced to leave their aging Issei parents in camp at the mercy of a government that had already proven its disregard for basic human rights. Finally, every eligible female who signed would be indicating her willingness to serve in the Armed Forces.

With typical lack of sensitivity Director Robertson fanned the embers of anger by threatening the internees with dire consequences if they did not respond as expected. He was under pressure from Washington to produce as many volunteers as Hawaii. He editorialized in the camp newspaper, pressured the block managers and chairman and even declared that the questionnaire was mandatory for the Issei. The last was a blatant falsehood.[15] Overnight, the volunteer effort for the Army and the work leave program for the WRA were in shambles, and all trust in either organization evaporated. Camp apathy was now camp anger.

On February 6, 1943, an Army Registration Team headed by Lt. Ray McDaniels visited Heart Mountain. The team included three sergeants, one of whom was a Nisei, Kazunobu Tanaka.[16] McDaniels was scheduled to speak at block meetings called specially for the registration process. The sergeants would then seek volunteers for the 442nd.

At the first major meeting, the facility was filled with Nisei men. A small group of them headed by a former UCLA senior, Frank Inouye, had been meeting for the purpose of opposing the registration process.[17] They intended to disrupt the meeting by challenging the government's right to recruit volunteers without first clarifying and restoring the Nisei's constitutional rights.

McDaniels opened the meeting by reiterating Stimson's line: "Our mission . . . (is) to return you to a normal way of life . . . . Its fundamental purpose is to put your situation on a plane which is consistent with the dignity of American citizenship. Not all Japanese Americans are loyal to their government . . . (and) individuals who will not accept any obligation to the land which gives them their opportunity . . . are the disloyal ones."[18]

When McDaniels completed his address, Frank Inouye, spokesman of the dissidents, read his own "manifesto" to the assembled Nisei. He pointed out that earlier draftees in the Army had suffered degradation and discrimination. He then attacked the illogical policies of the government which had relocated one-hundred thousand Japanese at the point of a gun and now asked many of these same Japanese to take up arms for military service. He concluded by demanding that the U.S. Government acknowledge the Nisei's rights as Americans before asking for their military enlistment.[19]

The "manifesto" was greeted with universal enthusiasm and acceptance among the Nisei. Thereafter, every attempt by the Army team to continue its registration process proved futile. McDaniels repeatedly asked for an opportunity to rebut the accusation, in vain. At that meeting, in full view of the Nisei and the WRA, the Army's volunteer registration effort collapsed.

THE HEART MOUNTAIN CONGRESS OF AMERICAN CITIZENS

Following the manifesto, Inouye called for the formation of an elected central body to pursue the purposes outlined in his speech. That evening each block elected two representatives. On February 11, the first meeting of the group was held. All members were Nisei and all were males. Among them were Kiyoshi Okamoto and Paul Nakadate, who were later to become prominent in the Fair Play Committee (FPC).[20] A chairman (Inouye) and secretary (Nakadate) were elected and the assembly adopted the name Heart Mountain Congress of American Citizens. At this meeting the delegates submitted fourteen resolutions which were eventually distilled into four main subjects:

1. Clarification of Nisei citizenship status.
2. Publicizing of clarification by the U.S. President, the Secretary of War and the Attorney General.
3. Postponement of further registration until clarification was obtained.
4. Implied consent of the Nisei to serve in the armed forces upon clarification of their citizenship status.[21]

The discussion of these resolutions to the block meetings raised an issue that occupied the next Congress meeting: why register at all? Many Nisei in camp did not wish to serve in the Armed Forces as Question 27 demanded, but they did not wish to lose their American citizenship. After considerable debate the Congress recommended a qualified "Yes" to item 27. This was felt to be the most expedient means of attaining the Congress' main goal: clarification of Nisei citizenship status. Unless the men indicated their willingness to serve, they would have little bargaining power with the federal government.[22]

During this period of discussion and debate, camp activities came to a virtual standstill. Frank S. Emi, a radical opponent of the volunteer movement, posted hand-printed copies of his answers to Questions 27 and 28 on mess hall doors and other public places. "Under the present conditions and circumstances," he said, "I am unable to answer these questions."[23] Kiyoshi Okamoto appeared at a gathering and urged the crowd to resist all recruiting activities in camp. There should be no appeasement of the authorities, he argued, as long as the Nisei were illegally detained.[24] The camp administrators regarded these activities with alarm. When the executive council of the Congress asked for use of telephones to contact the other nine internment camps, it was refused. The administration also tried to prevent the camp newspaper from covering the Congress. Guy Robertson threatened to invoke the espionage and sedition laws against those seeking to derail the registration process.[25]

In spite of this opposition, the Congress proceeded with its agenda. On February 19 it sent a formal petition to President Roosevelt. It also sent telegrams to the other nine camps urging them to do likewise.[26] The petition was never acknowledged by the President or anyone else. The Nisei would wait another fifty years to obtain the U.S. government's apology and restitution.

The WRA/Army registration process would eventually proceed but not before the Congress gained a significant victory. The Army, faced with dwindling support for its volunteer efforts in the camps, announced that Questions 27 and 28 could be answered with qualified or conditional responses.[27] Instead of the fifteen-hundred volunteers it had sought, the Army received only 805 from all the camps. At Heart Mountain, where two-thousand volunteers were expected, only thirty-eight came forward, and nineteen were eventually inducted.[28] And overshadowing these paltry numbers, eight-hundred camp Nisei renounced their citizenship.[29]

Thus, the Heart Mountain Congress had a singularly unexpected result. The body had been formed to protest the registration process and clarify Nisei rights. What emerged was a massive vote for repatriation to Japan. The Congress leaders, Rikio Tomo, Clarence Nishizu and Frank Inouye, were appalled at the unexpected outcome, but there was little they could do.[30] They and the delegates chose to interpret the Army's acceptance of conditional responses to Question 27 and 28 as a moral victory. At best, however, it was an incomplete victory, since the other resolutions went unanswered.

Perhaps the most significant outcome of the Congress was that its work was carried on by a more militant Nisei group called the Fair Play Committee, headed by Kiyoshi Okamoto and Paul Nakadate. This new group took up the anti-draft banner when the Army's volunteer program collapsed.

THE HEART MOUNTAIN FAIR PLAY COMMITTEE: BEGINNINGS

The Heart Mountain Congress died after the camp residents reluctantly complied with WRA/Army questionnaire registration. However, its basic premise was vindicated: Army recruiting in the camps would not succeed unless Nisei citizenship status was clarified. Faced with this stand, Secretary of War Stimson decided on January 20, 1944, to reimpose the Selective Service Act on all eligible Nisei males. Their previous 4-C, or enemy alien, status was revoked.[31]

The Fair Play Committee began as the Heart Mountain Fair Play Committee of One, and the "one" was Kiyoshi Okamoto. From the beginning he had been a fierce critic of the volunteer program, and now he started his crusade against the drafting of camp Nisei. He spoke to anyone who would listen and circulated anti-draft flyers. He was soon joined by Frank Emi, who had earlier posted his own anti-volunteer thesis, and Paul Nakadate, another well-educated and literate Nisei who had been the Congress secretary. The issues that Okamoto and his colleagues raised were similar to those raised by the Heart Mountain Congress: opposition to military service without restoration of Nisei civil rights; clarification of those rights, and elimination of racial discrimination within the military.[32]

As the Nisei learned of their vulnerability to the draft, interest in the Fair Play Committee rose. On January 26, 1944, three-hundred residents met to formally launch the FPC. Okamoto and Paul Nakadate were elected chairman and vice-chairman. Eventually some 275 became dues-paying members.[33] Okamoto rapidly expanded the FPC's operations beyond Heart Mountain. In February he contacted a Denver attorney, Samuel Menin, for legal advice on the draft issue.[34] He communicated with James Omura, an editor of the bi-lingual Denver *Rocky Shimpo*, a paper that was read in the camps.[35] Omura, like Okamoto, had been a militant critic of the Government's relocation policies.

The Heart Mountain Congress had been a camp-wide elected body. The FPC was a grass-roots organization, but it had several advantages over the Congress. First, it was focused on the issue of the Selective Service Act as it applied to the camp

Nisei. Second, it sought to test the legality of drafting the Nisei. The FPC urged drafted Nisei not to appear for pre-induction physical examinations, and before long the test case was pending. Third, the FPC had the full support of the *Rocky Shimpo* and did not have to depend on the WRA-sponsored and censored *Heart Mountain Sentinel*. Finally the FPC had the benefit of legal counsel almost from its inception.

On March 1, 1944, nearly four-hundred Nisei adopted an FPC resolution calling for a boycott of the entire induction procedure.[36] In an effort to defuse the volatile situation, the elected camp community council offered a petition to President Roosevelt again asking for restoration of the Nisei's civil rights.[37] The FPC was unimpressed and considered the petition an administration-inspired ploy. The members called for the removal of Director Guy Robertson.[38] The militant and uncompromising stand of the FPC brought dividends. By the end of March, seventeen percent of the Nisei males ordered to report for their physicals refused to do so.[39]

This flagrant opposition to the Selective Service Act could not be overlooked, and on March 30 federal authorities had Okamoto removed to the Tule Lake camp in northern California, where dissident Japanese were kept.[40] He was soon joined there by Paul Nakadate and the rest of the FPC leadership.

The following month those Nisei who had refused to appear for their physicals were arrested. Federal agents raided Omura's Denver newspaper office and seized records.[41] By May, the FPC was defunct. In that same month sixty-three "draft resisters" from Heart Mountain were indicted by a federal grand jury in Cheyenne, Wyoming.[42] This was followed by the largest mass trial in the state's history. On June 26, 1944, Federal District Judge T. Blake Kennedy found all sixty-three guilty of conspiracy against the Selective Service Act and sentenced all of them to federal prison.[43]

The government then arrested seven FPC officers and James Omura, the *Rocky Shimpo* editor, for violating the same Act. Omura was later found innocent, but the seven officers were imprisoned.[44] In November, A.L. Wirin, a distinguished American Civil Liberties Union lawyer who had defended seven of the eight co-defendants, was able, through appeal to the Tenth Circuit Court, to have the district court's decision overturned on a technicality. The seven former FPC officers were released.[45]

SUMMATION

The Fair Play Committee members were not alone in contending that the application of the Selective Service Act to the Nisei was hypocritical and prejudiced. A Federal District Court judge presiding over the trial of one-hundred draft resisters from the Poston, Arizona, Camps, sentenced the group to a one-penny fine without imprisonment. In Northern California Federal Judge Louis A. Goodman dismissed the indictments against twenty-seven internees charged with draft resistance, and declared, "it is shocking to the conscience that an American citizen be confined on the grounds of disloyalty and then, while so under duress and restraint, be compelled to serve in the armed forces or be prosecuted for not yielding to such compulsion."[46]

In reflecting years later on the dilemma of the Nisei draft resisters in the camps, U.S. Senator from Hawaii, Daniel K. Inouye said, "would I have volunteered (for the 442nd) if my family was in that 10' x 12' cubicle (in camp)? We look back now—they (the draft resisters) had greater courage, maybe."[47] In 1947, by executive order President Harry Truman pardoned all of the imprisoned draft resisters.[48]

The Fair Play Committee, the Heart Mountain Congress, the ten WRA relocation centers, are now distant and almost forgotten memories. What historical significance do they possess? Were the protests, petitions, and mass meetings of that period merely empty gestures of a downtrodden minority? Kiyoshi Okamoto and the FPC sought to establish a legal principle and precedent: that only U.S. citizens in full possession of their constitutional rights were eligible to be inducted into the armed services. That issue was never really addressed. Instead the Cheyenne court chose to focus on the FPC's part in the "conspiracy" to resist the draft. The narrow question before it was: had the FPC members taken overt action which led to the refusal of the Nisei to appear for pre-induction physicals? Despite evidence that the FPC had not condoned resisting the draft, *per se*, its leaders were nevertheless summarily sentenced to imprisonment along with the sixty-three other defendants. The number later increased to eighty-five. Since more than two-hundred other Nisei from the other relocation centers also refused to honor their induction notices and were not jailed, it appears that the FPC members were subject to harsher treatment because they tried to present an organized and united resistance to the Selective Service Act. In actuality they had been exercising their right to free speech, a right protected under the Bill of Rights in the American Constitution. This issue was also not addressed by the Cheyenne court for obvious reasons. The government needed an object lesson for those in camp who wished to resist the draft, and the FPC was the unfortunate victim.

What impact did the FPC have on history, or even on the life of the Heart Mountain Relocation Center? Did the fact that fewer than one-hundred men followed their leaders into prison and that their cause would soon lose its hold upon many Nisei constitute a major miscalculation on the part of the committee's leaders? It could be argued with the benefit of fifty years' hindsight that the committee and its leadership did what it believed was right. Instead of acquiescing to the demands of the Selective Service Act, they stood and opposed the Act with the only weapons at their disposal: their outrage over the enforced relocation and their right of free speech. That they went to prison and that more young men did not follow them is irrelevant. In the truest tradition of American dissent, they stated their views calmly and fearlessly and never stooped to the race-hatred and polemic of their captors. They were Americans just as the men of the 442nd and 100th were Americans, serving the same ultimate goal: the defense and adherence to the democratic principles upon which the Constitution was founded.

What had been forgotten but should be remembered is the reason the Tenth Circuit Court of Appeals reversed Judge Eugene Rice's sentencing of the Fair Play

Committee's seven leaders.
Judge Bratton wrote:

> In respect of the issue as to whether the appellants acted with honesty of pur-
> pose and innocence of motive in a good faith effort to bring about a test case
> to determine their exempt status under the Selective Service Act, Judge Rice
> had erred by not considering the right of American citizens to question or to
> refuse to comply with laws they considered unconstitutional.[49]

By that ruling the FPC leaders were completely exonerated and their persistent efforts vindicated even if the underlying issue of the legality of drafting the Nisei
in the camps was never addressed.

EXHIBIT A
FAIR PLAY COMMITTEE
"one for all - all for one"
WE SHOULD KNOW

The Fair Play Committee believes that the first duty of every loyal citizen is to protect and uphold the Constitution of the United States. The cornerstone of this instrument of our government is JUSTICE, LIBERTY, FREEDOM, AND THE PROTECTION OF HUMAN RIGHTS. The desecration of any one of these is a direct attack upon the fundamentals that molded our democratic institutions.

Abraham Lincoln said . . . "If by the mere force of numbers a majority should deprive a minority of any Constitutional right, it might in a moral point of view justify a revolution." The Fair Play Committee do not intend to start a revolution but we demand judicial and orderly procedures in the molding of our destinies.

If we are American Citizens of this Nation by right of birth and Constitutional grant, then, let it be decided once and for all without equivocation our positions as members of the Nation by a rectification of our evacuation, our concentration, our detention, our pauperization by Judicial Pronouncement and Congressional act, and restoration of our freedom, liberty, and all rights as guaranteed by the Constitution.

By the granting of these, we will know of a cause and a country worthy of our blood and our lives, and we need never feel ashamed to look the enemy in the eye. The granting of these will not only liquidate the injustices of the past, but it will guarantee assurances to the other minorities who otherwise may face a similar fate in the future. It is in accord with principles that motivated the Declaration of Independence, the War of Rebellion, the Boston Tea Party, the Constitution, the Bill of Rights and the Proclamation for the Emancipation of Slavery.

The Fair Play Committee believes it has a right to ask first a clarification of our status, and full restoration of our rights, and abolishment of the discriminatory features of the Selective Service as applied to Japanese Americans, before being drafted into the armed forces.

THIS ABSENCE OF CLARIFICATION OF OUR STATUS, RESTORATION OF OUR RIGHTS, AND LIFTING OF DISCRIMINATORY RESTRICTIONS AGAINST US IS THE KEYSTONE OF OUR INDECISION TO ANY PROPER ORIENTATION OF ATTITUDE TOWARDS THE PRESENT PROGRAM OF DRAFTING US FROM THIS CONCENTRATION CAMP.

Thus, to be drafted or not to be drafted, or to loyal or disloyal, are not the questions at issue. To us, the very fundamental of Democracy is at stake. If Democracy and Freedom is to exist in this Country, then we must uphold the ideals and principles of the Constitution and right the wrongs committed to a minority group.

EXHIBIT B
FAIR PLAY COMMITTEE
"one for all - all for one"

"No person shall be deprived of life, liberty, or property, without due process of law, nor private property be taken for public use without just compensation." Article V Bill of Rights.

"Neither slavery nor <u>involuntary servitude</u>, except as punishment for crime whereof the party shall have been <u>duly convicted</u>, shall exist within the United States, or any place subject to their jurisdiction." Article XIII Bill of Rights.

We, the Nisei have been complacent and too inarticulate to the unconstitutional acts that we were subjected to. If ever there was a time or cause for decisive action, IT IS NOW!

We the members of the FPC are not afraid to go war—we are not afraid to risk our lives for our country. We would gladly sacrifice our lives to protect and uphold the principles and ideals of our country as set forth in the Constitution and the Bill of Rights, for on its inviolability depends the freedom, liberty, justice, and protection of all people including Japanese-Americans and all other minority groups. But have we been given such freedom, such liberty, such justice, such protection? NO!! Without any hearings, without any due process of law as guaranteed by the Constitution and Bill of Rights, without any charges filed against us, without any evidence of wrongdoing on our part, one hundred and ten thousand innocent people were kicked out of their homes, literally uprooted from where they have lived for the greater part of their life, and herded like dangerous criminals into concentration camps with barbed wire fences and military police guarding it, AND THEN, WITHOUT RECTIFICATION OF THE INJUSTICES COMMITTED AGAINST US NOR WITHOUT RESTORATION OF OUR RIGHTS AS GUARANTEED BY THE CONSTITUTION, WE ARE ORDERED TO JOIN THE ARMY THRU <u>DISCRIMINATORY PROCEDURES</u> INTO <u>A SEGREGATED COMBAT UNIT!</u> Is that the American way? NO! The FPC believes that unless such actions are opposed <u>NOW,</u> and steps taken to remedy such injustices and discriminations <u>IMMEDIATELY,</u> the future of all minorities and the future of this democratic nation is in danger.

Thus, the members of the FPC unanimously decided at their last open meeting that until we are restored all our rights, all discriminatory features of the Selective Service abolished, and measures are taken to remedy the past injustices thru Judicial pronouncement or Congressional act, we feel that the present program of drafting us from this concentration camp is unjust, unconstitutional, and against all principles of civilized usage, therefore, WE MEMBERS OF THE FAIR PLAY COMMITTEE <u>HEREBY REFUSE TO GO TO THE PHYSICAL EXAMINATION OR TO THE INDUCTION</u> IF OR WHEN WE ARE CALLED IN ORDER TO CONTEST THE ISSUE.

We are not being disloyal. We are not evading the draft. We are all loyal Americans fighting for JUSTICE AND DEMOCRACY RIGHT HERE AT HOME. So, restore our rights as such, rectify the injustices of evacuation, of the concentration, of the detention, and of the pauperization as such. In short, treat us in accordance with the principles of the Constitution.

If what we are voicing is wrong, if what we ask is disloyal, if what we think is unpatriotic, the Abraham Lincoln, one of our greatest American Presidents was also guilty as such, for he said, "If by the mere force of numbers a majority should deprive a minority of any Constitutional right, it might in a moral point of view justify a revolution."

Among the one thousand odd members of the Fair Play Committee, there are Nisei men over the draft age and Nisei girls who are not directly affected by the present Selective Service program, but who believe in the ideals and principles of our country, therefore are helping the FPC in our fight against injustice and discriminations.

We hope that all persons whose ideals and interests are with us will do all they can to help us. We may have to engage in court actions, but as such actions require large sums of money, we do need financial support and when the time comes, we hope that you will back us up to the limit.

ATTENTION MEMBERS! FAIR PLAY COMMITTEE MEETING SUNDAY, MARCH 5, 2:00 P.M. BLOCK 6-30 MESS. PARENTS, BROTHERS, SISTERS AND FRIENDS INVITED.

EXHIBIT C

FAIR PLAY COMMITTEE
"one for all - all for one"
Questions and Answers on the Fair Play Committee

Q.   What's this Fair Play Committee about?
A.   The Fair Play Committee (FPC) is organized to inject justice in all the problems pertaining to our evacuation, concentration, detention and pauperization without hearing or due process of law, and oppose all unfair practices within our center, State, or Union.
Q.   How do you think it can do just that?
A.   By educational process; the use of the press; thru the courts; or if the FPC cannot do it itself, it will work jointly with or thru outside organizations.
Q.   Who can join this organization?
A.   Citizens only.
Q.   What has the FPC actually done and what is it doing now?
A.   We have retained the service of a Caucasian attorney, and have instructed him to write to Attorney General Biddle for a clarification of our rights as loyal American citizens and as the government has admitted their mistake for our evacuation, detention, concentration, etc; how is the government going to rectify those unconstitutional acts committed against us. Also, the FPC is giving the community, service to those who went to appeal their classification at Block 1 - 4 - D. This location is temporary. No charge is being made.
Q.   What does the FPC think is the right thing for any loyal American citizen to do in our present status?
A.   The FPC believes that the first duty as loyal American citizens is to protect and uphold the Constitution of the United States. THE CORNERSTONE OF THIS INSTRUMENT OF OUR GOVERNMENT IS JUSTICE, LIBERTY, FREEDOM, AND THE PROTECTION OF HUMAN RIGHTS, AND THE DESECRATION OF ANY ONE OF THESE IS A DIRECT ATTACK ON THE FUNDAMENTALS THAT MOLDED OUR DEMOCRATIC INSTITUTION.
Q.   Is this an objectors group?
A.   No. It definitely is not an objectors group, but we would like to present both sides of this draft issue.
Q.   What does the FPC think about this present draft program?
A.   The FPC believes we have a right to ask that the discriminatory features in regards to this selective service be abolished, or status be clarified, and a full restoration of our rights of our beings before being drafted. THIS ABSENCE OF CLARIFICATION OF OUR STATUS, RESTORATION OF OUR RIGHTS, AND THE LIFTING OF DISCRIMINATORY RESTRICTIONS IS THE KEYSTONE OF OUR ATTITUDE TOWARDS THE PRESENT PROGRAM OF DRAFTING US FROM THIS CONCENTRATION CAMP.
Q.   Why can't we contest the whole issue after the war?
A.   Because if we know of a cause and a country worthy of our blood, then we need never feel ashamed to look the enemy in the eye. And by the granting of these it will not only liquidate the injustices of the past, but it will guarantee against any future inroads upon the Constitution and its principles. It will guarantee assurances

135

to the minorities who otherwise may face a similar fate in the future.

Q.   Do you think that the FPC can succeed in its aims?

A.   No guarantee can be made. But, this is the crucial test. If we are successful, it would have been worth every sacrifice we would have made for the right of Niseis and all minorities to enjoy the right and privileges accorded to them in the principles and ideals of the Constitution. To those of you whose heart, whose interest, and whose ideals are with us in these critical times, please lend us your support, morally and materially as this is the only way we can succeed in achieving our aims.

OUR FINANCE COMMITTEE WILL BE AROUND FOR DONATIONS. ANY AMOUNT WILL BE APPRECIATED.

Notes

1. "Summary of the Heart Mountain Community," an analysis by the War Relocation Authority, folder M1.00 of the Japanese-American Evacuation and Resettlement Records (BANC MSS 67/14c), 1, Bancroft Library, University of California, Berkeley (hereafter cited as Bancroft Collection).

2. Ibid.

3. Ibid. "Center Living Conditions: Mess Halls," September 21, 1942, 1-4.

4. Ibid.

5. Ibid. "Community Organization," 4.

6. Ibid. "Center Living Conditions," 1.

7. *Heart Mountain Sentinel*, December 5, 1942.

8. *Heart Mountain Sentinel*, November 21, 1942.

9. Douglas M. Nelson, *Heart Mountain: The Story of an American Concentration Camp* (Madison: State Historical Society of Wisconsin, 1976), 86-87. *Heart Mountain Sentinel*, January 9, 1943.

10. "Community Organization," BANC MSS. See also Nelson, *Heart Mountain*, Director Guy Robertson to Dillon S. Myer, April 4, 1943.

11. Nelson, *Heart Mountain*, 98.

12. Diary notes of John A. Nelson, February 7, 1943. This lengthy handwritten diary covers almost the entire period of the Heart Mountain Relocation Center. The original copy is stored at the American Heritage Center, University of Wyoming.

13. *Heart Mountain Sentinel*, January 28, 1943.

14. Nelson, *Heart Mountain*, 98.

15. Ibid., 101-02.

16. Frank T. Inouye, "Odyssey of a Nisei; A Voyage of Self-Discovery," 1992, unpublished memoirs, Volume II, 79-80.

17. Ibid.

18. Ibid., 80.

19. Ibid., 80-82. Edited versions of the "Manifesto" are to be found in Nelson, *Heart Mountain,* 104-05, and in Dillon S. Myer, *Uprooted Americans* (Tucson: University of Arizona Press, 1971), 73; and the *Heart Mountain Sentinel,* February 13, 1943.

20. This meeting and subsequent actions of the Congress are documented in a special report, "Registration at Heart Mountain," Community Analysis Section, Heart Mountain Relocation Center, February, 1943. From the Collection of Michi Nishiuri Weglyn.

21. Ibid., 3-4

22. Inouye, "Memoirs," 84.

23. Frank S. Emi, "Draft Resistance at the Heart Mountain Concentration Camp and the Fair Play Committee," 2-3. A paper presented at the Fifth National Conference for Asian American Studies, Washington State University, March 24-26, 1988.

24. Federal Bureau of Investigation Sedition Report on Fair Play Committee, April 24, 1944, written by A. T. Hansen, Community Analyst at Heart Mountain, 3-4. For Okamoto's consistent position on Nisei involvement in any relocation camp activities, including draft resistance, see Fair Play Committee Bulletin No. 3, 19-20.

25. Registration, 6.

26. Nelson, *Heart Mountain,* 106.

27. Ibid., 107.

28. Ibid., 111.

29. Ibid., 112.

30. Inouye, "Memoirs," 84.

31. Nelson, *Heart Mountain,* 119.

32. FPC Bulletins 1, 2 and 3 in FBI Report, 17-22.

33. Nelson, *Heart Mountain,* 122.

34. FBI Report on FPC, 6.

35. Nelson, *Heart Mountain,* 121.

36. Ibid., 125.

37. FBI Report, 8-10.

38.Nelson, *Heart Mountain*, 128.

39. Ibid., 132.

40. FBI Report, 52.

41. Nelson, *Heart Mountain*, 138.

42. Ibid., 140.

43. Ibid., 141-42

44. Ibid., 145. The seven FPC leaders included Kiyoshi Okamoto, Paul T. Nakadate, Frank S. Emi, Ken Yanagi, Sam Horino, Minoru Tamesa and Ben Wakaye.

45. "Opinion by the Tenth Circuit Court of Appeals in Heart Mountain Conspiracy Case," Judge Bratton presiding, A.L. Wiren, attorney for defendants. Jack Tono Collection.

46. Emi, "Draft Resistance at Heart Mountain," 16.

47. *Rafu Shimpo*, April 13, 1992.

48. Nelson, *Heart Mountain*, 150.

49. Bratton, "Heart Mountain Conspiracy Case," 4.

Nisei Soldiers:
Their Contribution to Post-World War II Japanese American Rights

Sam Fujishin

THE EVACUATION

December 7, 1941—what a devastating day! No one realized what an impact this would have on all of us, nor did we know that we would be incarcerated behind barbed wire fences with guard towers five months later. It opened up a new page in the history of us Americans of Japanese ancestry.

December 7 fell on a Sunday, and though the next day was a school day, many of us Nisei—second generation Japanese Americans—were apprehensive about attending. At my high school in Kent, Washington, about twenty percent, or twenty-five students out of my junior class of 125, were Nisei. The school superintendent anticipated problems and we Nisei appreciated him calling a special assembly as soon as school was in session. At the assembly, the superintendent told the students that the Nisei were just as "American" as anyone else and equally loyal. He made it known to the non-Nisei that we should be treated fairly. His address relieved a lot of tension and the student body from that time forward got along as if nothing had happened.

In April of 1942 we were ordered by the government to prepare to leave for an "assembly center." My family was given two weeks to prepare. Like many of the Japanese American families in the Seattle area, ours was just beginning to enjoy the prosperity earned by our parents' twenty to thirty years of hard work in their adopted country. Nevertheless, we sold a recently acquired new car for half what we paid for it, as well as many of our belongings for ten cents on the dollar. Some of our possessions we were able to store in an old building on the farm we were then renting.

We were a family of eight and when we were ordered to report to the train station to leave for the assembly center my father was in poor health suffering from heart problems. An ambulance came to our home to transport him to the train and he was allowed a Pullman car so he could lie down during the journey. We were sent initially to Pinedale, California, about seven miles from Fresno. We spent the hottest part of the year there, May through August, and many of the older Issei, or first generation Japanese Americans, had difficulty coping with the 110 to 120 degree weather. Some suffered from heat stroke, and my father's weight dropped to about ninety pounds. In August we were transferred to the Tule Lake Relocation Center in northern California. The temperatures were more tolerable there for the older people, and my father slowly regained weight and recuperated from his heart problem. Our entire housing block at Tule Lake celebrated his return to good health with a watermelon bust!

At Tule Lake I re-enrolled in school as a high school senior. There were a number of difficulties at the school that year, largely due to a lack of supplies, poor facilities, and a month-long teachers' strike. These disruptions led me to conclude that my time was not being productively spent in this school environment, and I decided to quit temporarily and go with my older brother Mike to work in the fields of Idaho, where labor was in short supply. My plan was to labor in Idaho until the work slowed in the fall, then finish my high school diploma there. I looked forward to the prospect of earning money to send to my family in the camp as it would help provide them with many of the necessities which they could not afford at that time.

In July of 1943, however, I received a high school diploma in the mail along with a letter from the Tule Lake School Superintendent, H. M. Harness. After I had left Tule Lake, he had sent for my transcripts from the high school I had attended in Kent, Washington. He learned that I was two credits short of meeting the California high school graduation requirement. In his letter he said that under the circumstances, he thought it appropriate to waive the two credits and place me on the roll of the 1943 graduating class of Tri-State High School at the Tule Lake camp. It always seemed ironic to me that I never earned a single credit from the high school at Tule Lake, and yet I am proud to have a diploma from an accredited California high school.

During the summer of work in Idaho the War Department decided to designate the Tule Lake Relocation Center, where my family was housed, as a segregation camp where those Japanese Americans who wished to renounce their American citizenship and be repatriated to Japan would be assembled. Residents of the other nine relocation camps who made this choice would be sent to Tule Lake, and those at Tule Lake who decided to stay in this country would be sent to one of the other centers. This development alarmed my older brother and me, because we knew that if this decision was left to our elderly parents and younger brothers and sister, they might decide to stay at Tule Lake simply to avoid moving again.

My older brother Mike had been designated as head of the household because of his ability to speak English and due to the infirmity of my father. He went immediately to Tule Lake and made arrangements for the family to leave. It was decided that they would be moved to Minidoka in Idaho, or Heart Mountain, in Wyoming. My family was eventually moved to Heart Mountain where my brother and I joined them in December of 1943 after finishing our labor contract with the Amalgamated Sugar Company in Idaho.

That winter the War Department decided that Nisei would be drafted into the armed forces. The all-Nisei 442nd Infantry Regiment was formed and was already proving itself an outstanding unit but it was incurring heavy casualties and was badly in need of replacements. On March 1, 1944, I received my greetings from the President of the United States, by way of the Powell, Wyoming, Draft Board No. 1, to report for my preinduction physical examination. On March 7, a bus-load of approximately thirty of us Nisei from the Heart Mountain camp went to take our physicals at Fort Warren in Cheyenne. As it turned out, the doctors administering the physicals were Navy physicians who had been at Pearl Harbor on December 7. They were very bitter and opposed to the idea of Japanese Americans serving in the armed forces. As a result, I was the only one among this first group of inductees to pass the physical exam.

We stayed the night at Fort Warren and many of the inductees called their families to tell them that they would not be going into the service. When we returned to Heart Mountain the next day, the camp director, Guy Robertson, called all of us into his office. He said that there had been rumors around the camp that the American military would still not accept Japanese Americans for military service. I spoke up at that meeting and said that the rumors were untrue, as I had passed the physical and intended to serve when called. My orders came at the end of March, 1944, to report to Fort Logan in Denver, Colorado, for induction.

During this period there was an organization at the Heart Mountain camp known as the Fair Play Committee. The committee met two or three times a week at different places in the camp to persuade prospective draftees not to report for physicals or for induction when called. When my orders for induction came, my father said he wanted me to attend a meeting of the Fair Play Committee before making a decision whether or not to report. That night we attended a meeting of the committee at an adjoining housing block. There were four or five members of the committee there and they informed those present that our incarceration in the camps was unconstitutional and until our constitutional rights were restored we had no obligation to serve our country. If the draftees stood together in their refusal to serve, there was little the government could do because we were already imprisoned.

On our way home that night my father asked what my decision was. There was no question in my mind that night, nor have I ever doubted since, that reporting for induction was the right thing to do.

My father was a quiet man, but when we returned to our barracks that night he showed me a 1-A card which he had treasured for many years. Before he was married, he worked for twenty years as a railroad foreman at Bear Creek, Montana, just a few miles west of the Heart Mountain Relocation Center. During that time, World War One broke out, and though he was an alien he volunteered for the army, passed his physical and was issued a 1-A card. Before being called to serve, the war ended. As he proudly showed me his card, he said he would pray that the war would be over before I had to go overseas also. From that night on, I was comforted in knowing that, though he never attempted to influence me, my father was proud of the decision I had reached. My father and my family later shared in the consequences of my decision as well, as they had to endure the taunting and ridicule of those at the camp who did not share my views.

There had not been, before that time, a service flag at the Heart Mountain camp, even though some Nisei had gone into the service before me.[1] Before I departed for Denver, the Camp Director, Guy Robertson, procured a service flag and held a gathering at the headquarters building where I was honored in a small ceremony, with just a sprinkling of my friends and family, due to the tension existing at the camp over my agreeing to report for induction. Many stars were pinned to that flag after that day, but I regret that, looking through past copies of the *Heart Mountain Sentinel*, I was never able to find an article about the ceremony. I have only my own memories and the remembrances of friends and family to remind me.

Although I was technically drafted, I have always considered myself a volunteer. The reason for this feeling was that in January, 1943, the War Department sent questionnaires to all male and female Japanese Americans seventeen years of age and over. The questionnaire was to determine our loyalty to the United States. The questions that were most discussed from the "loyalty questionnaire" were the infamous questions "27 and 28" which read:

No. 27. Are you willing to serve in the armed forces of the United States on combat duty wherever ordered?

No. 28. Will you swear unqualified allegiance to the United States of America and faithfully defend the United States from any or all attacks by foreign or domestic forces, and forswear any form of allegiance to any Japanese emperor, or to any other foreign government, power or organization?

I answered those questions YES-YES. Some answered YES-NO, NO-YES or NO-NO. Most of those answering YES-YES, volunteered for the new Japanese American 442nd Regiment that was being formed in March 1943. I was only seventeen years old when I took the Loyalty oath, and was underage to volunteer. I know that if I had been of age when I took the oath, I would have joined the other volunteers at that point, so my decision to serve when called was from that time, for the most part, predetermined.

LIFE IN THE 442ND

At Fort Logan I joined about two hundred other Nisei from the Amache Relocation Center in Colorado. With two hundred men we had enough to form one company, and together we took the week-long train trip to Camp Blanding, Florida, for our seventeen weeks of basic training.

I had not been at Camp Blanding long when I received a letter from my sister, who wrote that my father had not been able to eat at the camp mess hall for a week because of being ostracized by a number of the center's residents. They felt that he was personally at fault for allowing me to report for induction. My mother took his meals to the barrack during this period, where he ate alone until people tired of ridiculing him and turned their attention to other matters. In a sense, my decision to serve was felt by him much more than myself. I was always confident that I had made the right choice and was surrounded by other soldiers who shared my view. My father, on the other hand, faced camp residents daily who believed that he had shared in a decision that would undermine their efforts to regain their constitutional rights. I have always respected him for enduring the social pressures that resulted from my decision.

My company of 200 stayed together through basic and the specialized training that followed it at Camp Shelby, Mississippi. The 442nd Regiment, already in Europe, was experiencing heavy casualties and, as a result, preparations were hurried to get us overseas as quickly as possible. In October we were sent to New York to board the Queen Mary, which had been converted to a troop ship. After landing in Glasgow, we were transported by train to Southampton where we boarded troop ships for the Channel crossing to France. On arrival at LeHavre, France, we heard on the radio that the 442nd was taking heavy casualties in the battle to rescue the Texas 36th Division, which had been labeled the "Lost Battalion" because it had been cut off behind enemy lines. As we received our combat gear and trucks were being prepared to take us to Bruyeres, there was a lot of quiet apprehension in the company. We contemplated what we would face in the days ahead. We spent the night in Bruyeres and moved out the following morning just in time to meet what remained of the 442nd Regiment walking towards us, having succeeded the day before in breaking through to the positions held by the greatly outnumbered Texans. As a nineteen-year-old soldier, I was shocked and moved by the appearance of the survivors of our Regiment. The few who could, walked past us looking dirty, tired, bearded and expressionless. The fact that my company arrived a day too late to engage in that battle was probably the major single factor that brought me back from my military service alive.

Because of the heavy losses in dead and wounded experienced by the 442nd in the fight around Bruyeres, the Regiment was pulled off the line and sent to the Maritime Alps in the South of France until enough replacements could be trained to bring it back to full strength. Military action there was sporadic, and in March of 1945 we moved to Marseille where we met one thousand new replacements. I was surprised to meet in that group a lieutenant who had helped in the training of my company at Camp Blanding, Florida.

The lieutenant, a fellow by the name of Goldstein, had the reputation of being the meanest, toughest, and most obnoxious training officer in the company. Many of us despised him and thought that he must have been prejudiced against the Nisei because of his Jewish heritage and associating the Nisei with the Japanese-German Axis war effort which resulted in atrocities against the Jewish people in Europe.

I could not resist asking him how it happened that he was shipped to our regiment, which he seemed to dislike so much. I will never forget his answer. He said,"Fujishin, I was tough on you boys in basic training because I wanted you to be as well prepared as you could be, both mentally and physically, for the situations you would meet in combat. I think I did my job well, and when I got my own orders to go overseas, I requested service in this unit because I believed that I had my best shot at surviving this thing with you folks because of the quality of the training you received."

I never saw Goldstein after that day, but I often wondered if he had bet right, and I would have like to have thanked him for his part in my getting home from my combat experience. My question was answered several years ago when his name appeared as one of the officers of the 442nd Regimental Veterans Organization in Los Angeles.

In July of 1945, I was part of a group of five hundred soldiers from the 442nd, then in Italy, who had the honor of bringing the Regimental Colors back to the United States. It was a very emotional experience for us all entering New York Harbor as we came into sight of the Statue of Liberty. We trained for two weeks at Fort Bevoir, Virginia, in preparation for a parade in our honor down Constitution Avenue in Washington, D.C. The weather on the day of the parade was dismal and rainy, but none of us seemed to notice the weather as President Harry Truman met us and affixed the 7th Presidential Distinguished Unit Citation Streamer to the Regimental Colors. It was the nation's highest honor for a combat unit—equivalent to the Medal of Honor for individuals. In his speech that day, Truman said: "I can't tell you just how much I appreciate the privilege of being able to show you just how much the United States thinks of what you have done. I think that Americanism is not a matter of race or creed, but of the heart." He continued by pointing out that the record of our regiment had reminded the nation that it should "stand for what the Constitution says it stands for: the welfare of all the people all the time."[2] At that moment, I think I was joined by five hundred other young men in my belief that despite all the second thoughts and agonizing doubts, at least for us, the decision to enter military service had been the correct one.

A POSTWAR STRUGGLE FOR JAPANESE AMERICAN RIGHTS

The difficult situation that developed whereby interned Japanese Americans had to make a decision regarding military service almost did not occur. At the outbreak of World War II there was not widespread support for allowing Nisei to enter military service. In fact, in 1942, several thousand Japanese Americans were summarily thrown out of various branches of the military solely because of their ancestry. Many Americans doubted the loyalty of Japanese Americans and some even felt that their attempt to enter the military was a carefully veiled plan to undermine America's military effort and commit traitorous acts.

In fact, the Federal Bureau of Investigation, Navy Intelligence and Army Intelligence today admit that there was not one single case of espionage against the United States by any person of Japanese ancestry before, during or after December 7, 1941. Between 1938 and 1955, ninety-one persons were convicted of spying in the United States, and while sixty-four of them were American citizens, not one was a Japanese American.

Nisei Soldiers

John J. McCloy, Assistant Secretary of War in the Roosevelt Administration, probably played the largest role in making Nisei service in the military possible. He went to General George Marshall and told him that young Japanese American men from Hawaii and the mainland had approached him, saying they wanted to serve in the military to prove their loyalty. McCloy suggested to Marshall that some arrangement should be made to allow this and urged the formation of the 442nd Infantry Regiment to serve in the European Theater. As a result of his efforts, McCloy was later awarded an honorary membership in the 442nd Regiment.

While the record of the Nisei in the 442nd is probably best known by the general public, the precedent set by McCloy's urging resulted in many Nisei also serving in the Pacific Theater. Over thirty-seven hundred Nisei served in the Pacific in the Military Intelligence Service. General Charles A. Willoughby, General Douglas MacArthur's top intelligence officer, estimated that the participation of Japanese American intelligence teams shortened the war in the Pacific by two years. Col. Sidney Mashbir, who headed the Allied Translator and Interpreter Section, estimated that the Nisei soldiers preserved "millions of dollars in materials and thousands of lives" as a result of their contribution to the war effort.[3]

Nisei military service set the stage for some ironic incidents during the war. When Mary Masuda returned to Santa Ana, California, from the Gila River, Arizona Detention Camp, she was accosted by local bullies who wanted her to leave the area. Her trip home was to receive the Distinguished Service Cross for her brother, Kazuo, who had been killed in Italy. General 'Vinegar' Joe Stillwell went to the Masuda home to present the award. In his speech, Stillwell noted the accomplishments of the Nisei soldiers and said, "Those Nisei boys have a place in America, now and forever. We cannot allow a single injury to be done to them without defeating the purpose for which we fought." After the ceremony, Mary was not bothered again.[4]

In another incident, Frank Hachiya, serving in military intelligence, parachuted behind enemy lines to make maps of Japanese defenses. As he returned to American lines he was mistaken for a Japanese soldier and shot. He died three days later. In the meantime, the local American Legion Post at his hometown of Hood River, Oregon, was removing the names of fourteen Japanese American servicemen, including Hachiya's from the town's honor roll. When the town learned that Hachiya had been awarded the Distinguished Service Cross, posthumously, the embarrassed townspeople restored the names.[5]

The evidence strongly supports the view that the actions of the Nisei soldier in World War II contributed to an acceleration of full legal rights for Japanese Americans. On December 18, 1944, the United States Supreme Court, in *Ex Parte Endo*, ruled that loyal American citizens could not be detained in detention camps against their will. The government, anticipating this ruling, announced that restrictions on the activities of Japanese Americans were being lifted across the country. In 1949 the California Alien Land Law of 1920 was wiped off the books and the Walter-McCarren Immigration and Naturalization Act allowing Japanese aliens to become citizens was passed in 1952. The Alien Land Law had been on the books for 29 years and the law denying citizenship for all but "free white persons" had survived since 1790. The fact that most discriminatory laws against Japanese Americans were, for the most part, invalidated within seven years after a war that stirred up considerable anti-Japanese sentiment indicated that other forces were at work casting a positive light on Japanese Americans in this country.[6]

Congressional testimony in the 1980s on the bills to provide financial redress for Japanese-Americans relocated and interned during World War II seems to bear this out. Congressmen in both the House and the Senate often referred to the record and sacrifices of the 442nd Regiment to support the view that those in the relocation camps were "loyal Americans." The Honorable Jim Wright, then House Minority Leader from Texas and a co-sponsor of the House Bill, pointed out that many Texans of the 36th Division owed their lives to the men of the 442nd. Representative Mike Lowery from Washington noted that 14,500 Washington residents of Japanese ancestry were interned without "one day in court" and many of those same Washington residents were "fighting members of the famous 442nd Regiment and died or received injuries to protect those constitutional liberties." Perhaps the most moving testimony was from Hawaii Senator Daniel Inouye, who was himself a captain in the 442nd Regiment. Inouye had lost an arm in military service and was a recipient of the Distinguished Service Cross. Inouye testified that of the 200 mainland Japanese Americans from internment camps going through the ranks of his company, all but about twenty were either wounded or killed in action. Inouye asked his Congressional colleagues to remember "those from the internment camps who proudly and courageously demonstrated their last full measure of devotion in the defense of their country and although these men will not receive the benefits from the provisions of this bill, I am certain that they will gratefully rest in peace." On August 10, 1988, President Ronald Reagan signed the Civil Rights Restoration Act, which provided that an official apology from the nation be sent to each surviving internee along with a check for $20,000.

As Mike Masaoka, the National Affairs Consultant for the Japanese American Citizens' League, pointed out in Congressional testimony, "The War Authority tried to combat unreasonable prejudice of Japanese Americans during the war, but what did more than anything to check discrimination and ill treatment was the reports given to the public on the operation of the Japanese-American units of the U.S. Army—the 100th Battalion and the 442nd Infantry Regiment. The unparalleled records of these two organizations in the army made sound impressions. They brought home to the neighbors of the Japanese Americans that these were Americans also."

Roger Daniels, a historian of the Japanese American experience, has posed the question of whether there is more heroism in resistance than in patient resignation, whether or not the "passive submission" advocated by the Japanese American Citizens' League was the proper response during the war for free men to respond to

148

injustice and racism. In looking back, the response of the Nisei and our parents was as much shaped by cultural forces as by conscious decision making. All Nisei of my generation can remember our parents guiding our upbringing by the words "fu-ga-wari," "gaman," and "shikata-nai." "Fu-ga-wari" suggested to us the importance of never doing anything that would bring "shame" upon the family, while "gaman" reminded us that one should remain stoic in the face of hardship. Perhaps the last word, "shikata-nai," was the most important in shaping the response of Japanese Americans to the order resulting in internment. The closest English translation of this term is probably that there are things in life that "cannot be helped." When one is confronted by these situations in life, the correct course of action is to accept its inevitability, and do all that you possibly can to make the best out of a bad situation.

Nevertheless, I believe that the combination of cultural forces and conscious decision making, largely by the Nisei soldier, that drove the Japanese American wartime experience, brought us to the best possible outcome in a "bad situation." To quote Masaoka, again, "If not for the JACL's constructive cooperation in the first instance and the heroic gallantry of the Nisei servicemen of the 100th, 442nd and the Military Intelligence Service thereafter, there probably would have been no place for the various tests that were made. In a sense the conduct of the evacuees and the hero-ics of the Nisei GI's made possible the freedom to attempt such efforts at [changing] the laws."

CONCLUSION

In 1994, at the 51st Anniversary Reunion of the 442nd Regiment in Las Vegas, Nevada, Wendy Hanamura, a news reporter from San Francisco whose father was a veteran of the 442nd, spoke to the group. Hanamura was a Sansei, and she had returned to Bruyeres with many 442nd veterans in October of 1994 to commemorate the 50th Anniversary of the Battle of the Lost Battalion. She is currently putting together film footage and interviews for a documentary on the military victory in Europe for the Public Broadcasting System which should be completed in May, 1995.

Hanamura, in her talk, related an interview she had recently conducted with historian Eric Saul. In the interview, Saul said:

> Because of the 442nd we have redress, because of the 442nd, Ronald Reagan signed a bill apologizing to Japanese-Americans, because of the 442nd you can be a television reporter in 1994, because if you hadn't proved that Japanese are American no one would want to see you on televi-sion, no one would let your kids enter the best colleges in America.

Hanamura concluded her address by stating, "What you guys did changed history and that's the story we need to tell."

Though I believe that Saul and Hanamura are right in their assessment of the role of the 442nd in the postwar struggle for Japanese American rights in this country, I cannot honestly say that any of us in the 442nd could have predicted this at the time we were actually serving in the military. While that service seems positive, in retrospect, at the time, like anything in life, it was a mixture of good and bad. There was the good feeling that, at least for us, we were doing the right thing to serve our country, but, on the other hand there was the bad side—the criticism our families faced for our decision and of course the terrible suffering and deaths of many who served with us.

Even World War II itself was a confusing mix of negative aspects and positive rewards. For my father, the internment camp experience destroyed his health and spirit, so he was never able to really work again or recover financially from his wartime losses. As for me, as a 442nd veteran I was able to qualify for an Oregon veteran's loan and purchase a farm and home. Because of the war I went to the Treasure Valley on the Idaho-Oregon border to do seasonal farm work, and there met my wonderful wife of forty-six years, Itsie. I give her much of the credit for raising four wonderful children, all of whom are married to wonderful spouses, resulting in nine wonderful grandchildren. As Lawrence Welk would say, "Wonderful, Wonderful!" For what more could a person ask?

I was honored to have been asked to participate in this program. Nevertheless, I very nearly refused the invitation. I am not an academic person accustomed to these kinds of presentations and it would have been much easier to say "no" than "yes." After some thought, I decided it was important that I come. I needed to come to represent the 50,000, many of them Issei, who were interned but were not alive to receive a letter of apology from President Reagan along with a check for $20,000. I needed to come to represent many of my friends in the 442nd with whom I trained and fought, but who never had the opportunity to come back to this country like me to raise a family and watch their children enjoy the rights and freedoms for which we fought. I am among the fortunate, and the very least I can do for the Issei and my fallen comrades is to tell their story—lest it be forgotten.

I guess people of my generation have a simpler, old fashioned patriotism, because when I hear that patriotic song by Lee Greenwood, "I'm Proud to be an American," I get goose bumps, because I too am proud to be an American.

[Editor's] Notes

1. Sam Fujishin was the first internee drafted directly out of the Heart Mountain Relocation Center. The army had previously asked for volunteers but received a very limited response.

2. Bill Hosokawa, *Nisei: The Quiet Americans* (1969; reprint, Niwot: University Press of Colorado, 1992), 410-11.

3. Hosokawa, *Nisei*, 399.

4. Hosokawa, *Nisei*, 414.

5. Hosokawa, *Nisei*, 398, 414-15.

6. Hosokawa, *Nisei*, 450-55.

Sergeant Ben Kuroki's Perilous "Home Mission": Contested Loyalty and Patriotism in the Japanese American Detention Centers

Arthur A. Hansen

"The best-known single sentence to come out of America's part of World War II," the writer Samuel Hynes remarked in 1995, "is not from a general's dispatch or a politician's speech. It is three words from a common soldier whose name stood for every soldier: 'Kilroy was here.'"[1] If in spring 1944 Hynes a Marine pilot in America's so-called "good war"[2] had visited any of the three federal detention centers for evicted West Coast Japanese Americans at Heart Mountain, Wyoming, Minidoka, Idaho, or Topaz, Utah, he might well have heard voiced this very similar declaration: "Kuroki was here."

If asked to explain this utterance, virtually anyone in the imprisoned population likely would have given the same general rejoinder. Technical Sergeant Ben Kuroki was a twenty-five-year-old Nisei or second-generation Japanese American who was born and raised in Nebraska. Following Pearl Harbor, he swapped his peacetime life as a potato farmer and truck driver to become, arguably, the first person of Japanese ancestry in the U.S. Army Air Corps. Overcoming massive institutional prejudice, Kuroki served as an aerial gunner on a B-24 Liberator bomber for thirty missions (five more than required) over North Africa and Axis Europe, for which he was decorated with two Distinguished Flying Crosses and an Air Medal. Then shortly after rotating back to the United States in early 1944 and being billeted in Santa Monica, California, Kuroki was denied a scheduled appearance on the popular Ginny Simms radio show. Not long after this rebuff, however, 700 members of the posh Commonwealth Club gave Kuroki a thunderous ten-minute standing ovation after he spoke to them at a luncheon in San Francisco's Palace Hotel. Following this triumph, *Time* magazine lauded Kuroki as an American hero. The same NBC radio program that only a month earlier had denied him airwaves access because of his ancestry, now welcomed him as their featured guest. When public acclaim for Sergeant Ben Kuroki had peaked, the War Department decided to capitalize on his celebrity by ordering him to go on morale-building, public relations visits to Heart Mountain, Minidoka, and Topaz, three of the ten Japanese American detention centers administered by the U.S. War Relocation Authority (WRA).

If pressed for details about the Nisei sergeant's reception in the three camps he visited in 1944, the incarcerated Japanese Americans would have told a mixed tale. Many would have narrated accounts resembling those that appeared in the *Heart Mountain Sentinel*, the *Minidoka Irrigator*, and the *Topaz Times* that Kuroki had been received in a manner befitting Japanese America's first and, at that time, only World War II military hero: regaled in public and private gatherings, wildly cheered and fawned over, and figuratively presented with a key to each camp. Many other inmates, though, would have countered that, official hoopla notwithstanding, Kuroki was widely felt to be a naive "outsider" foisted upon them by the U.S. government, the WRA, and the Japanese American Citizens League (JACL). Ben Kuroki, in the minds of these internees, had been used as a mouthpiece to combat the resistance to the military draft that had mushroomed within all ten WRA centers, most dramatically at Heart Mountain, after the War Department reversed its earlier wartime policy of considering Japanese Americans unfit for military induction, and reinstituted selective service for Nisei on January 20, 1944.

This article will revisit, review, and reconceptualize Ben Kuroki's so-called "home mission" of 1944, paying particular attention to his week-long tour of Heart Mountain in late April of that year. The emphasis here is not on filling factual gaps in this colorful story, but rather in opening up the gaps between the established facts to support a new interpretation of them. I have sought to stake out a view broad enough to embrace and even nurture opposing perspectives. I have also taken pains to resist indulging an analysis that, however viscerally satisfying, is grounded in and sustained by highly selective perceptions and interests.

I first became intrigued by Ben Kuroki's Heart Mountain-Minidoka-Topaz "home mission" when preparing for a 1988 interview with Brown University social psychologist, James Sakoda,[3] a bilingual Nisei who had conducted participant-observation fieldwork at the Minidoka center for the University of California, Berkeley-sponsored [Japanese] Evacuation and Resettlement Study (JERS).[4] In reading Sakoda's wartime correspondence with the JERS project director, Dorothy Swaine Thomas, I found this captivating reference in a May 2, 1944, letter:

> One . . . item . . . current [at Minidoka] is Ben Kuroki's visit. Thus far it has been highly pathetic because of the lack of response on the part of the people. The Isseis [immigrant-generation Japanese Americans, ineligible for U.S. citizenship] are highly incensed by his statement that he is going to bomb Tokyo, while the Niseis don't dare show too much enthusiasm. I was very much depressed the first day to notice the lack of appreciation of Ben's stand, even though I felt that there were things that he had yet to understand which the people felt deeply.[5]

Sakoda's only other mention of Ben Kuroki and his Minidoka visit, made in a May 15 letter after Kuroki had departed the Idaho center for the Topaz camp in Utah, was still more enticing:

> Ben Kuroki was given a poor reception here, and Acre [Acree], the Reports Officer, just about broke his neck trying to make it seem as though Ben received a "roaring" welcome. Ben made a hit with the younger kids, but was being called all sorts of names by the Isseis. I'm afraid the visit here

confused him quite a bit, and [I] hope that he doesn't become another [Charles] Lindbergh. . . . Ben Kuroki said that he got a poorer reception here than he did in Heart Mountain. And this was considered the most "loyal" center of all.[6]

Even though quite removed from my primary research interest at this time on Nisei social scientists in JERS, I duly highlighted the relevant passages about Kuroki's Minidoka visit in the Sakoda-Thomas correspondence and incorporated a query about it into the schedule of questions for my impending interview with Sakoda. I also consulted several standard volumes on the Japanese American Evacuation (JAE) to add to my small stock of knowledge about Kuroki.

The most useful source was *Nisei: The Quiet Americans* by Bill Hosokawa, a wartime editor of the *Heart Mountain Sentinel*. First, Hosokawa linked Kuroki with the JACL by describing how Kuroki and his brother Fred, along with some fifty other Rocky Mountain Nisei, had been attending an organizing meeting of a new JACL chapter on the morning of December 7, 1941, in North Platte, Nebraska, when FBI agents burst into the room and arrested the presiding JACL official, Executive Secretary Mike Masaoka. Second, Hosokawa explained how, following that meeting, Kuroki's Issei father had unhesitatingly offered him this advice: "'Enlist in the Army, Ben, America is your country. You fight for it.'" Third, Hosokawa related how, after Kuroki's 30 missions in the European theater, he had waived his eligibility for rotation to a safe job in the United States and "insisted on and received an assignment in the Pacific [where he] flew 28 more combat missions in B-29 bombers, many of them over Tokyo." Finally, Hosokawa alerted me to the existence of a biography on Kuroki: "The story of his heartbreaking efforts to be accepted in the armed forces, to win the right to fight for his country, to overcome the wartime stigma attached to his ancestry, is told vividly by Ralph G. Martin in his book, *Boy From Nebraska*."[7]

I did not, unfortunately, get around to reading Martin's celebratory 1946 biography of Kuroki before recording my interview with Sakoda. As the published transcript of our conversational narrative makes clear, our discussion about Kuroki, though revealing, had been quite brief.

S: I know when Ben Kuroki, who was a flyer, came to Minidoka, he got very cold treatment.

H: You said [in your ERS correspondence with Dorothy Thomas] he even got a worse one [reception] at Minidoka than he did at Heart Mountain.

S: Yes.

H: And at Heart Mountain, he got pretty rough treatment, because they had the [organized] anti-draft movement there.

S: . . . . I talked with Ben Kuroki [when he came to Minidoka] . . . . It's very interesting that, because Minidoka had a lot of volunteers [for the Army's special combat team that had been organized in early 1943], there were some deaths also. While deaths were announced [at Minidoka] and they had ceremonies for the deceased, I don't think I ever discussed the death of a soldier with anybody. It was as though it was something that nobody wanted to talk about. Maybe the [Issei] parents of the [Nisei] soldiers felt a little guilty about the situation. . . . It would be an interesting topic to pursue, actually, because it was very important for the family.

H: I think another interesting topic for somebody to write on is this Ben Kuroki thing. I think your account of it in your correspondence [for JERS] . . . is real interesting, because he [Kuroki] apparently took a tour around the different camps, and [the reception given him represents] kind of an index of where the [various] camps [he visited stood] at that particular time on a very important issue, the reopening of selective service to the Nisei.[8]

It was also unfortunate that as part of my preparation for interviewing Sakoda I had not consulted two other books alluding to Kuroki's wartime activities: historian Roger Daniels's *Concentration Camps USA* and redress leader William Hohri's *Repairing America: An Account of the Movement for Japanese-American Redress.*[9] Both books deal with Kuroki in the context of the draft resistance movement at the Heart Mountain camp. Moreover, both discuss the subsequent imprisonment in federal penitentiaries of Heart Mountain Fair Play Committee (FPC) leaders and members for refusing to countenance the drafting of Japanese Americans from behind barbed wire prior to the government restoring or at least clarifying their Constitutional rights as U.S. citizens. Finally, both books connect Kuroki's actions vis-á-vis Heart Mountain in 1944 to the policy initiatives of the "accommodationist" JACL leadership.

In his book, Roger Daniels couples Kuroki's 1944 visit to Heart Mountain with a request from the JACL's headquarters that Roger Baldwin, American Civil Liberties Union (ACLU) head, make public his mid-April 1944 letter to FPC head Kiyoshi Okamoto. In that letter Baldwin disassociated himself and the ACLU from the FPC and admonished Okamoto that, while the draft resisters assuredly had a strong moral case, they had no legal case whatsoever. Furthermore, Baldwin warned Okamoto that "men who counsel others to resist military service are not within their rights and must expect severe treatment." The second accommodationist JACL action that Daniels ties in with Kuroki involves the Nisei sergeant essentially echoing the position toward the FPC leadership voiced by the JACLer-dominated *Heart Mountain Sentinel*. First, Daniels notes that, after a federal district judge, in June 1944, found sixty-three Heart Mountain draft resisters guilty of refusing induction and sentenced them to three-year federal prison terms, the *Sentinel* had "argued that those who encouraged the draft resisters not to report `deserve penitentiary sentences even more than those convicted.'" Then, having explained that a few months later the seven FPC leaders were declared guilty in the same Cheyenne courtroom for "unlawful conspiracy to counsel, aid, and abet violations of the draft" and handed down two to four-year prison sentences, Daniels quotes a post- verdict interview that Kuroki, a non-testifying government witness at this trial, granted the *Wyoming State Tribune*: "'These men are fascists in my estimation and no good to any country. They have torn down [what] all the rest of us have tried to do. I hope that these members of the Fair Play Committee won't form the opinion of America concerning all Japanese-Americans.'"[10]

William Hohri's narrative in *Repairing America* more pointedly conflates Kuroki's actions toward the FPC with JACL directives. Hohri vivifies this association through citing the testimony that Jack Tono, a former Heart Mountain FPC member and convicted draft resister, presented in 1981 at the New York hearing of the Commission on Wartime Relocation and Internment of Civilians. After telling how, in early April 1944, the FBI had rounded up the sixty-three Heart Mountain draft resisters and deposited them in an assortment of county jails pending their mass trial, Tono lauds Abraham Lincoln Wirin, a southern California ACLU lawyer who broke ranks with that organization's national office to represent the resisters at their trial. Tono then draws an invidious distinction between the ACLU and the JACL:

> I shall never forget the Union for their gutsy services. My admiration and esteem for the organization is beyond what I can relate in words. Others have left us high and dry: mainly the Japanese American Citizens League. We were expecting this group to give us their full support, but instead [they] turned their back on us. To this day, I still feel the knife in the back.

Tono's testimony describes how two prominent JACL leaders visited the resisters in jail shortly before their trial and used scare tactics to try to change their minds about resisting the draft: "If you go to prison, you'll get beat up with a two-by-four." After divulging how the JACL persisted in making life difficult for the resisters even after they had gone to prison, served time, and become eligible for parole, Tono momentarily shifts his wrathful attention to the heralded aerial gunner from Nebraska: "Our great war hero, Kuroki, labeled us 'fascist' in the Wyoming newspaper." Having tossed the JACL and Kuroki into the same trash bag, Tono then scathingly remarks: "For all of these two-faced coins we have the appropriate phase: 'the yellow Uncle Toms.'"[11]

Scrutinizing Daniels's and Hohri's accounts made me bemoan not having been familiar with Kuroki's 1944 camp tour when in 1984 I had interviewed another

Nisei, James Matsumoto Omura.[12] Omura had been tried with the seven FPC leaders for conspiring with them to violate the Selective Service Act in his capacity as the English-section editor of the Denver-based *Rocky Shimpo* (a charge for which he was cleared on grounds of freedom of the press). Minimally, Omura would have been able to shed a great deal of light on Kuroki's attendance at that Cheyenne trial as well as the Nisei war hero's post-trial defamation of the FPC leaders. Moreover, because Omura was a staunch opponent of the JACL's wartime role who was then engaged in writing a memoir centered on that topic,[13] Omura could have illuminated any connection between Kuroki and the JACL. Sad to say, moreover, I never communicated with Omura about this situation in the decade that separated our interview with his death in June 1994.

However, it was not until after Omura's death that I seriously turned my attention to Kuroki's controversial 1944 junket. As noted earlier, in my 1988 interview with Sakoda I had commented upon how that tour might be an interesting subject for someone, not myself particularly, to research and write up. It seems that, unconsciously, I had been bitten by the Kuroki bug. For when doing research on Sakoda at the Bancroft Library the very next year I reproduced every entry related to Ben Kuroki in the voluminous field-work journal Sakoda maintained at Minidoka for JERS.

Just prior to Kuroki's arrival at Minidoka, in a journal entry dated May 2, 1944, Sakoda surveyed the camp's Issei population about the situation. One Issei man told Sakoda: "I don't like what he [Kuroki] said [at Heart Mountain] about going to bomb the Japs. You know, he could have just said that he would do his best if he went to the Pacific to fight. After all, he's a Japanese, too." Said one Issei women, rather sarcastically, "It's all right for him to say that he's going to bomb Tokyo because he's an American citizen." More sympathetically, another Issei woman rejoined: "You shouldn't say things like that because if he were in Japan, he would make a good Japanese soldier. You should appreciate the fact that he's a splendid soldier." Two other Issei woman objected to Kuroki talking about bombing Japan. One of them remarked that he was being used as a tool by the government, while the other one referred to him as "*baka*" (fool). Another Issei woman, one who had sons in the U.S. Army, was more charitable: "You can't help what he says because [coming from Nebraska] he's lived only among Hakujins [Caucasians]."

Sakoda covered Kuroki's arrival at Minidoka in rich detail, but before logging his entry, he vented his personal views about the Nisei's hero reception: "I feel very sad as I write this, sad for the bitterness that some people feel and their inability to sympathize with the feelings of others. I don't mind Isseis calling Kuroki all sorts of names, but for some Niseis to do the same thing makes me want to cry." Sakoda then turned to describing Kuroki's actual arrival at the Minidoka site. It is sufficiently poignant and significant to warrant reiteration:

Ben was scheduled to come in through the gate at 10 a.m. I went out to the Ad[ministration] Area a little before 10, and met [Elmer] Smith, the Community Analyst, and his staff standing around, too. I stood talking to them most of the time, looking around to see what was going on. Some of the Isseis working in the Ad[ministration] Area were poking their heads out of doors, curious, it seemed, to see what was going on. However, most of the people who were standing along the main road leading to the gate were Niseis. From the direction of Block 22 some boys and girls were walking up towards the gate. Some Caucasians were intermingled in the crowd.

A little after 10 a car drove up to the gate, and Sargeant [sic] Kuroki stepped out, and shook hands with [Harry] Stafford [the project director] and others. He was dark and smiled warmly. The rest of the time he seemed greatly embarrassed, not knowing what to do with himself. He was placed in a jeep. The girls crowded around him noticeably, probably to get a good glimpse of him. A small applause went up, and I clapped, too. Not because he was a hero or anything, but because he was one of us Niseis. He was just as bewildered as the rest of the Niseis by the treatment the Japanese were receiving. His outlook was different from those of most of the people in the center, perhaps, but he was risking his life for what he believed to be our cause. The applause was weak, and there was practically no cheering. One Nisei was saying: "Let's take a look at our hero." He [this same Nisei] also remarked that he was shoved out of the office by his Caucasian supervisor. Some girls were saying: "Gee, he's cute." Another remarked: "He looks sick." The reception was cool. There were only several hundred persons out to greet him, and most of the people only stared at him, dumbly. Some Isseis hung on the fringes of the crowd, looking on rather disinterestedly. It was little wonder that Sergeant Kuroki looked embarrassed. As the parade moved down the main road, music was furnished by the Boy Scout band and a public address system. The jeep on which Ben Kuroki rode was followed by passenger cars with Caucasian and evacuee dignitaries sitting in them. [One staff member] had his car filled with evacuee office workers. On one bus rode the inductees [into the Army].

The community analysis staff followed the parade to the high school, where students lined both sides of the road. There were some clapping, but no loud cheering. After the parade went by the students streamed back into their class rooms.

As the welcoming parade serpentined through the Minidoka camp, Sakoda collected additional reactions to Kuroki. One Nisei referred to him as a "baboon." When this Nisei's wife obligingly said, "I don't have to go to see that guy. My husband is just as good as him," the Nisei man quickly retorted: "Don't compare me with that guy, I'm better than him." One Issei dismissed Kuroki as an *inu* (dog); while others referred to him as the "*Chosenjin*" (Korean). Still another Issei said: "He's just being used as a tool by the government. They want to get Niseis to go to the Army."[14]

Reading these journal entries by Sakoda made me extremely curious as to what extent the ambivalent reception Kuroki allegedly received at Minidoka had been foreshadowed in his just-completed visit to Heart Mountain, the WRA hotbed of draft resistance. To answer this question, I consulted a new study of Heart Mountain, a 1992 interview with the aforementioned outspoken draft resister Jack Tono, particularly relevant issues of the *Heart Mountain Sentinel*, contemporary reports by the camp's director, Guy Robertson, and community analyst, Asael Hansen, covering Kuroki's visit, and assorted Wyoming newspaper accounts of the FPC trials.[15]

Simultaneously, I wrote letters of inquiries to a number of FPC resisters, including Jack Tono.[16] I also made contact with the Japanese American National Museum in Los Angeles about Ben Kuroki's whereabouts and was informed that he was living in the southern California community of Ojai. After reading Kuroki's biography and entries about him in biographical reference works, I learned that he had graduated in 1936 from Hershey High School and from the University of Nebraska in 1950, and thereafter had pursued a career as a newspaper editor in Nebraska, Michigan, Idaho, and California. The North Platte, Nebraska, librarian confessed to having never heard of Ben Kuroki, and furthermore could find nothing in her library relating to him. But from the University of Nebraska's archives I was told that, beyond majoring in journalism at the Lincoln campus, Kuroki had minored in English, philosophy, and political science. From the Nebraska State Historical Society I received a newsletter featuring a transcript of the talk Kuroki had delivered in 1991 at the opening of the Museum of Nebraska's exhibit on Nebraska and World War II.[17] Having mined this document for biographical facts, I then scanned the Heart Mountain, Minidoka, and Topaz camp papers before, during, and after Kuroki's tour for relevant information.

In summer 1994 I wrote Ben Kuroki informing him of my research focus and requesting that he permit me to transact a two-day combined life-history and topical interview with him. Several weeks later, Kuroki responded by telephone. In a deep yet soft voice, Kuroki said, "I really don't want to do this interview. I was hoping that my 1991 talk at the Museum of Nebraska was my final hurrah." To which I meekly responded, "I really wish you would consent to do this interview with me." Pausing momentarily, Kuroki replied: "Okay, I'll do it, but it will have to be a one-day interview, not a two-day one like you suggested in your letter." It was then arranged that I would interview him at his Ojai, California, home on October 17, 1994. In a follow-up letter, I asked him to prepare a schematic time line of his life for use by me as an interview guide. I also supplied him with personal and professional facts about myself. Earlier, I had told Kuroki that I was a sociocultural historian, not a military historian. Now I supplemented this point: "Owing to a congenital problem with my legs and feet, I was declared 4-F and was even dismissed from otherwise mandatory participation in ROTC during my college years. So I am anything but a war hero like yourself."[18]

In spite of our differences, Ben Kuroki and I really hit it off during our full-day interview. I found him to be one of the most decent men I have ever known: considerate, cooperative, frank, reflective, self-effacing, and conscientious. That day we covered in-depth his life both before and after World War II, information that was noticeably absent from the documents I had read about him in preparation for the interview. Owing to my comparative ignorance about military and aviation history, what the interview communicates about Kuroki's experiences as an aerial gunner on B-24s and B-29s is manifestly inadequate. Those who consult this interview will not discover a substantially different Ben Kuroki from that presented in Ralph Martin's biography, but hopefully Kuroki's life will now be seen as possessing greater complexity.

As to Kuroki's "home mission," we had three "dialogues" that I think were quite enlightening and hence merit attention here.

(DIALOGUE # 1)

H: Now, Heart Mountain's background was that when they had recruited volunteers for the combat team in early 1943, there were very few from Heart Mountain who volunteered to join, and there was some resistance to the recruitment itself. Then, in early 1944, the only organized draft resistance movement in the WRA camps took place at Heart Mountain. I know that when you went there, one of the things you did was to talk to this draft resister group, the Heart Mountain Fair Play Committee. Apparently there was a certain amount of sparks generated by this encounter, leastwise from what I can tell from my research.

K: Yes. (chuckling)

H: But I want you to tell me about this, because I've seen things and heard things from other people who were on the other side of the podium at that time. What are your recollections of the Heart Mountain experience?

K: Well, I [will] never forget one incident. Of course, I was advised that they were a dissident group and that they were also having special guards to avoid any problems there. But I remember getting up and speaking to the group, and one thing that I remember most was that I told them that "If you think Japan's going to win this war, you're crazy." I said, "They're going to get bombed off of the map." And I heard some hissing and booing. (chuckling) I never quite forgot it. But nothing else really happened, no problems.

H: I guess the situation for the Issei who were in the camp was this: first, that they had been stripped of so many things, and then the idea that they might be stripped of their kids; but also [apparently] there were a lot of Issei who truly felt that Japan was going to win that war, even in 1944 when most people would say it was inevitable that they were going to lose. It didn't take a person like yourself to say that to them. But they still had this power to suspend their disbelief and think that Japan's victory was going to happen.

K: Oh, very definitely. Yes, I certainly agree with that. I think that some of those dissidents might have even, you know, been disloyal to the U.S. and returned to Japan if they had not been interned. I mean, you can't say for sure. But it was a terrible experience, and in a way I couldn't blame some of them for feeling like they did. I mean, golly, you lose everything that you ever worked for in life, and have it all taken away. And your being a citizen of this country, to have that sort of thing happen, I don't know how I would have reacted in this same situation. It's quite a thing.

(DIALOGUE # 2)

H: When you were at Heart Mountain, then, the draft resisters baited you a bit, I think, and you responded in kind. Some of them to this day nurture certain grievances against you. One thing you were quoted as saying in a Cheyenne, Wyoming, newspaper was that "These men [the Heart Mountain draft resister leaders] are fascists in my estimation and no good to any country."

K: (chuckling)

H: You were very gung-ho at that time, obviously. You re-upped [for five more flights in Europe over the required twenty-five] and then you also fought to go and fight in the Pacific Theater. So, I mean, you had a strong perception about what your role was. And I suspect for the draft resisters it wasn't simply a matter, as their opposition claimed, that they were draft dodgers, but there was a perception, too, that, if you have citizenship rights, one of the ways to honor them is not to put up with having the government put you behind barbed wire and then draft you into a segregated unit in the

Army and tell you that "this is a wonderful reward."

K: Yes.

H: You've probably thought about these things over the years. I know the Japanese American community has wrestled with who to honor and who to dishonor, and they're finally reaching the conclusion that, you know, we were all involved in this situation together and we responded with our various perceptions of Americanism in different ways and courses of action. Do you feel a bit different now from how you did at the time, or not, towards those Japanese Americans who resisted the draft? I guess my question is this: Do you still continue to see them as draft dodgers rather than draft resisters?

K: Well, I think in most cases I can sympathize with their viewpoint. However, I believe that not all of them were patriotic. Some were using the loss of rights as an excuse. Some were out and out loyal to Japan not many of them and had they not been interned, I think they would have gone back to Japan. Whatever, I'm glad that the draft resisters' position did not prevail at the time the 442nd [Regimental Combat Team] was organized. If theirs was the dominant reaction, the splendid record of the 442nd may have never been. And the Congressional reparations bill and national apology may likewise have never been because I feel that [the] latter would never have reached first base without the achievements of the 442nd and the contributions of the Nisei in the Pacific intelligence units.

(DIALOGUE # 3)

H: Before you went to the three [WRA] camps . . . you had gone to Salt Lake City for awhile, and there you met with some of the leaders of the Japanese American Citizens League.

K: Yes.

H: Had you joined the JACL at that time when you were in North Platte, Nebraska, for that fateful recruitment meeting held on December 7, 1941? Or were you still not a JACL member at the time you went to Salt Lake City in 1944 and met with the JACL leaders?

K: I don't think they ever got the chapter started in North Platte because Mike Masaoka got jailed and nothing was done, as I remember.

H: So did you become a JACL member afterward? One thing I've read recently said that you'd been a long-time JACL member, but then it didn't go on to say when you joined the organization.

K: I don't remember where I joined the JACL, but I know I was with the JACL for a long time.

H: Did you feel that you were coached in any way as to what you should be talking about when you were in these camps [in 1944] by the War Department, the War Relocation Authority, or the Japanese American Citizens League? Because those three groups were intertwined in certain respects.

K: No, absolutely not. I did not have any instructions from the government, and I don't remember anybody else ever giving me any instructions.

H: Were you reluctant to undertake your tour of the three camps, or were you anxious to do it? I mean, compared with going on a bombing mission? (chuckling)

K: Well, a little of each, I guess. I was still a dirt farmer from Nebraska at that time and I wasn't really cut out for something like that.

Right after my interview with Kuroki, I received two letters written by high-profile Heart Mountain personalities containing information about Ben Kuroki's wartime visit to that camp. The first was by Bill Hosokawa, the *Heart Mountain Sentinel's* founding editor and a postwar JACL leader who authored a series of popular histories encompassing the World War II experiences of Japanese Americans.[19] "As for Ben Kuroki," wrote Hosokawa,

I was gone by the time he visited Heart Mountain, but the Sentinel's stories indicate he was lionized as a hero and he had a tremendous impact on the youngsters in the camp. I met him after the war. I would say he was respected and admired by the overwhelming majority of Nisei. Today, perhaps Sansei and Yonsei [third- and fourth-generation Japanese Americans] would not recognize his name, but Nisei would go out of their way to shake his hand whereas they would have little interest in any of the No-No boys. I would guess, without having made any sort of study or survey, that among many Nisei he is looked on as a greater hero than the individuals who went to court to challenge the evacuation. Ben is living quietly in retirement north of Los Angeles and has avoided the limelight, mainly I would guess, because he is at heart a farm boy who prefers the quiet life.[20]

The second letter was from the late Frank Inouye, an early resistance leader at Heart Mountain and a vocal critic of the WRA, the JACL, and the *Heart Mountain Sentinel*.

> When Ben [Kuroki] appeared in [Heart Mountain] camp as part of his tour . . . , I was struck by his "un-military" persona. Altho' he was in uniform and his visit had been preceded by considerable publicity in the "Sentinel," I saw nothing unusual or commanding about his appearance or speech. He appeared to be what he was: a Nebraska farmer's son, in uniform. . . . As the first Nisei war hero, his visit should have elicited enormous pro-volunteer support in camp. That it didn't was due in large measure to the thorough mistrust the camp residents had for anything the WRA and the US military advocated.
>
> Altho' Ben was accorded the full courtesies due a visiting celebrity, including interviews and speaking engagements, my impression is that, while many Nisei admired him for his heroic missions, few identified with him personally. He was, to most of us, a rather remote and distant figure, more of a manipulated robot than "one of us."
>
> One reason for this lack of emotional linkage with Ben is that for all of us in camp, the war was a very distant and barely felt experience. We saw ourselves as its victims and our isolation worked against any personal identification with it, except in general terms.[21]

Several convicted Heart Mountain draft resisters responded by post to my appeal for assistance. One who did so with alacrity was Mits Koshiyama. Even though he was in jail at the time of Kuroki's Heart Mountain visit, Koshiyama harbored strong feelings both about that occasion and Kuroki himself. "I believe that, from what I hear from those who were there," stated Koshiyama,

> that he was well received in Heart Mountain Camp. Imagine, a parade, people waving the flag, Boy Scouts in uniform in a concentration camp. Could make a good TV drama which could show how a small group (the Japanese American Citizens League) with the help of the War Relocation Authority can control a helpless majority. Also can you imagine a person coming into a camp and be[ing] blind to the fact that these innocent people were incar-

cerated behind barbed-wire fences, [plus] watch towers with armed guards. He should have protested the treatment his fellow Japanese-Americans were forced to endure. All he thought was that he was such a great war hero that he became blind to the injustices dealt to a group of unfortunate people. I wonder what he went to fight for.[22]

Koshiyama also referred me to another Heart Mountain draft resister, George Nozawa, whom he termed "our historian." So I wrote to Nozawa for help. In my letter I reviewed for him what I had learned from James Sakoda's wartime reports about Kuroki's mixed reception at Minidoka i.e., that the children idolized him, the teenage girls were captivated by him, but the Nisei men of draft age and their Issei parents were very cool toward him (both because their sons were being placed at risk and because many of them truly believed that Japan would win the war and punish those who participated in the war effort of the United States). I also relayed the information that in advance of Kuroki's Minidoka visit, the word apparently had gotten out that in a speech at Heart Mountain Kuroki had declared that "he wanted to bomb the rice out of his dishonorable ancestors in Japan."[23]

In his reply letter, Nozawa expressed general agreement with Sakoda, but took exception to his observation that many Issei parents believed Japan would win the war and punish all those who had abetted the U.S. war effort. "The Isseis that objected to the draft," maintained Nozawa, "based [their objection] on the fact that it was insensitive and unfair for the Government to take their sons when the future of the family was in total disarray. Come hell or high water they would be needed to help reestablish the family first and foremost; then talk of drafting."[24]

I also heard from Frank Emi, one of only two surviving members among the seven FPC leaders:

> You asked if there was any "relationship" between Ben Kuroki and the [draft] resisters. As far as I know, there wasn't any relationship, communication, or dialogue between the resisters and Ben. The consensus of the resisters was that he was just a Nebraska corn-husker with J.A. features who was completely insensitive to, and without any understanding about the injustices committed to the J.A.s, and was just being "used" by the military for propaganda purposes.

> You also mentioned that rumor has it that I "detested" him. I did not "detest" him. I respect the fellow for his military accomplishments, but I certainly felt back then, and still do now, that he was very insensitive and stupid to come into concentration camps where American citizens of Japanese ancestry were incarcerated and emasculated of all constitutional rights, and foist his "flag waving" bullshit tactics on the inmates. Talk about "chutzpa." He was the proverbial "goat" that lead the mindless, and unthinking "sheep" to slaughter.[25]

At this juncture in my research, I received a passel of letters from former Heart Mountain inmates that were embedded with nuggets of information pertaining to Ben Kuroki and the Wyoming stop on his 1944 camp tour. "Ben Kuroki's visit to Heart Mountain," wrote Kara Kondo, "may have occurred shortly before, or after my leaving camp. It's hard to recall, but I was not directly involved in any of the activities concerning his visit. . . . That we were aware of his accomplishments and proud of his heroism and acclaim, I recall. But, we were looking for 'positive' images of all kinds that might counteract the 'reasons' for our internment."[26]
From Rose Tsuneishi Yamashiro came this recollection:

> I remember that I was 13 or so at the time he visited Heart Mt. I was tremendously proud of all the young men who were in the armed forces from our camp. Among them, of course, were my brothers serving in the South Pacific. Another young man was Ted Fujioka our first student body president who was killed in Italy at age 18 so when I heard that Sgt. Kuroki would be visiting Heart Mt., I was very proud because we all had heard about the Nebraska farm boy who had flown so many missions in Europe. I remember being surprised to learn that he was born in Nebraska. I just did not realize there were many JA's outside of California. His brief story made a big impression on the student body to whom he spoke. He seemed to be such a mild mannered man to have gone on so many bombing missions. He was well received by the students but as I recall there was no big fanfare. He was treated very much like a celebrity, and I remember being very proud of him because he had survived so many bombing runs. I've often wondered whatever happened to him.[27]

Judge Lance Ito's parents, Jim and Toshi Ito, wrote to me at the height of the sensational O.J. Simpson murder trial to say that neither of them were still in Heart Mountain at the time of what they styled Kuroki's "recruiting mission."[28] Their letter also told me about a movie that another Heart Mountain internee, Eiichi Sakauye, had shot of Kuroki's visit. Finally, there was a letter from Ike Hatchimonji informing me that a portion of the Sakauye film had been incorporated into a 1994 documentary video, *Something Strong Within*,[29] shown in conjunction with the Japanese American National Museum's exhibit "America's Concentration Camps." "My recollections about Kuroki and his visit," Hatchimonji ruminated,

> are quite fresh because I was in the Boy Scout drum and bugle corps and the big parade and ceremony held in his honor. He was considered a war hero because of his many missions as a tail gunner in the U.S. Army Air Corps, including flights over the Ploesti oil fields in Rumania. Guy Robertson, the HM camp director [,] made a speech and introduced Kuroki. Looking back, I'm sure Kuroki's visit was intended as a promotional event to encourage

Nisei to join the service. As an impressionable teen-ager, [I thought] Kuroki was a hero even though I didn't realize the irony of being interned while a fellow Nisei made such a name for himself.[30]

I also heard from two other Heart Mountain draft resisters, Tak Hoshizaki and Yosh Kuromiya, both of whom told me that they were in jail when Kuroki arrived at the camp. Hoshizaki conjectured that the purpose of Kuroki's visit was perhaps "to counter the draft resistance occurring in camp."[31] Kuromiya was more expansive:

> It seems our cooperation with the evacuation effort, rather than to clear us of any suspicion of sinister intent, made it even more convenient for the government to question our loyalties. We were no longer Japanese American Citizens of the United States; we were merely "Evacuees." Obviously, Sergeant Kuroki's loyalty and patriotism was regarded as superior to ours and qualified him to act as role model to us, the disenfranchised.
>
> I can only imagine the coming of Sergeant Kuroki, resplendent in all his glittering medals, glorifying his overseas exploits and promoting the familiar JACL accommodationist line. No doubt the term loyalty and heroism were used a lot. What this had to do with evacuation, detention and the U.S. Constitution, I don't know. Nor do I know what his real message was. Perhaps, "You too can join the Air Force and drop a few bombs on white folks in Europe." Ben Kuroki, in a word, was irrelevant.[32]

As one whose published writings over the years had squared in most particulars with the sentiment and line of argumentation enshrined in Yosh Kuromiya's letter,[33] it was very tempting for me to agree that probably Ben Kuroki was irrelevant. But to accept this evaluation involved, leastwise by implication, my also accepting that the 3,000 people who greeted him when he arrived at Heart Mountain and the more than 700 from that camp who did board the bus for their draft physical (385 of whom were accepted for induction, among whom 11 were killed in battle and another 52 wounded) were also irrelevant. Nor could I unstick from my mind the image and the memory of Ben Kuroki himself; in no way had my interaction with this human being given me occasion to conclude that he was, as some of his detractors then and now claimed, a "fool," "tool," "war monger," or "dog." I did think that his perception on the draft resisters was grossly wide of the mark in 1944 and remained so fifty years later when I talked to him on tape about his experiences at Heart Mountain.

I also felt that, in spite of his being a free moral agent, much of what Ben Kuroki said and did during his home mission of 1944–his protestations to the contrary notwithstanding–was guided and goaded on by the War Department, the WRA, and the JACL. As Kuroki explained to me during our interview, his famous speech before the Commonwealth Club had not been written by him, but for him by Staff Sergeant

Bob Evans. "Hell," confessed Kuroki, "at that time I couldn't even write sentences, I don't think." That speech was printed by the JACL and given mass circulation in print and in a dramatized radio program. When Kuroki came to Heart Mountain and the other two camps in 1944, he was shepherded around by the camp's administration and JACLers associated with the internee government and newspaper. What he saw was filtered for him in such a fashion that it was extremely difficult for him to view the members of the Fair Play Committee as anything other than fascists, troublemakers, and traitors. Nor could he call upon his Japanese American background, having never lived in a Japanese American community, to help him achieve a profound perspective on the problem that the draft resisters posed for his sense of Americanism.

If people of Japanese ancestry were "strange" in Nebraska, Kuroki was estranged from them and their ways. In his interview with me, Kuroki made it clear how much he loved his family, even ending our interview by reading into the record a moving published eulogy that he had written about his father. Still, Kuroki told me that as a youngster he "was always . . . a little bit uncomfortable, especially whenever our family would go into North Platte or a place like that. Because when my parents met another one of the Japanese neighbors, they would converse very loudly in Japanese and bow and all that stuff. People would walk by and they would stare at them, and it was very uncomfortable for me." He also divulged to me that,

> having grown up with the kids around Hershey, and going hunting and playing basketball, when the war broke out I felt terrible. I mean I hated being Japanese. But whatever it was, I had the right indoctrination, the right schooling, and whatever democracy had done for me was so deep that there wasn't any doubt in my mind that I was going to defend the United States against Japan. And there had to be something like that in all internees who came out of those camps, because, man, they were treated badly.

I sensed that Kuroki's fierce patriotism, whether expressed in his desire to risk his life as an aerial gunner on a bomber or in lecturing the FPC members at Heart Mountain about the inevitable outcome of the war, had a great deal to do with his socialization in Nebraska and his being courted by chauvinistic chaperons during his 1944 tour of duty in the United States. Surely it also must have had a lot to do with what Kuroki had experienced in the Army Air Corps, something that I had not inquired into in any detail. Although I have an aversion to reading, talking, or teaching about war, I knew that I could not be fair to Ben Kuroki or the cause that he represented at the camps unless my research was broadened to encompass his military service.

The complete details of my research in this area are not especially important, but it did include reading a new history of the Army Air Corps in World War II (Geoffrey Perret's *Winged Victory: The Army Air Forces in World War II*), a revisionist survey of American participation in that war (Michael C. C. Adam's *The Best War*

Ever: America and World War II), and a remarkable and very personal book by a historian haunted by the death of his uncle in the last American bomber shot down over Germany in World War II (Thomas Childers, *Wings of Morning: The Story of the Last American Bomber Shot Down Over Germany in World War II*).[34] I also supplemented my reading by talking at length to an uncle who had been a P-38 pilot in the war and later suffered such severe amnesia attacks that it required forty-four shock treatments to unscramble his brain. I spoke, also, with my mother-in-law, who had lost her brother, an aviation machinist's mate, to the war when his plane crashed in the Aleutian area. I even watched anew the 1949 film *Twelve O'Clock High*, reputedly the best motion picture made about the role of the Army Air Corps in World War II.

My combined reading, conversing, and viewing made me painfully aware of the courage it required and the toll it took on one's nerves to go on bombing missions. Flying, as Ben Kuroki did, in an unpressurized aircraft at over 30,000 feet with temperatures frequently dipping below 35 degrees Fahrenheit was certainly no picnic. Until mid-1944, the life expectancy of a bomber and crew was fifteen missions, and a flyer like Ben Kuroki had only one chance in three of surviving a tour of duty.

Sometimes the problem was oxygen deprivation, which could lead to blacking out and death. With temperatures well below zero, sweat and blood would freeze and clog a flyer's oxygen hoses. There was, too, an ever present danger of frostbite. The crew wore electrically heated flight suits, but if the electrical system shorted out or was damaged in combat, a crew member could freeze to death. To compensate for this contingency, the men wore layers of bulky clothes for warmth. But this clothing caused them to be ever more cramped than they already were in their claustrophobic quarters; often, too, it prevented them from escaping a burning plane before it exploded. With good reason, the Germans referred to the American heavy bombers as "flying coffins."

The biggest problems of all was not, as might be expected, enemy fighter planes like the Germans' new Me 262 jets, but flak ground-based enemy anti-aircraft fire. When on bomb runs, the sky sometimes became so thick with flak, it was said, that you could walk on it. At such times, it seemed impossible to fly through this wall of flak unscathed. But somehow, defying the odds, Kuroki and his bomber team did, and lived to tell about it.

Ben Kuroki's "team" on the bomber were ten men who had lived, trained, and done virtually everything else together. In the 1942 book that John Steinbeck was commissioned to write for the U.S. Army Air Corps, he noted that "the ties between members of a bomber team are tighter than those of nearly any organization in the world" [because] "the men know one another as few men ever get acquainted, for they will be under fire together. They will play together after a victory. They will plan together and eat and sleep together on missions. And finally there is the chance that they may die together."[35]

What does all this have to do with Ben Kuroki, the resisters at Heart Mountain, and their differing views of loyalty and patriotism? I found a provisional answer to this question through reading a now all-too-neglected 1956 book authored by the late Morton Grodzins, *The Loyal and the Disloyal: Social Boundaries of Patriotism and Treason*. When writing this book, Grodzins was the chair of the political science department at the University of Chicago. But much of the book's insight derived from Grodzins's World War II years of employment with JERS, an experience which led to his controversial book about the JAE entitled *Americans Betrayed*.[36]

According to Grodzins, there is customarily a face-to-face group that serves "to define and to clarify abstract goals in terms of day-to-day activity." In a democratic state, groups such as these are the sources of life's principal joys, as well as the objects of one's primary loyalties. The mere existence of such groups affords chances for sharp clashes between national and other loyalties. Paradoxically, however, these other group loyalties are also the most crucial foundation of democratic loyalty. "The welter of non-national loyalties," explains Grodzins, "makes a direct national loyalty a misnomer. It does not exist. Loyalties are to specific groups, specific goals, specific programs of action. . . . One fights for the joys of his or her pinochle club when he or she is said to fight for the country."[37]

Ben Kuroki's "pinochle club" during World War II his primary reference group, if you will was his bomber team. It is true that the Japanese American subculture was also an important reference group to him, but it remained largely a reference group of his imagination and not one deeply grounded in day-to-day activities. So his loyalties as an American were mediated and shaped far less by his ethnic subculture than by his interactions with his fellow bomber crew members. Moreover, his acceptance in that tight military subculture of ten, both as a crew member and as a real American, was perennially provisional, always subject to proving and reproving. For this reason, once his bomber's required 25 missions were over, Kuroki alone refrained from throwing his hat up into the air in a celebratory salute to survival. Instead, he decided to implore his superiors to allow him to fly on five more perilous missions (on the final one of which he almost lost his life).

When Ben Kuroki returned to the United States and was asked to go on still another mission, this time a home mission to Heart Mountain, Minidoka, and Topaz, he did not hesitate to discharge his duty as a good aerial gunner and American. When on this mission, he continued to reference his sense of loyalty to his bombing team and its objectives, which were to destroy the enemy, first in Europe and then in the Pacific. Although a shy man, he could unabashedly tell some thirty thousand people of Japanese ancestry, two-thirds of whom were American citizens, that he fully planned, once his home mission was over, to fly on still more missions, this time in planes carrying bombs to be dropped on his ancestral country, including his Issei mother's hometown of Yokohama.

In the camps he visited, this message (as we have seen) was received well by some inmates, but not by others. Those who were receptive to Kuroki's message were those whose pinochle club was not a bomber team, but Asian Americans whose national status was provisional like Kuroki's and constantly in need of validation, even if this should require the shedding of their blood. But there were also inmates at these camps Kuroki visited, like the members of the Heart Mountain Fair Play Committee, whose loyalty to the United States was mediated by their participation in an organization whose position made it clear that, while they were willing to shed their blood for the nation, they would only do so once the United States started to treat them as citizens rather than prisoners and saboteurs. Given his brittle sense of loyalty and patriotism, when Ben Kuroki encountered these men and this message at Heart Mountain, he could only see in them what he most feared that others would see in him—not only an American who had the face of people living in a reviled enemy nation, but also someone whose loyalties squared with these people.

During his home mission in 1944, whether on the Ginny Simms Show, before the elite throng at the Commonwealth Club, or within the barb-wire girded confines of three American concentration camps, Kuroki reiterated the point that the war the United States was waging against fascism overseas was worthless unless intolerance was conquered at home. But Kuroki failed to see that the FPC members, whom he saw as draft dodgers rather than draft resisters, were his allies, and not his foes, in this two-front fight. These men in the FPC at Heart Mountain were deeply attached and fundamentally adjusted to American ways; nonetheless, they felt deeply that the Evacuation was an affront to America as they conceived it should be. They risked being thought of as disloyal Americans precisely because of their impassioned Americanism. They, like Ben Kuroki, are courageous American heroes whose deeds, like his, should be both remembered and revered.[38]

Notes

1. Samuel Hynes, "So Many Men, So Many Wars: Fifty Years of Remembering World War II," *New York Times Book Review*, April 30, 1995, 12.

2. See Samuel Hynes, *Flights of Passage: Reflections of a World War II Aviator* (New York and Annapolis, Md.: Frederick C. Beil and the Naval Institute Press, 1988), and Studs Terkel, *"The Good War". An Oral History of World War II* (New York: Pantheon, 1985).

3. See Arthur A. Hansen, ed., *Japanese American World War II Evacuation Oral History Project-Part III, Analysts* (K. G. Saur: Munich, Ger.: 1994), 342-457. This edited collection of selective interviews in the Japanese American Project of the Oral History Program at California State University, Fullerton, included four other titled parts: Part I, *Internees* (1991); *Part II, Administrators* (1991); *Part IV, Resisters* (1995); and *Part V, Guards and Townspeople* (1993). Parts I and II were published by Meckler of Westport, Connecticut, while Parts III-V were published by K. G. Saur of Munich, Germany. Hereafter citations of interviews in this collection will be to the appropriate titled part.

4. For a discussion by Sakoda of his ERS work, see "Reminiscences of a Participant Observer" and "The 'Residue': The Unresettled Minidokans, 1943-1945," in Yuji Ichioka,

ed., *Views from Within: The Japanese American Evacuation and Resettlement Study* (Los Angeles: UCLA Asian American Studies Center, 1989), 219-84.

5. See James Sakoda to Dorothy Thomas, letter dated 2 May 1944, folder W 1.32, Japanese American Evacuation and Resettlement Study Records, 1930-1974, Japanese Evacuation and Resettlement Study [JERS], Bancroft Library, University of California, Berkeley [BL-UCB].

6. Sakoda to Thomas, May 15, 1944, ibid.

7. See Bill Hosokawa, *Nisei: The Quiet Americans* (New York: Morrow, 1969), 226-27; 419-20. For the Kuroki biography, see Ralph Martin, *Boy From Nebraska: The Story of Ben Kuroki* (New York: Harper & Brothers, 1946).

8. James M. Sakoda, interviewed by Arthur A. Hansen, in Hansen, *Analysts*, 427-28.

9. Roger Daniels, *Concentration Camps USA: Japanese Americans and World War II* (New York: Holt, Rinehart and Winston, 1971), and William Minoru Hohri, *Repairing America: An Account of the Movement for Japanese-American Redress* (Pullman, Wash.: Washington State University Press, 1988).

10. Daniels, *Concentration Camps USA*, 104-29. As Daniels explains (p. 117, fn. 25), for his treatment of events at the Heart Mountain center he draws heavily upon the 1970 M.A. thesis, "Heart Mountain: The History of an American Concentration Camp," done under his direction by Douglas W. Nelson. Virtually unchanged, this thesis was published with the same title in 1976 by the State Historical Society of Wisconsin for the University of Wisconsin Department of History.

11. As cited in Hohri, *Repairing America*, 172-73.

12. James M. Omura, interviewed by Arthur A. Hansen, in Hansen, *Resisters*, 131-335.

13. This memoir, "A Shattered People," is currently being edited for publication by the present author.

14. See James Sakoda Journal (May 2, 1944), passim, folder R 20.81, Tule Lake Relocation Center, JERS, BL-UBC.

15. Mike Mackey, "Heart Mountain Relocation Center: Both Sides of the Fence" (master's thesis University of Wyoming, 1993); Jack Tono, interviewed by Jean Brainerd, December 1992, State of Wyoming Department of Commerce. Both the thesis and the interview, plus the reports and the newspaper articles, were supplied me by Mike Mackey, one of the organizers of the 1995 Powell, Wyoming, conference where I presented an earlier version of this study.

16. Arthur A. Hansen to Jack Tono, November 19, 1944. This letter to Tono, regretfully, went unanswered.

17. "Ben Kuroki Opens World War II Exhibit," *Historical Newsletter* (Nebraska State Historical Society), 7 (January 1992): 1-3.

18. These two letters to Kuroki, dated August 28, 1994 and September 13, 1994, along with numerous other letters between us, are on file with the transcript of our October 17, 1994, interview in the archives of the Oral History Program at California State University, Fullerton.

19. In addition to *Nisei*, cited above in fn. 8, see Bill Hosokawa, *JACL in Quest of Justice: The History of the Japanese American Citizens League* (New York: Morrow, 1982) and Robert A. Wilson and Bill Hosokawa, *East to America: A History of the Japanese in the United States* (New York: Morrow, 1982).

20. Bill Hosokawa to Mike Mackey, September 24, 1994.

21. Frank T. Inouye to Mike Mackey, September 29, 1994.

22. Mits Koshiyama to Arthur A. Hansen, October 28, 1994, in response to Arthur A. Hansen to Mits Koshiyama, October 23, 1994.

23. Arthur A. Hansen to George Nozawa, October 31, 1994.

24. George Nozawa to Arthur A. Hansen, December 9, 1994.

25. Frank Emi to Arthur A. Hansen, January 14, 1995, in response to Arthur A. Hansen to Frank Emi, November 19, 1994 and January 11, 1995.

26. Kara Kondo to Mike Mackey, January 5, 1995.

27. Rose Tsuneishi Yamashiro to Mike Mackey, January 5, 1995.

28. Jim and Toshi Ito to Mike Mackey, January 5, 1995.

29. Directed by Robert A. Nakamura, this documentary is based upon internee-shot footage within the ten War Relocation Authority centers.

30. Ike Hatchimonji to Mike Mackey, January 8, 1995.

31. Tak Hoshizaki to Mike Mackey, January 22, 1995.

32. Yosh Kuromiya to Arthur A. Hansen, February 3, 1995, in response to Arthur A. Hansen to Yosh Kuromiya, January 25, 1995.

33. See, in particular, Arthur A. Hansen and David A. Hacker, "The Manzanar Riot: An Ethnic Perspective," *Amerasia Journal 2* (Fall 1974): 112-57, and Arthur A. Hansen, "Cultural Politics in the Gila River Relocation Center 1942-43," *Arizona and the West* (Winter 1985): 327-62.

34. Publication data, respectively, for these works are: (New York: Random House, 1993); (Baltimore: Johns Hopkins University Press, 1994); and (Reading, Mass.: Addison Wesley, 1995).

35. John Steinbeck, *Bombs Away: The Story of a Bomber Team* (New York: Viking, 1942), 154-55.

36. Morton Grodzins, *Americans Betrayed: Politics and the Japanese Evacuation* (Chicago: University of Chicago Press, 1949). For the controversy over this book, see Peter T. Suzuki, "For the Sake of Inter-university Comity," 95-123, in Ichioka, *Views from Within*.

37. Morton Grodzins, *The Loyal and Disloyal: Social Boundaries of Patriotism and Treason* (Chicago: University of Chicago Press, 1956), 28-29.

38. The initial version of this paper was presented on May 20, 1995, for the "Japanese American History: The Heart Mountain Experience" conference held at Northwest College in Powell, Wyoming. I am especially thankful to one conference organizer, Mike Mackey, not only for providing me lodging, transportation, and word-processing facilities during the conference, but also for abetting preparatory research for my presentation by putting me in touch with numerous key informants and sending me a variety of relevant primary and secondary sources.

Part V

Recollections of Heart Mountain from Area Residents

Evacuees arriving at Heart Mountain. Since internees were only allowed as much luggage as they could carry, they had to purchase clothes and household items at their own expense after arriving at camp.

Recollections of Heart Mountain

Peter K. Simpson

I am a fourth generation Wyomingite whose family home has been in Cody, Wyoming for more than eighty years. Born in Cody in 1930, I lived in that town all of my growing up life and attended the public schools there. I need to paint a picture here because I think it is important to show how I felt at the time World War II broke out and the Heart Mountain Relocation Center was constructed. I think it is important and instructive in terms of what it was like to come to grips with a cultural chasm of many, many miles, not just the physical distance between Heart Mountain and Cody. It was an educational experience, perhaps outstripping anything that I had learned in the school system at the time and I want to revive that for the reader.

My great-grandfather came to the Territory of Wyoming in 1864. He was of English descent. He married a Scotch-Irish woman named Eliza Ann McCarthy whom he met at South Pass City. He was on the Conner expedition to Tongue River. He was stationed at Fort Phil Kearny and was a Settler's Store owner and operator, carrying supplies like tobacco and incidentals and other things to the soldiers at the various forts. After the so-called Indian wars had been completed, he was appointed the first "Boss Farmer" on the Wind River Reservation, near Lander and Riverton.

He had eight children, four of whom intermarried within the Shoshone Tribe, so I have many cousins on the reservation. My grandfather was a cowboy and a self-taught man who had been kicked out of the eighth grade for watching a public hanging. Later, due to an interest in the law, he began studying Latin. He was enamored with this Latin teacher who was working at the mission at St. Stevens on the Wind River Reservation. In time they married and moved to Meeteetsee, a small cattle town thirty-six miles south of Cody. He practiced law in the Bighorn Basin and moved to Cody sometime prior to 1910 where he and my grandmother raised their family.

My father grew up in Cody and attended the public schools there. Eventually he married the daughter of a coal mine owner in Sheridan, Wyoming who was of Dutch descent. Hence my first name Peter and a middle name which many thought was Japanese: K, double O, I, Kooi. It is pronounced "Coy." Many of my friends pronounced it "Kuwee" and equated it with Oriental descent. It means "a cage for birds," strange birds as it turns out. From Kooi comes the word "decoy," which has to do with fooling ducks here in Wyoming.

My early childhood was a pleasant one. We lived in a rather large house by community standards. It was depression time and there were friends of my parents who did well and there were friends who were caught in the depression's whirlwind of down-turned economies and did not do well. The effects of the Great Depression were quite evident in Cody. It was probably typical of towns in Wyoming. However, we survived, Dad practiced law and did well. The only discrimination I can ever remember was the result of my father's ill-advised purchase of two Packard bikes for my brother Al and me when we were eight and nine-years old. Some of my "friends," whose families were not doing so well, gave me the worst damn licking I had ever had in my life. There was a little bit of have and have not in that game. But it was better than getting licked by the sons of opposing attorneys when Dad argued a case in court.

So it was a comfortable childhood in a very homogeneous town. A little red school house was my initial acquaintance with the public school system and not until I was in my teens was another school built on the east side of town which divided us a bit. The middle-class orientation of the town and its homogeneity gave us a view that, in the larger world, was at least parochial if not in many ways mistaken.

There were no Oriental citizens in the town of Cody when I was growing up, at least in my memory. I recall only one black citizen. Her name was Amanda. The daughter of a railroad conductor, she worked for many of the people in town as a domestic and babysat Al and me on more than one occasion. She was a tolerant and wonderful woman. I recall one night when our parents were visiting friends up the South Fork of the Shoshone River, she accidentally got us locked out of the house. The dear old lady sat with both of us, one on each knee, on the porch until just after midnight when our parents came home. She told us stories and gave us some cause to avoid alarm.

The biggest cultural differences I ever knew were the differences between Powell and Cody. We took it out on each other on the football field and basketball court, and whenever they would allow us to beat them, we would gloat, which was only right. The setting then was one of small town America, small western-town America, small Wyoming-town America.

When the war broke out I was eleven and my brother Al was ten. The common causes and the common enemy which brought us together were all that anyone talked or thought about. In many ways it was a unifying factor and in many ways, like it did across America, it produced an economic upturn. The depression years began to fade and the cause of all-out war was upon us.

My father was Defense Council Chairman, which was simply the head of civil defense for Park County, Wyoming. Dad ran as a Republican for the United States Senate in 1940 but was defeated by the incumbent Democrat, Joseph C. O'Mahoney, in a race that was not even close. It was a landslide with Franklin Roosevelt at the helm and an impending crisis. My father was disappointed by that loss and doubly disappointed when he also found he could not rejoin the Army. He had been a young lieutenant in World War I. Since he was not taken into the Army in World War II, he focused his attention on the home front. My most vivid early memories were of things he did and activities my parents were involved in on the so-called "home front" in the little town of Cody. You would not imagine there would be an immense amount of fervor, but the intensity of the war effort permeated that small town like it did every other community in America.

Recollections

I remember the parties given for returning service men who came home on furloughs, men we looked up to as young boys—Socks Freeman, Hugh Brown, Jack Evans, Bill Barker, Elwood Smith, and many others. I remember those parties quite vividly. The soldiers always looked splendid in their uniforms. Two of them died in the Pacific, one was a prisoner of war in Germany and two others died in the Battle of the Bulge.

I remember too, (this is part of painting the picture of the culture which Al and I grew up in,) civil defense exercises, and Al and I could actually play a part. There were black outs. If you can imagine it, we actually went through the exercise of blacking out the town when the siren downtown on the First National Bank building wailed out a warning of upcoming disaster in the middle of the Rocky Mountains, 1000 miles from the coast. We would dutifully put on our "CD" arm bands, Al and I, and because Dad was in this impressive position we could actually go out and help check to see if any light was leaking from windows in our neighborhood. It was like sneaking out after curfew. We had a lot of fun doing that and one night we even swore that we saw an incendiary balloon floating across the moon. In fact, there had indeed been balloons launched with the general notion that some might drop or fall in forested areas. I do not think that we ever saw such a thing, but at eleven or twelve your imagination can run riot. We reported the balloon siting dutifully, and I think they just as dutifully ignored it.

The third, and by far the most powerful, memory that I have of the entire war was the visits that I took, as a young boy, to the Heart Mountain Relocation Center. I do not think there is a soul in Park County who can ever forget it. It is surprising that the center was not better known in Wyoming. It seemed a major part of our lives. My first experience related to Heart Mountain came when I was walking down the street one day. As an eleven or twelve-year-old I can remember the sign in Merle Rank's barber shop—it was a big sign that said, "No Japs Allowed." I can remember seeing them elsewhere in Cody too. So my first memory as a young boy in that fiercely patriotic, homogeneous town with stories and propaganda coming across the airways, in the newspaper and on Movie-Tone News was fear and concern, maybe very much like the Scots in the northern part of the British Isles when their parents wanted them to be good, would say "Watch out, or the Vikings will get you." There was something of that in the air for us early on in the war.

The fierce patriotism of Wyomingites was reflected in the high percentage of young men and women who went to the service. It was nearly the highest percentage rate per capita in the nation. In this isolated little state, with its parochial concerns, it had a wellspring, very powerful sentiments related to the war and we were participants in that sentiment.

It seemed like an inordinately threatening thing to have a Japanese relocation center put up just a few miles from the hometown. Most of us, and this seems incredible looking back on it, but most of us as young kids growing up were actually encouraged and even soothed by news that there would be military police and protective barbed wire around the camp. We were curious enough to take trips out after it was built and saw the barbed wire and the guard towers firsthand, in front of us. It made one clear impression on both Al and me, as twelve and eleven-year-olds at that time, that we needed to be protected and that the internees were alien and potentially hostile. That is what the camp symbolized and what it conveyed. When I hear of the protest, by the internees, to the construction of the barbed wire fence around the camp, I can empathize with them. They knew what the symbol would mean as well.

I am an Episcopalian and was an acolyte, together with Al, in the Episcopal church (The little poker church in Cody, the one that was built when Buffalo Bill and five cronies got together in a poker game and decided the pot had gotten so big that they ought to try to do something good with it rather than give it to one of their rap-scallion friends who might win. So they decided that the winner should put the money toward the construction of a church. To assuage the conscience of those renegades they built the Episcopal church. There must be a place in heaven for people who do the right things for the wrong reasons). I was shocked to hear our minister, John McGlaughlin (who we would have literally followed to the moon), when he said, "Boys, I want you to help pack up the vestments, sacred vehicles and utensils. We are going to go out to the relocation center and hold a service." I could hardly wait to grab Mom and Dad afterwards and say, "This guy is going to take us out to the alien camp. We are in mortal peril." My parents were surprisingly complacent. I thought, "Where is the protection when you really need it?"

Two days later we were in a car on our way down that old dirt, graveled, partly paved farm road. I will never forget going through the gate and coming into what seemed like an absolutely alien, strange, horrifying and difficult world. We stuck very close to the minister and to each other. We did not want to offend anybody. I remember unconsciously bowing more than I have ever bowed in my life, before or since.

We went to a very plain, tar-papered recreation hall. There was a table at one end of the hall, and as I recall, no windows. We put a cross on the table and gathered things together. I remember sitting up close, right in the front. I sat stock still and watched as the congregation came in. As the service progressed, I was fascinated to see that not only did everybody there speak the same darn language I did, they actu-ally knew the service better than I did. It was during this interesting cross-cultural experience, and I remember in my nervousness, that I made a major mistake. You had to give the wine to the minister first and the water second. In my nervousness, the water went first, and I remember a wry guy, probably in his fifties, looking at me and giggling. After that Sunday, it was never quite as easy to fit the people of the Heart Mountain Relocation Center into the stereotype of the enemy abroad.

We went four times to do that in the space of one year. I found that by the fourth time (there were six of us who were acolytes in the church) we were compet-ing with each other to see who might be able to go to the camp because of the inter-esting stories we would bring back. We would tell other kids what it was like and it fascinated them. Eventually John McGlaughlin made sure that not only the six acolytes went, but many of the younger members of the congregation as well. He was a smart guy. He knew that if the children and young teenagers went to the camp there would be lessons taught that he might not be able to teach the older members of the congregation. The older members of the congregation were split concerning the trips we had been taking to the camp. Some of them approved of it. Others disapproved, but were silent, while others who disapproved were very vocal.

The next most vivid experience in my education as a thirteen-year-old was the result of another great youth leader, Glenn Livingston (an elementary school is named for him in Cody), he was the Scoutmaster of Troop 250 in Cody. He was a remarkable man. Glenn Livingston did the same thing as John McGlaughlin. He said, "Men of Troop 250," (we always snapped to attention) "we are going to have a jamboree at the Heart Mountain Relocation Center." "What?" "We are all going to go out there and we are going to spend an entire day at the relocation center with the Boy Scouts of Troop 379."

We were going to go out and have a jamboree with Troop 379 at the Japanese relocation center. We arrived at Heart Mountain at eight o'clock in the morning. It seemed to take forever to reach the relocation center and it probably did in the old cars with the roads the way they were. The first speaker was the Scoutmaster from Troop 379 and again, to the astonishment of many young men who had not had the advantage of going to the camp with their minister, the guy spoke perfect American English. That was a big revelation for some of Troop 250's most stalwart members. Next, Glenn Livingston gave a talk. Both Scoutmasters made an impression on us because they both spoke about the preparation of young men for life and about the war in very patriotic terms.

Following the initial talks by the Scout leaders, we worked on merit badges. I remember a very skillful young Japanese boy who must have been practicing tying rope knots out in California. It was more than a little bit embarrassing that a guy from the "Cowboy State" could not do the first damn knot and this guy was spinning them out like he could do them in his sleep. We exchanged projects, did merit badges and had quite a morning. I did notice that we stayed pretty close to our Caucasian Cody friends and the Japanese stayed pretty close to theirs. We seemed to be making formal exchanges rather than informal exchanges. I am not sure whether it was planned or how that worked out, but it did help us to ease into the events of the day.

By noontime we were sitting pretty much mixed together in the recreation hall over a hot meal. In the afternoon we broke up into less formal groups and I was paired with a young Japanese American who liked art and so did I. He drew a picture of Tarzan that was terrific. We then went outside and tossed the football around. It could have been out there on Bleistein Avenue in Cody. It was cold and there was snow on the ground. It looked just as God-forsaken at the camp as it did in Cody. My Japanese friend had a dandy sense of humor. He said at one time during the ball throwing, "I'm so cold, even my goosepimples got goosepimples." I laughed like he was Bob Hope. I thought that was the funniest damn thing I had ever heard. I followed him around the rest of the day waiting for his next one-liner.

After tossing the football around, my friend took me to one of the tar-paper shacks and we went inside. His mother was making tea but she also had hot chocolate and cookies. I remember how gracious she was and how good the hot chocolate tasted after our tossing the football. After the hot chocolate my friend took me a few yards down along the front of the tar paper barrack and we went into another room where his grandmother lived. My friend's grandmother was a very dignified little lady. Though the outside of the barrack was poor and bedraggled looking, the inside was a scene of Oriental opulence with tapestries hanging on the walls and a little shrine in the front of the room. It was almost like a religious experience. Though she could not speak English, my friend told me that his grandmother said she was glad I was there and that she hoped I was enjoying the day. Meeting my friend's family was a memorable experience.

That night, after the dinner, they had games including Blind Man's Bluff, which must have been played differently in California than we had ever played it in Wyoming. Instead of just touching the person, the guy in the middle, who was wearing the blindfold, was armed with a rolled up newspaper that he would use to take whacks at the people who touched him. If you could not get away, you would get clubbed with the newspaper. One particular guy and I did very well at that game until we came across a little Japanese fellow who I think only weighed 120 pounds. He was not very big. At twelve years of age I was taller than everybody, but I was certainly not as mature. The little guy, to my horror, had hair on his legs. He was stocky and armed with this damn newspaper, and he beat the hell out of me. I had a terrible time. I did not want any part of him after that and my friend had disappeared. I do not know where he went; he might have set me up. After the game ended the little guy peeked out from under his blindfold. I can still see that goofy grin on his face, when he saw red nose and watering eyes.

I had at least six experiences at the relocation center. The last one, and perhaps the most telling, did not have anything to do with conversations or with an interconnection with anybody at the relocation center. It was a trip that Mom and Dad had to take to Heart Mountain for an errand. I remember that when we came to the gate on our way home, Dad stopped the car and got out to talk to somebody. As we sat waiting in the car I looked over my right shoulder and saw a soldier and his girlfriend standing under the guard tower. He had one arm around her. He had a red Fifth Army patch, on his shoulder (my favorite army). I will always remember that picture. I can see it not just in memory, but in Technicolor. The red patch, that fellow with sort of a jaunty look, looking at a kid in a car, a proud look, smiling, and I involuntarily waved. He did not wave back; he just smiled as we drove away.

That might have been the beginning of the first independent, intellectual, challenging political and philosophical thought that I had about this whole thing. That thought stemmed from six experiences, a friend in the camp, a Boy Scout beating, a church muff and an occasion of discontentment and unsettling feelings. It dislodged my comfortable stereotyping and left me, for the first time, without a ready-made answer to questions of national right and wrong. I grew up in those years, and my growing up became conscious that day. I have only one regret out of all of that. I wish I would have kept my Boy Scout friend's name so I might have kept in touch with him. My brother, however, did find one of his Boy Scout jamboree friends, Norm Mineta. He and Al shared the experience in the Congress of the United States where Norm, the former Mayor of San Jose, serves as Congressman from California. They have a fast friendship to this day.

I found myself at UCLA recently looking at relocation pictures in an exhibit there. I was looking mostly at the faces of people in the photos to see how visibly the tragedy might have been written on them. Though I never saw it in their faces, I could see tragedy in every grain of the pictures.

The distance between Cody and Heart Mountain was twelve and one-half miles, but it seemed like the longest trip in the world for a young boy between two cultures and two separate times.

Remembering the Heart Mountain Hospital

Velma Kessel

I grew up on a homestead at Deaver, Wyoming, approximately fifteen miles from Powell. Following my graduation from Deaver High School I attended the Deaconess Hospital Training School for registered nurses in Billings, Montana. After the completion of nurses training I went to work for the Yellowstone County Hospital in Billings. I was employed there until October of 1942 when, due to the construction of the Heart Mountain Relocation Center between Powell and Cody, Wyoming, I was given the opportunity to work closer to home. From that time until May of 1945 I was employed at the Heart Mountain Hospital as a registered nurse supervisor. My pay, as a Caucasian worker, was $1,800 per year. The Japanese doctors and nurses who worked at the hospital were paid $228 per year.

The hospital was located in the northwest corner of the Heart Mountain Relocation Center. It consisted of seventeen barracks connected by a long hallway. The hallway allowed for each barrack building, or ward, to be evacuated and then isolated in case of fire. The hallway, which had windows on each side, was not heated. It was like an oven in the summer and was frigid cold during the winter months. The hospital had 150 beds, which was about average for a hospital located in a community of ten thousand people at that time. The hospital was self contained with steam heat, laundry and kitchen facilities.

The first barrack was used as the front office for the hospital. Doctor Irwin (the Chief Medical Officer), the hospital administrator, head nurse, Public Health nurse and social worker, all had offices in the first barrack. The remainder of the building was used as a waiting room for the hospital. The second barrack was divided up into private rooms and was used as the Doctors' quarters. This barrack also contained a bathroom with showers, a small kitchen and a larger room at the end of the building which was designated as the lounge. However, during the early months of the camp's operation the lounge contained no furniture. Furnishings for the lounge area were built later at the camp's wood shop. These quarters were used by the doctors when they were on call for obstetrics or for an emergency.

The nurses' quarters were set up in a manner similar to those of the doctors' with showers, one bathtub and a larger lounge area. These, however, were our permanent quarters. My room had one window (without curtains), one light bulb hanging from the ceiling in the center of the room and an army cot with one blanket, two sheets, one pillow and pillowcase. I had an empty nail keg which I used as a stool and stacked my uniforms on the floor. On my first trip home to Deaver my dad built a crude vanity for me. It was made from two orange crates with a board across the top. When I returned to camp I brought a hammer and pounded nails into the wall so that I had a place to hang my uniforms.

Ward Four was the OB ward and nursery. It had two private rooms, a large open ward, a small diet kitchen with refrigerator, stove and table, linen closet, medicine room, labor room and delivery room. Very little sedation was given during labor and then drip ether was administered for episiotomy. Following childbirth, mothers remained in the hospital an average of eight to ten days. The supervisor of the OB ward was a middle aged registered nurse of Japanese ancestry. She was very efficient and, unless you had a delivery during the 3:00 p.m. to 11:00 p.m. or 11:00 p.m. to 7:00 a.m. shift, she was in charge.

Ward Five was the first ward opened at the hospital. Once construction of the remaining wards was completed and those wards were properly equipped, Ward Five was designated as the pediatrics ward. It contained several private and double rooms, a small diet kitchen, medicine room, linen closet and a nurses' desk where the charting was done. Initially, when the ward was first opened, no beds or cribs were available so we were forced to use army cots. At that time it was necessary for one of the parents to remain with a hospitalized child in order to help keep him or her in the cot. The supervision of pediatrics fell to Gladys and Arvella Atwill. Both were registered nurses who came to Heart Mountain from the Children's Hospital in Denver, Colorado. Doctor Ito was the pediatrics specialist.

The illnesses we treated were typical of what would have been seen in any other hospital at that time. We cared for children with pneumonia, croup, sore throats, ear aches, flu and diarrhea. We made mustard plasters in wash basins to put on the chests of the little pneumonia patients, and for diarrhea we used the water that rice had been cooked in. The accidents were also typical and several come to mind. One little boy ran barefooted through hot ashes from one of the mess halls and received severe burns. A little girl fell off the barrack steps and broke her arm, while another little boy swallowed a box of X-Lax and had to have his stomach pumped.

There were also two rooms at the end of Ward Five which were used for the treatment and care of soldiers stationed at Heart Mountain. Doctor Irwin always treated and cared for the soldiers. They were treated for typical illnesses and occasional accidents. One soldier, for instance, was treated for a fall he took while trying to climb into one of the guard towers. After arriving at the emergency room and receiving stitches to his face, the soldier was admitted to Ward Five.

On one occasion five armed soldiers were admitted to Ward Five and as I made my rounds during the 3:00 p.m. to 11:00 p.m. shift one of the soldiers was assigned to go with me since I was the only Caucasian in the hospital. There was a strike in the kitchen. I do not know exactly what happened but as I recall, it had something to do with the reclassification of workers. The evening trays were late and the nurses aides had to go to the hospital mess hall and get them. Thankfully, by noon the following day the strike ended and the soldiers returned to their base camp.

Ward Six was the surgical ward. Mrs. Harvey, a registered nurse originally from Denver, was the nurse supervisor in surgery. She was also in charge of all the sterile supplies used in the OB department, the clinic and the hospital. The men's surgical area was on one end of the ward with the women's area on the other. In between the two surgical areas was a utility room, diet kitchen, medicine room, linen closet and a nurses' desk where the patients' charts were kept. We did appendectomies, thyroidectomies, hysterectomies, tonsillectomies and gall bladder and breast surgeries. There were also surgeries on internees involved in accidents. One young man was working for a farmer near Cowley, Wyoming and was accidentally shot by a resident of the area who had been hunting birds. The gunshot victim was brought back to Heart Mountain where he was operated on. He survived his wound and the surgery. By the middle of 1944, 848 surgeries had been performed at the Heart Mountain Hospital with tonsillectomies and appendectomies being the most frequent.

Ward Seven was set up as the men's and women's medical ward. Ward Eight was eventually used as the women's medical ward leaving Ward Seven for the men. However, when the camp first opened, Ward Eight was used to care for evacuees with communicable diseases. As evacuees disembarked from the trains each individual had his or her eyes, ears, nose and throat checked for communicable diseases. Only four patients were admitted to Ward Eight. In the men's and women's medical ward we treated pneumonia, pleurisy, cancer, cardiac problems, diabetes, stroke, high blood pressure, ulcers and depression. Elderly patients liked to stay on Wards Seven and Eight because they did not have to go out into the cold to get to the mess hall or latrine and they received tender loving care.

Like the other wards, men's and women's medical contained a utility room, diet kitchen, linen closet and nurses' station. Miss Wolford, a registered nurse from California, was in charge of Wards Seven and Eight. In addition to these duties, Miss Wolford taught classes for the training of nurses aides and orderlies from the evacuee population. The classes covered how to make beds, give bed baths, back rubs and how to take a patient's blood pressure, temperature and pulse rate.

Ward Nine was divided into an isolation ward and mental ward. Miss Leonard was the registered nurse in charge of Ward Nine. She had been an army nurse in World War I and ran the ward like an army hospital. We had a good number of TB patients in the isolation ward. The only treatment we had at the time was rest and plenty of fresh air. One young man in isolation was suffering with TB and also had a broken leg. He was so bored that we taught him how to knit. Little Emico was a favorite patient of mine. She was sixteen years old and suffering with tuberculosis. I used to visit with her and buy crochet thread for her.

In the mental ward there was one padded cell for individuals who were violent to themselves or others. We had some mental patients in the ward but those we could not treat were transported to the state hospital in Evanston, Wyoming. Across from Ward Nine was a supply ward and the morgue. The camp had an agreement with funeral homes in Cody and Powell so the deceased were not in the morgue for very long.

The hospital mess was supervised by Miss Wade, the dietitian. In addition to serving meals to all of the hospital employees three times a day, Miss Wade was also responsible for serving the needs of the patients, many of whom had special dietary requirements. Meals were made for patients who were diabetics and those who were on soft food, liquid, non-fat or no salt diets. Miss Wade also trained the aides who worked in the diet kitchens on each ward. The aides set up the trays, delivered the meals to each ward and cleaned up afterwards.

The next barrack was the ward for emergency services. The ward contained a room for the ambulance drivers and emergency and surgery rooms. There were eight ambulance drivers at the hospital and they had a number of duties. They would take the aides on the 3:00 p.m. to 11:00 p.m. shift home and pick up and deliver the aides working the 11:00 p.m. to 7:00 a.m. shift to the hospital. The ambulance drivers also delivered formula to the mothers of new-born babies. The kitchen on Ward Eight made the formula for the new-borns and it was delivered by the ambulance drivers every four hours. This was necessary because there was no refrigeration in the barracks where the internees lived. A mother, working through the doctor, would tell the formula kitchen how many bottles her baby would require in a twenty-four hour period and the ambulance drivers would see to it that the bottles were delivered. In addition to these duties the ambulance drivers answered an average of thirteen emergency calls per day.

Those who came through the emergency room during the winter months were most frequently treated for frostbite. In the summer months patients arriving at the emergency room were usually treated for bee stings and burns. All patients had to first come through the emergency room or the clinic before they could be admitted to the hospital.

The next ward contained the x-ray department, dentist offices, the eye clinic, outpatient clinic and a complete pharmacy. When the large x-ray machine was installed I was asked if I would be interested in being the x-ray technician. Since I had no interest in that area the hospital administration trained eight young men from the camp to serve as technicians. When the dental and optical clinics first opened they did a brisk business. Early on, the dental clinic cared for an average of 600 patients weekly while the optical department saw nearly 900 patients per week.

The hospital also had a clinical laboratory where numerous test were run. Laboratory workers made nearly 175 analyses weekly. The pharmacy was supervised by a Japanese American pharmacist. The pharmacist was responsible for all of the drugs used in the hospital and the clinic and for seeing that prescriptions were properly filled. Hundreds of prescriptions were filled each week.

The outpatient clinic had private examining rooms and a large waiting room. It was a very busy place. By the middle of 1944 more than nine thousand people had gone through the clinic with many being admitted to the hospital. Patients we were unable to treat were transported to Billings, Montana. The hospital saw an average of 133 patients per day. During the time the center was open, 552 babies were born at the Heart Mountain Hospital and 185 deaths were recorded in the camp.

At one time, according to the *Heart Mountain Sentinel*, we were the largest and best equipped hospital in the state of Wyoming. By the middle of 1943 the

Heart Mountain Hospital

Caucasian staff included eight registered nurses, a dietician, Public Health nurse and social worker. The head nurse had been a missionary in Japan and spoke Japanese fluently. She frequently visited with the elderly patients. The nurses wore white uniforms with the nurses aides and kitchen aides wearing blue dresses and white pinafores. We were proud of the hospital and took pride in our appearance. The first autumn when the camp opened and the weather turned cold, the evacuees were issued surplus navy "pea coats." Evidently one size was supposed to fit all. The aides, who were small in stature, were completely lost in the coats.

The Public Health nurse, Doris Keese, trained four Public Health aides, all of whom helped to relieve some of the congestion at the clinic by making house calls. Keese and her aides checked on patients who were recuperating at home, swabbed sore throats and took care of cuts and bruises. Hospital personnel assisted the Public Health Department in giving diphtheria shots to pre-school children and physical examinations to elementary and high school students.

During the summer of 1943, fourteen cases of Rocky Mountain Fever were reported in Wyoming. As a precaution, agricultural workers, firemen, police officers, motor pool employees, Boy Scouts, Girl Scouts and hospital personnel, were all inoculated. All totaled, 980 shots were given. Though it caused a certain amount of anxiety among the evacuees, Rocky Mountain Fever was never a real problem at Heart Mountain.

The hospital was a world unto itself. Halloween and Christmas parties, along with numerous dances, took place in the hospital mess hall for all medical staff employees. Many farewell parties for hospital employees were also held there. We ate in the hospital mess hall when we were on duty, but to find out what was going on in camp we would eat at the administration mess hall when off duty.

During the years that I worked at the Heart Mountain Hospital I met and became friends with a number of the evacuees. On one occasion my mother and I took two young Japanese women with us to Billings on a shopping trip. When we registered at the hotel the clerk refused to talk to the girls. He asked me if they were from the "Jap Camp" in Wyoming. I said that we were from the Heart Mountain Camp. He then wanted to know if the girls could be trusted. I told him that they were American citizens, so he said they could stay if I would be responsible for them. We had to have a connecting door between our rooms. Today I would tell that clerk where to go, and we would find another hotel, but times were different then and I was a proper young lady, so we stayed.

On several different occasions I took young ladies from Heart Mountain to my home and to church in Deaver. They were always accepted as my friends. Sometimes I took the aides from the hospital to Cody to the theater and I remember seeing signs in a few stores that said, "No Dogs or Japs Allowed." I do not remember any such signs in Powell. There were two Japanese families who farmed near Powell before the war and they were highly respected. Maybe that made a difference.

My dad worked for the Shoshone Irrigation District at Deaver and on one occasion they needed an additional worker for a few weeks. My dad asked if I knew anyone at the camp who might be willing to work for him. I told a young man at Heart Mountain about the job and he worked for the irrigation district for a couple of weeks. When he came back to camp he told me that the employees at the district could not pronounce his name so they just called him "Shoshone." My dad thought he was a remarkable young man, a good worker and an excellent ambassador for Heart Mountain.

In April of 1943 I was married in Billings. Since my husband was stationed overseas I continued working at the Heart Mountain Hospital. By 1944 many of the nurses aides had relocated, either moving with their families, enlisting in the military or going off to college. At that time we closed Ward Eight and moved women's medical back to one wing of Ward Seven. In December of 1944 President Roosevelt said that the evacuees could return to the West Coast and that the camps would close in 1945. As the population at Heart Mountain declined, additional wards were closed. Wards Four and Five were the last to close. The evacuees appreciated the care of the doctors, nurses and hospital staff as was evident by the many thank you notes published in the *Heart Mountain Sentinel*, the camp newspaper.

In May of 1945 I left Heart Mountain to join my husband who had returned from overseas and was stationed in Florida. I enjoyed my experience at the camp and the chance to work with very professional and qualified individuals. I am honored to have this opportunity to pay tribute to the five Japanese doctors and the medical staff who did not relocate, but stayed in camp to give professional care to the residents of Heart Mountain. They were dedicated men and women.

Part VI

Re-Reading the Archives and Sources

for Future Research

The Okano family posing in front of their apartment. Evacuees at Heart
Mountain, as with those interned in other relocation centers, persevered and
tried to make the best of their situation.

Re-Reading the Archives:
The Intersection of Ethnography, Biography & Autobiography in the Historiography of Japanese Americans During World War II

Lane Ryo Hirabayashi

INTRODUCTION:
STUDYING THE LIVED EXPERIENCE OF MASS INCARCERATION

In studying what might be called the "lived experience of mass incarceration," I submit that important work still remains to be done. If we take a camp like Poston, (officially known as "the Colorado River Relocation Center"), near Parker, Arizona, there are literally tens of thousands of pages of archival material available on this camp, alone. Almost all of these data were written between 1942 and 1945 by Euro- and Japanese Americans who were "on the scene."

Poston is distinct, to be sure, in that it was the site of no less than three major research projects: the Bureau of Sociological Research (BSR), set up by John Collier, Sr., head of the Office of Indian Affairs, which operated exclusively at Poston; the Japanese Evacuation and Resettlement Study (JERS), a University of California research project directed by Professor Dorothy S. Thomas, which had six field sites, one of which was Poston; and, the "community analysis section" of the War Relocation Authority (WRA), which deployed anthropological and sociological field workers in all ten of the War Relocation Authority camps.[1] Combined, these research projects entailed data collection on every conceivable aspect of the experience of mass incarceration.[2] Today, fifty years after the end of World War II, both the materials written by project employees, as well as a plethora of different kinds of collected documents including letters, diaries, and reports, largely written by Japanese Americans, have become an increasingly valuable resource, as time passes by and memories fade.

Specifically, I have found that oral history work of Nisei, such as I have done off-and-on for the past twenty years, is useful up to a point, but in the final analysis is limited if not misleading on certain topics. The archives may be one of the only vehicles now available to explore Issei political participation in the camps, if only because many of the Issei who played leadership roles are no longer with us. One of the things that I have been able to discern from BSR, JERS and WRA archival materials is that there may have been more "political participation" on the part of the Issei than the extant literature reveals, or that Nisei may have known about, let alone have remembered.

In exploring this point, I want to begin by outlining the methods I have found useful in assessing archival materials in the JERS collection. I will also introduce and outline two specific examples that provide evidence of previously unacknowledged dimensions of informal political organization at Poston, at least as far as the published secondary literature is concerned.

METHODS

How can we best approach the archival materials produced by the staff members of projects such as the BSR, JERS and the WRA's "community analysts?"

One step is a matter of common sense, and involves processes of "triangulation."[3] At one level, this is a matter of "data triangulation" which requires that one compare archival data and interpretations to the extant literature and assess the degree to which a given point corresponds to what has already been established and put on the record. When there is little or no extant literature on a given point, the process can become painstaking; for example, one may have to search out individuals from whom supplementary oral history interviews can be taken in order to clarify facts or points at issue. In any case, once basic data are retrieved, the challenges of interpretation begin.

In my research on Poston, the fact that there were three projects in operation there, employing more than a dozen researchers, as well as additional sources such as reporters for the camp "newspaper," the *Poston Chronicle*, also means that there are plenty of points at which the interpretation of a particular datum can be cross-checked. Researchers represented a range of situations and perspectives, so one can often find more than one point of view on the record (in the archives as well as in the secondary literature) in regard to major events. Comparing materials at these levels involves elements of both "methodological triangulation," or comparing bodies of data on the same topic that have been arrived at via different research methods, and "investigator triangulation," or the use of data generated by different observers.

Another significant point at a methodological level is that archival materials can be most effectively utilized if we have a full understanding of exactly who the BSR, JERS and WRA researchers were. Now this is one thing if we are considering professional scholars whose lives and accomplishments are often recorded in everything from *Who's Who in America* to the popular media, let alone in professional forms such as in biographies, *festschrifts*, obituaries and so forth.

If we take, by comparison, the two JERS field workers in Poston, Richard S. Nishimoto and Tamie Tsuchiyama, it is significant that while other researchers have drawn from his fieldnotes and field reports repeatedly over the years, virtually nothing was ever written about Nishimoto's life until 1987.[4] Tsuchiyama's life has never been studied or documented, to the best of my knowledge, until I began working on this task a couple of years ago.

Now, the JERS archival materials on Poston are largely a matter of the research that Nishimoto and Tsuchiyama carried out, on site, between 1942 and 1945. I like to think of their research methodology as fundamentally ethnographic. Tsuchiyama and Nishimoto, that is, were engaged in fieldwork, an approach to data collection and socio-cultural description that revolves around observing, talking to and often living with a group of people over an extended period of time.[5] On the basis of his first-hand research, Nishimoto, in particular, left a large and fascinating body of fieldnotes and field reports, that are supplemented by a voluminous personal correspondence. When one includes similar materials generated by Tsuchiyama, these two JERS researchers alone left thousands of pages of raw data which, in my opinion, have not yet been fully tapped.

In order to get a handle on what they've left us, however, we very much need to know who they were, what questions framed their work and what conceptual and analytic predispositions and commitments "drove" their research, so to speak. Once we have a handle on such information, I propose that we, who read their field notes some fifty years after the fact, are in a much better data position to control for the conscious and unconscious biases that necessarily frame the production of knowledge.[6]

Specifically, how can we fully utilize the field notes and filed reports of Tamie Tsuchiyama unless we know something about her background—especially those early personal and educational experiences that helped to form her sensibilities? As it turns out, Tsuchiyama was a Nisei, born in Kauai, Territory of Hawaii, in 1915. On one hand, Tsuchiyama had exposure to Japanese language and culture at home and at Japanese language school for eight years. On the other hand, she went through her elementary, secondary, high school and college (two years at UH, anyway) in an educational system that strongly emphasized assimilation and "Americanization."[7] If one knows this much about Tsuchiyama, one is in a much better position to understand her sometimes openly derogatory and hostile response to more traditional, conservative members of Poston's Japanese American community.

Above and beyond this, my formal training as a socio-cultural anthropologist makes me keenly aware that the specific networks that a field worker develops in order to gain access and information are critical to the kinds of data and interpretation that result.[8] To wit: the information gathered through a process of ethnographic fieldwork is predicated on a set of relationships, and I submit that these, the "social relations" of production, lie at the foundation of knowledge in socio-cultural anthropology, Thus, a field worker's relationships to researched "others" must be understood before someone else's fieldnotes and field reports can be effectively utilized for subsequent research purposes.[9]

Although this is not all there is to say about issues of "method," these points will suffice for now. Let us turn to Richard Nishimoto and Tamie Tsuchiyama, and consider how and why their field research on the political set-up and informal political processes of Poston are still a rich source of insights which haven't been integrated into the literature.

NISHIMOTO AND TSUCHIYAMA

Tsuchiyama was already an advanced graduate student in the department of anthropology when the U.S. entered World War II. Although she was close to finishing her dissertation, and could have actually petitioned to rejoin her family in Hawaii in 1942, she returned to Los Angeles where she had done one year of undergraduate work at UCLA. For the period of about two months, she lived with an old friend, Edith Kodama and her family. There, Tsuchiyama observed the initial process of mass removal, and was so moved that she tried to do what she could to help others during this period of shock and crisis. At the same time, her letters reflect a growing interest in formally studying the impact of mass incarceration on the Japanese Americans who were affected by Executive Order 9066. Eventually, Professor Robert Lowie, the eminent anthropologist and Tsuchiyama's professor and mentor, linked her up to Dorothy Thomas and the JERS project. Tsuchiyama eventually decided to go to the Santa Anita Assembly Center with the Kodama family, and from there, she went off on her own to work as a field researcher in what was initially a camp administrated by the Office of Indian Affairs: Poston, Arizona. Tsuchiyama, however, had relatively little field experience. In the final analysis, I don't think that she knew what she was getting into—especially in terms of the amount and kinds of stress that doing fieldwork on a forcibly incarcerated population was going to entail for her.[10]

Richard Nishimoto was an *oya no yobiyose*. He was born in Japan and, while his parents emigrated to the U.S. and tried to set up a business in San Francisco, Nishimoto stayed behind and completed his secondary level education in Tokyo. His parents then "called" for Nishimoto and, because his parents had done relatively well, Nishimoto was able to enroll in and graduate from San Francisco's Lowell High School. Deciding to continue his education, Nishimoto applied to and graduated from Stanford University with a degree in engineering. Unable to obtain any kind of job in this profession, Nishimoto gravitated to Los Angeles, where he worked in different capacities, got married, and wound up in the produce business before the war. Moving up to East L.A., where his family joined his wife's sister's family, the Nishimotos were removed directly to Poston without being processed through an "assembly center." In this fashion, Nishimoto was able to remain in this single camp from 1942 to late 1945, which was an unusually long period. Small wonder that such an individual would attract the attention of the various scholars in Poston, seeking Japanese American field assistants for their research projects. Nishimoto, after all, was a well-educated, fully bi-lingual, and bi-cultural Issei, who had a penchant for both research and writing.[11]

What makes the data that Nishimoto produced for the JERS project even more unusual is, first, that he left a good deal of autobiographical data in his field notes and reports. (By the way, Nishimoto died in late May, 1956, and other than what wound up in the archives, almost none of his personal papers were preserved.) On this basis, we know a good deal about his background, as well as his activities and thoughts during the time he carried out fieldwork for JERS.

Second, between 1942 and 1945, Nishimoto became an increasingly important community leader and power broker within Poston's Unit I. In this sense, a good deal of Nishimoto's research entails a combination of ethnography and auto-ethnography: that is, Nishimoto would also include accounts of his own positions and actions as an integral part of the political processes he studied and described at Poston.[12] This dimension makes Nishimoto's corpus very distinctive from the research generated by the typical Nisei field worker who was employed by the BSR and JERS, or who worked as an assistant, gathering data, for WRA community analysts. By comparison, these Nisei were younger and, although they were well educated, their command of Japanese wasn't as strong, and I sense that they were more detached from their compatriots both before and during the war. None, to my knowledge, came even close to Nishimoto in terms of his status as a "community leader."

JERS FIELDWORK AT POSTON

When Tsuchiyama arrived on the scene, it is important to remember that things were very much in flux in regard to her assignment. Although she was supposed to have worked for the JERS project in Poston, Dr. Alexander Leighton recruited her almost immediately to work for the BSR. Tsuchiyama was actually allowed to work for both research projects in the beginning, although she quit the BSR after three months of employment there.[13]

Tsuchiyama's letters indicate that she already knew Nishimoto prior to the war. Nishimoto certainly knew about Tsuchiyama when she arrived at Poston. Correspondence and fieldnotes indicated that he was concerned that she might be an F.B.I. operative. Nishimoto considered Tsuchiyama a potentially "dangerous enemy," and he had joined the BSR himself in order to keep an eye on her.[14]

By November, 1942, Tsuchiyama had written to Dorothy Thomas indicating that she had made a tremendous breakthrough. Tsuchiyama said that she had gained the trust of the "real" leaders behind the strike, and that they were freely sharing inside information with her. A subsequent letter indicates that Tsuchiyama had finally won the confidence of Nishimoto, whom she characterized as "one of the two most powerful political leaders in camp."[15]

As of late 1942, Tsuchiyama had built a preliminary foundation for her fieldwork in all three units of Poston, but it is also very clear that Nishimoto's role as a community leader in camp gave him a special value to her, in terms of providing access to information that Tsuchiyama couldn't otherwise obtain, In sum, Nishimoto became Tsuchiyama's "key informant," and this relationship must be "read back in" to Tsuchiyama's field notes and reports if the most effective use is going to be made of them.

INFORMAL POLITICAL ORGANIZATION IN POSTON

Let me offer a brief overview of key aspects of two unpublished JERS doc-

uments as an illustration of how background biographical and autobiographical information allows us to better appreciate and evaluate the contributions of the
Tsuchiyama-Nishimoto research team.

In early 1943, Tsuchiyama wrote a fascinating research report, entitled "The
Visit of the Spanish Consul." Three points about this report are especially relevant
here.[16]

First, in 1942, Issei leaders appealed to the Spanish Consul, Sr. Francisco de
Amat, to inform the Japanese government that the conditions and treatment of people
of Japanese descent in Poston were poor in some cases, and unacceptable in others.[17]

Second, even before Nishimoto was hired on to the JERS project in order to
be Tsuchiyama's Issei assistant, his role as a key informant was well established.
Thus, Tsuchiyama's ethnographic reports are quite useful in terms of understanding
Nishimoto's thoughts and activities as a community leader.

Third, "The Visit of the Spanish Consul" manuscript establishes that there
was an informal political structure in place at Poston, that, unbeknownst to Euro-
American authorities and researchers alike, was based on pre-World War II community organization, and was dominated by Issei, or first-generation Japanese
Americans. This deserves further explication.

We know from his autobiographical accounts that Nishimoto had a pretty
wide exposure to both urban and rural Japanese American communities throughout
California, since he had worked and lived in diverse areas such as San Francisco,
Vacaville, Colusa, Palo Alto, Los Angeles, and Gardena, among other locales.
Whether in rural or in urban settings, when numbers permitted, there were a stock set
of groups often formed by the first generation Issei. These ranged from the more par-
ticularistic regional associations (or *kenjinkai*), through rotating credit associations
(*tanomoshi*) and mutual aid groups (*kumiai*)—which might be formed on a variety of
bases from "common point of origin," common endeavor, propinquity in the U.S., or
a combination of the above—to more universalistic organizations like the Japanese
Association of America (or, *Nihonjinkai*). Undoubtedly, because of his different
work experiences in diverse settings in California, Nishimoto was fully aware of the
full range of such institutions that knit Japanese American individuals and families to
the larger community.

One also learns from Tsuchiyama's report that Nishimoto had a formulated
analysis of the informal political organization of the pre-war Japanese American communities. From Nishimoto's vantage point, in order to fully understand the politics
inside of a given Japanese American community, one had to identify the local *yushi*—
a Japanese term, literally meaning "public spirited" individuals, which we can gloss
here as "community leaders" as long as it is noted that such persons achieved their
status on the basis of service, rather than on the basis of authority or command *per
se*. In short, because of their "good works" on the behalf of their compatriots, yushi
were disproportionately influential within their local communities.[18]

Beyond this, it must be remembered that when people of Japanese descent were subject to mass removal, if nuclear or extended family members were living in the same point of origin, family units were basically moved together. Similarly, in many cases, members of pre-war communities from a particular point of origin were often kept together and processed through the same "assembly center," and ultimately assigned to the same WRA camp. Furthermore, in the Poston case, people from the same pre-war areas often wound up being assigned "apartments" in barracks in the same block. If they were a large group, or otherwise didn't fit into a single block, they might also be situated in contiguous blocks.

Tsuchiyama's report indicates that Nishimoto used both his knowledge of the organization of pre-war communities, as well as of the regionally-based set up of housing in Poston's barracks, blocks and quads, in order to identify key yushi inside the camp. Because of their pre-war prominence, many yushi apparently remained influential among community persons from their respective areas of origin on the West Coast. What is more, it is notable that *none* of the yushi sought or played a role in Poston's formal political institutions, whether the "Issei Advisory Board," or the "Central Executive Council." According to Tsuchiyama, yushi preferred to remain well out of the limelight since, in some cases, prominence as a "leader" resulted in an initial period of incarceration, without one's family, in special "internment camps" run by the U.S. Justice Department.

Tsuchiyama's report details, at some length, Nishimoto's broader political methodology in the early days at Poston when he was still consolidating his power base. Basically, Nishimoto would target the key yushi throughout Poston's Unit I, and would focus in on them in an attempt to sway them to his point of view. If successful, Nishimoto could usually count on the yushi to bring their following into line and entire blocks could be deployed to influence the formal decision-making structure of Poston's self-governmental set up. In this manner, Nishimoto fashioned himself into a major "opinion leader" in Poston.[19]

In short, as wholly dependent as I believe Tsuchiyama to have been on Nishimoto for the data and insights that make up this report—and this is another patent limitation that must be "read" back into the text—I propose that "The Visit of the Spanish Consul" provides the basis for some interesting hypotheses. The most important are: (1) as early as 1942 the Issei had been able to re-introduce elements of the pre-World War II political organization into camp settings such as Poston; and (2) awareness of this informal and apparently hidden dimension of camp politics does not appear to be evident in the archival contributions of Euro-American bureaucrats or researchers on the scene, let alone in the secondary literature.[20] These two points, then, offer a new perspective that can be utilized to re-read as well as to reinterpret creatively the archival records and extant secondary literature, alike.[21]

RE-READING POPULAR RESISTANCE AT POSTON:
THE ALL CENTER CONFERENCE

For reasons that I cannot go into here, Tsuchiyama ended up leaving Poston in late 1943, in order to go to Chicago to write up her field notes. In the nine months that followed, she produced virtually nothing, and Dorothy Thomas basically ended up firing her.[22] By agreement, however, Nishimoto remained in Poston, and when Tsuchiyama left, he became the primary and sole JERS field worker in that camp.

In 1944, Nishimoto began work on a series of three longer papers, focusing on topics such as the loyalty questionnaire, selective service and "relocation;" in other words, to put it in a nutshell, various events and processes related to the WRA's policy (1944-1945) of encouraging Japanese Americans to leave Poston so that the camp could be shut down. These reports are complex and multi-faceted, and Nishimoto ended up drafting them as a trilogy—an interrelated set of papers on the order of four hundred pages in all. I will only focus on the penultimate report, which treated what is sometimes referred to in the literature as "the All Center Conference."[23]

Although a misnomer, the idea behind the All Center Conference emerged in response to the War Relocation Authority's decision, in early 1944, to close all of the camps except for Tule Lake, by the end of 1945. Keep in mind here that, as this announcement was made, many recalled that Milton Eisenhower, the first director of the WRA, had originally stated that camps would remain open "for the duration" [i.e., of the war], plus fourteen days. Suddenly, in December, 1944, with the war in full progress, WRA authorities announced that they wanted to close nine of the WRA camps within the year—again, with the sole exception of Tule Lake, which was where all of the so-called disloyals and renunciants had been confined after 1943.

In response to this announcement, Japanese Americans in at least four of the WRA camps—including Topaz, Utah; Poston, Arizona; Heart Mountain, Wyoming; and Amache (a.k.a., Granada), Colorado—proposed a meeting of popularly-elected representatives from each of the WRA camps. "Examination of the facts," and "opportunity for discussion" were the two stated purposes of the proposed conference. In hindsight, it is clear that the main agenda was actually to see if there was any way to prevent the WRA from arbitrarily and precipitously closing the camps. In short, anger over the WRA's plans in regard to camp closures generated a popular movement whose fundamental tenant was the assertion of Japanese Americans' rights.

The conference began in Salt Lake City, Utah, on February 16, 1945, at ten in the morning. In the end, there were elected representatives from only seven of the ten WRA camps. The camp at Jerome, Arkansas had already been closed, Tule Lake was not included, and the block managers at Manzanar declined to send representatives because they felt apparently there wasn't any point.

Nishimoto's report on the conference shows that the representatives who did come presented impressive analyses of the general situation facing the seventy-thousand or so souls who were left in the WRA camps by 1945. To begin with, representatives—including those from Heart Mountain, by the way—prepared a concise summary of the injustices and losses suffered as a result of mass incarceration. Representatives pooled information and estimated that between sixty-five and seventy percent of the people who remained in the camps were basically unable to leave unless they were provided with "more assistance and tangible proofs of guarantee," as Nishimoto put it.

In order to illustrate some of the finer points of the delegates' analysis, let me summarize some key points from Nishimoto's report. The research that the delegates carried out revealed that about fifteen percent of the Japanese Americans wanted to and were able to re-enter the larger society. Representatives from each participating camp agreed that no one intended to discourage such individuals or families and that, in fact, everything possible would be done in order to facilitate their departure. Another fifteen percent of the camp populace was regarded as being *unable* to leave due to factors that ranged from advanced age, impoverished financial conditions, debilitating emotional and psychological problems and so forth.

It is most significant that the All Center representatives collectively agreed that the majority of the population, some sixty-five to seventy percent in all, *did* want to leave camp. The representatives also agreed unanimously that, before these folks could re-enter the larger society, the federal government needed to provide them with: (1) more financial assistance (and remember here that, at this point, the government was only offering $25 and a train ticket back to one's point of origin); and (2) guarantees that the government would actively protect their rights and safety once they left camp.

The conference ended with an evening meeting, February 25, 1945. Despite some differences, representatives were able to agree on many points. They drafted a nine page, single-spaced document that featured an extensive list of grievances and demands. The document—which incidentally is preserved both in Nishimoto's report, as well as in the All Center Conference proceedings, a copy of which I found in the JERS collection—was signed by all of the representatives and then sent directly to Washington, D.C., to then President Franklin D. Roosevelt, Dillon Myer, director of the WRA, as well as to the Department of Justice, the Department of the Interior, the War Department and both houses of Congress.

In examining the demands issued by the All Center Conference, then, it is clear that the Japanese Americans left in camps by 1944-45 were angry about the entire process of war-time removal and incarceration. Demands were also an expression of resentment toward a plethora of administration miscalculations and misjudgments such as had occurred with the so-called loyalty questionnaire and the imposition of compulsory selective service. Demands also reveal that, whatever their contempt for the WRA camps, the Japanese American community did not want to be unconditionally forced to leave them in response to an imposed deadline that many felt to be both premature and certainly misconceived.

Thus, the All Center Conference proposal points to the fact that by 1945, Japanese Americans who were still incarcerated felt a sense of outrage and injury. Second, the community as a whole was able and willing to identify the federal government as the source of the original problem. Third, the community as a whole held the federal government accountable for losses as well as for the protection of individual constitutional and human rights as the remaining Japanese Americans left camp.

This, then, was a popular mass movement. At Poston, in particular, Nishimoto made much of the fact that the election of representatives was held in an open and democratic fashion. Finally, it needs to be emphasized here that, as a popular movement, the All Center Conference represents a form of collective empowerment that goes above and beyond the efforts of specific individuals who are sometimes identified as heroes—some of whom even advocated the concept of monetary reparations during the 1940s—or small groups of men and women who went out on a limb to resist mass incarceration in general, or selective service, in particular. Even if one acknowledges that some of Nishimoto's interpretations are problematic, the above point provides the basis for valuable insights.[24]

For example, it has often been proposed that the redress movement dates from the 1970s.[25] I would argue that the larger significance of Nishimoto's report on the All Center Conference is that it reveals how and why the redress movement can be seen as reflective of the struggles of the larger Japanese American community from 1942 on, and, perhaps even from the earliest struggles of the Issei in this country for self-respect and self-determination. The All Center Conference also indicates that Japanese Americans still in camp by 1945 were far from a passive or, alternatively, pro-Axis, population—portrayals that appear in both the secondary literature and in the popular imagination.[26]

In summary, now that the central goals of the redress/reparations movement have been accomplished we should continue to grapple with an on-going challenge: that is, to return to this key period and assess it yet again with fresh eyes. In doing so, I suggest that we be especially conscious and critical of familiar images that, in the final analysis, may be misleading.

IMPLICATION

In conclusion, I hope I have been able to offer support for my initial assertions that, first of all, the JERS, WRA and BSR archives offer unique materials for the assessment of the lived experiences of mass incarceration. Second, as rich as these archival holdings may be as primary source materials, they must be "re-read" both critically and with imagination. Third, it is imperative that we do more research about the men and women who wrote, collected and in some cases synthesized these materials, so that we are better able to utilize data, while at the same time controlling the various biases necessarily entailed in their creation.

Beyond this, let me offer one final point. Although more work certainly needs to be done on each one of the camps, I would guess that, between the books, articles, doctoral dissertations and M.A. theses that are available, we now have basic information on all ten of the WRA camps, as well as on many of the assembly centers, Justice Department internment camps and so forth. In short, while I wouldn't discourage the production of camp-specific monographs, it is clear that such accounts often repeat what is already well established, or document particular features which have little interest or relevance beyond the ideographic record.

I would say, then, that investigation of selected topics that *cut across various camps* is an approach that should be prioritized.[27] To what extent did informal political structures evolve in other WRA camps that were similar to what Nishimoto and Tsuchiyama described in Poston? I am also very curious as to how and why Japanese Americans at Topaz, Granada, Heart Mountain and Poston seem to have independently generated the idea of an all-center conference. Let me put this forward as an example of a multi-camp research project that might best be pursued by having a number of scholars studying camp-by-camp histories within a unified, comparatively-oriented, framework.

In short, by developing research agendas around themes that allow the WRA camps to be studied comparatively, we can explore broader perspectives on the various meanings of this period for Japanese Americans and Euro-Americans alike. In this fashion we may also be able to come to grips with an important project that the historian Richard Drinnon has introduced: framing research on the camps in order to illuminate processes of political, economic and socio-cultural oppression in North American history as a whole.

Notes

1. I am not able to go into the specific foci and goals of each of these three research projects here. Interested readers can obtain an overview by consulting the descriptive, and typically uncritical, overviews presented in the following sources: Alexander H. Leighton and Edward H. Spicer, "Appendix: Applied Anthropology in a Dislocated Community," in Alexander H. Leighton, *The Governing of Men: General Principles and Recommendations Based on Experience at a Japanese Relocation Camp* (Princeton, Princeton University Press, 1946), 371-97; Dorothy S. Thomas and Richard S. Nishimoto, *The Spoilage* (Berkeley: University of California Press, 1946), V-VX; and, "Appendix I: Annotated Bibliography of the Community Analysis Section," in Edward H. Spicer, et al., *Impounded People: Japanese-Americans in the Relocation Centers* (Tucson: University of Arizona Press, 1969), 301-16; et passim.

2. The Bureau of Sociological Research materials are archived, in part, at the University of California, and in full in the manuscript collections held by Cornell University. The Japanese Evacuation and Resettlement Study materials are archived at the University of California, Berkeley. The materials produced by the Community Analysis Section are held in the

National Archives.

3. Norman K. Denzin, *The Research Act: A Theoretical Introduction to Sociological Methods* (New York: McGraw-Hill, 1978). For an update on Denzin's related work and contributions, see "The Art and Politics of Interpretation," in *Handbook of Qualitative Research*, eds., Norman K. Denzin and Yvonna S. Lincoln (Thousand Oaks, CA: Sage, 1994), 500-15.

4. Richard Drinnon, *Keeper of Concentration Camps: Dillon S. Myer and American Racism* (Berkeley: University of California Press, 1987), 48-49.

5. An excellent discussion of the ins-and-outs of ethnographic field work, focusing on the production and analysis of field notes, is presented in Roger Sanjek, ed., *Fieldnotes: The Makings of Anthropology* (Ithaca: Cornell University Press, 1990).

6. This perspective, emphasizing the way that biases are necessarily and inherently a part of the production of knowledge in history and the social sciences, is drawn from Gunnar Myrdal, *Objectivity in Social Research* (New York: Pantheon Books, 1969).

7. Interested readers can consult the recent study by Eileen H. Tamura, *Americanization, Acculturation and Ethnic Identity: The Nisei Generation in Hawaii* (Urbana: The University of Illinois Press, 1994), for further details in this regard, especially Parts 2 and 3.

8. This is not a new observation, of course. A classic example is presented in G.D. Berreman, *Behind Many Masks: Ethnography and Impression Management in a Himalayan Village* (Ithaca: Society for Applied Anthropology, Monograph, No. 4, 1963).

9. Sanjek's point that even very-thoroughly written fieldnotes may actually entail "headnotes" that only the original author can fully flesh out, let alone interpret, adds an additional level to the challenges faced in trying to appropriate another person's research; Roger Sanjek, "Fieldnotes and Others;" Roger Sanjek, *Fieldnotes: The Making of Anthropology*, 324-40.

10. This conclusion is drawn from my forthcoming book in Lane R. Hirabayashi, *Field Work in an American Concentration Camp: Tamie Tsuchiyama at Poston, Arizona* (Tucson: University of Arizona Press, 1999).

11. I have presented an extended biography of Nishimoto in Lane R. Hirabayashi, *Inside an American Concentration Camp: Japanese American Resistance at Poston* (Tucson: The University of Arizona Press, 1995).

12. A number of anthropologists have surveyed such work under the rubric "auto-ethnography"; for one example, see David M. Hayano, "Auto-ethnography: Paradigms, Problems and Prospects," *Human Organization* 38 (1979): 99-104.

13. Hirabayashi, *Fieldwork in an American Concentration Camp*.

14. Edward H. Spicer, "R.S. Nishimoto," December 17, 1954, JERS.

15. Tamie Tsuchiyama to Dorothy S. Thomas, January 5, 1943, JERS.

16. Tamie Tsuchiyama, "The Visit of the Spanish Consul," is held in JERS collection at the University of California. This report is dated January 10, 1943.

17. Tamie Tsuchiyama, "The Visit of the Spanish Consul," 1-5. I am not able to discuss this important point here. Suffice it to say that, from the very beginning, Issei leaders and/or their spokespersons fully recognized the injustices of mass incarceration, and were able to formulate and present their protests and demands vis-a-vis the federal government and the War Relocation Authority to the Spanish Consul.

18. Tamie Tsuchiyama, "The Visit of the Spanish Consul," p. 10-25. The role of yushi as "leaders" goes beyond the domain of "personal influence" as delineated by Elihu Katz and Paul F. Lazarsfeld in *Personal Influence* (New York: The Free Press, 1955). Interestingly enough, Nishimoto's insights about yushi role in Poston's politics were developed independently of the research of the former scholars, carried out while they were members of the Bureau of Applied Sociological Research at Columbia University during the 1940s and 1950s.

19. In my view, Nishimoto's role as an "opinion leader" revolved around who Nishimoto claimed he knew, what he claimed he knew, and eventually, who he "was" within Poston's administrative and bureaucratic fields of power; see Gabriel Weimann, *The Influentials: People Who Influence People* (New York: State University of New York Press, 1994).

20. There are exceptions to this general rule; see, for example, the contributions of Arthur A. Hansen, including his classic study, "Cultural Politics in the Gila River Relocation Center, 1942-1943," *Arizona and the West* 27[1985]: 327-62.

21. For a good example of what I am talking about, readers need only compare Tsuchiyama and Nishimoto's descriptions of the political organization of Poston with those generated by a colleague who published the results of his field work immediately after the war: Leighton, *The Governing of Men*.

22. Hirabayashi, *Fieldwork in an American Concentration Camp*.

23. "All Center Conference and Director Myer's Visit," JERS. A surprising number of authors have briefly mentioned this conference, but few appear to have appreciated its significance. It is important to emphasize from the beginning, that—contrary to what was claimed by WRA analysts including John Embree or Edward Spicer, and even liberal doctoral students like Speier or Mossman in their Ph.D. dissertations some thirty years later—it *was not* that the Japanese Americans did not want to leave camp. Rather, the All Center representatives asserted that there were complexities that the WRA was glossing over, if not ignoring, in asking "the residue" to leave camp with the war in full progress.

24. I have found, over time, that two key caveats must be remembered when using Nishimoto's materials. First, he had a tendency to put himself at the center of events, whether these were events that he told Tsuchiyama about, or events that he described himself

in his field journal and reports. Second, Nishimoto's work sometimes appears to be too overly focused on his political enemies of the moment. "The Visit of the Spanish Consul" report, for example, describes Nishimoto's efforts to discredit Issei leadership whom he felt to be too "radical" without, in my view, allowing the latter any "benefit of the doubt."

25. Examples abound; here I will only cite William M. Hori's study, *Repairing America: An Account of the Movement for Japanese-American Redress* (Pullman: Washington State University Press, 1984), 29.

26. Admittedly, we should be careful not to overgeneralize about "Japanese Americans," "Nisei," or "resistance" in the WRA camps. The populace, generations, and orientations/activities in each regard, varied over time, place, and in response to extant conditions. Nonetheless, I am struck by the fact that one of the singularly important questions of the 1970s—namely, Sansei or third generation Japanese Americans, asking their second generation Nisei parents, "Why didn't you resist?"—was misconstrued. My reading of the archival record confirms, repeatedly, Gary Y. Okihiro's and Arthur A. Hansen's emphasis of the frequency and tenacity of resistance on multiple occasions and multiple levels.

27. Studies that have paved the way in this regard are Toshio Yatsushiro, *Politics and Cultural Values: The World War II Japanese Relocation Centers and the United States Government* (New York: Arno Press, 1978); Gary Y. Okihiro, "Japanese Resistance in America's Concentration Camps," *Amerasia Journal* 2[1973]: 20-34; Rita Takahashi Cates, Comparative Administration and Management of Five War Relocation Authority Camps, unpublished Ph.D. dissertation, University of Pittsburgh, 1980; and, Drinnon, *Keeper of Concentration Camps.*

Records at the National Archives—
Rocky Mountain Region Relating to the
Japanese American Internment Experience

Eric Bittner

The wartime removal of 110,000 Japanese and Japanese Americans living along the West Coast of the United States to internment camps situated in remote areas in the country's interior, formally initiated when President Franklin Roosevelt signed Executive Order 9066 on February 19, 1942, was a sweeping act that continues to have ramifications for individuals, families, communities and the national conscience. The relocation process carried out by the federal government resulted in the creation of many "official records" which can now be found among the holdings of the National Archives and Records Administration (NARA). The NARA, as the nation's record-keeper, is responsible for preserving and making available for research those documents created by federal agencies, offices, committees and courts that have continuing historical value. Records pertaining to the wartime relocation of Japanese Americans can be found throughout the NARA facilities nationwide—in the Washington D.C. area, the regional archives system, in Presidential Libraries, and on National Archives microfilm publications. The largest collection of records in the NARA's custody relating to Japanese American internment were created under Record Group 210, Records of the War Relocation Authority, held by the NARA facilities in Washington, D.C. and College Park, Maryland.[1]

This paper will deal specifically with those records which can be examined at the National Archives—Rocky Mountain Region, located in Denver, Colorado. The regional archives holds records that document the activities of federal agencies and courts in Colorado, Montana, New Mexico, North Dakota, South Dakota, Utah and Wyoming. Within these boundaries three relocation camps existed: Heart Mountain, in northwest Wyoming; Amache, at Granada, Colorado; and Topaz, in central Utah. Although records relating to all three of these camps can be found at the regional archives in Denver, due to space restrictions, this paper deals primarily with those records relating to the camp at Heart Mountain. However, parallel records for the Amache and Topaz camps are noted in context when applicable. All of the records described herein are available for public research and duplication without restriction.

Records at Denver relating to the saga at Heart Mountain, from the inception of the camp until after closure of the facility, were created by a variety of diverse federal agencies and can be found in several record groups among the NARA's holdings. For example, the camp itself was constructed on land administered by the Bureau of Reclamation as part of the Shoshone Project which was designed to bring irrigation water to land located in the arid basin between the Absaroka and the Big Horn Mountains in northwest Wyoming. During the existence of the Heart Mountain

Relocation Center many internees were employed in the construction of canals and other waterworks tied to the Shoshone Project. The War Relocation Authority (WRA) was created in March of 1942 to formulate and execute a program for the establishment and maintenance of the relocation centers. The Heart Mountain camp was constructed during the summer of that same year, and from that time until it closed, the center was under the administration of the WRA.

After the establishment and occupation of the relocation centers, internal strife, resulting from internees being made eligible for the military draft, resulted in some federal criminal prosecutions as a result of non-compliance with the Selective Service Act. The resulting district and appeals court case files are among the records held by the National Archives—Rocky Mountain Region and description of those records constitutes a major portion of this guide. Those court records are the most frequently requested documents held at Denver relating to the internment experience.

Finally, after the closure of the relocation centers in November of 1945, those sites underwent a transformation from wartime to peacetime use. Records relating to the dismantling of the camps, sale and removal of their buildings, and in the case of Heart Mountain, their subsequent occupation by homesteaders, can be found in records of the War Assets Administration, Federal Property Resources Service, and the Bureau of Reclamation.

RECORDS OF U.S. DISTRICT COURTS AND TENTH CIRCUIT COURT OF APPEALS

The defendants assert that inasmuch as they are American citizens by birth that they have been discriminated against by various acts of the Government in classifying them in 4-C which includes enemy aliens, and removing them from their places of residence to Relocation Centers, their loyalty to the United States Government has thereby been questioned without reason and that they should not be re-classified for service in the war at least until such time as their status of citizenship has been clarified.[2]

The most provocative records concerning Heart Mountain are 63 U.S. District Court criminal case files (#4928 and 4931-4992). The main case, *U. S. vs. Fujii* (#4928), contains documents that relate to the prosecution of Shigeru Fujii and others, all Heart Mountain internees, for non-compliance with the Selective Service Act. Fujii, along with his fellow defendants, had all originally registered at the beginning of the war with draft boards in their home districts on the West Coast and were classified "4-C" (a designation for enemy aliens), a status that exempted them from military service. During the course of their internment, Japanese Americans were re-designated "1-A" and told to report for pre-induction physical exams. Seeking to force a clarification of their citizenship status, each of them systematically refused to report for examination. The defendants were tried as a group in what became the largest mass trial in Wyoming's history.

Each of the case files include indictments, mandates, warrants, orders, returns, verdicts, notices of appeal and correspondence between the court and the defendant's original draft board. The case file for Shigeru Fujii also contains some transcripts of pleadings, a list of defendants, and various motions and stipulations relating to the defendants as a group. Also included are nearly one-half cubic foot of exhibit materials, which include items relating to the camp's "Fair Play Committee;" copies of the Denver, Colorado version of *Rafu Shimpo*, a Japanese American newspaper containing articles related to the trial; correspondence and formal essays written by the defendants and sympathizers within Heart Mountain and at other relocation camps; and a copy of U.S. Senate committee hearings relating to the evacuation of "enemy aliens" from the West Coast military zones.

The Fujii file contains ample documentation that District Court Judge T. Blake Kennedy was not sympathetic to the defendant's assertions that they should be exempt from the draft as a result of their detention at Heart Mountain. In one memorandum he writes:

> It has been seen that the discrimination exercised by the Government on account of their Japanese ancestry was legitimate, justified and legal as being within the Power of Congress and the President in war emergency . . . .The Courts have repeatedly asserted that the orders of the Boards of Selective Service have the substance of Congressional Acts and must be obeyed. It is evident that what they asserted in the matter of the clarification of their citizenship was in fact accomplished by the effect of the order which they disobeyed . . . . When, therefore, they were placed in 1-A and ordered to report for pre-induction physical examination, their pure American citizenship was established beyond question.[3]

The guilty verdicts handed down to the 63 defendants, as well as to other internees convicted of aiding the movement, resulted in two separate appeals to the U.S. Circuit Court of Appeals for the Tenth Circuit, sitting at Denver, Colorado. The regional archives holds documents from appeals by the draft resisters in Court of Appeals case file #2973, *Shigeru Fujii vs. The United States of America*, filed October 25, 1944. The file primarily contains copies of the original district court documents - indictments and verdicts, Judge Kennedy's memorandums, excerpts from testimony, and copies of correspondence between some of the defendants and their local draft boards.[4]

More extensive documentation of the appeals arguments can be found in the Court of Appeals Transcripts of Records and Briefs, which consist of bound volumes arranged by the date of filing. These transcripts duplicate much of what is contained in the appeals case file, but also include briefs by the appellant and appellee, statements, arguments, citations from precedent cases, and conclusions.[5]

In addition to Fujii and the other sixty-two draft resisters, prosecutions were pursued against eight other Heart Mountain internees for "Aiding or Abetting Persons to Evade Registration" by holding meetings and otherwise assisting the draft resisters. Court documents from this case can be found in U.S. District Court criminal case file #4930, *U. S. vs. Kiyoshi Okamoto et., al.* These men were also found guilty and like Fujii and the others appealed their sentence to the U.S. Court of Appeals. Transcripts of those proceedings can be found in appeals case files #3076-3082.[6] Documents included in both the Court of Appeals and District Court files are similar to those found in the Fujii cases.

Similar draft resistance cases occurred at Amache and Topaz, although apparently not to the extent seen at Heart Mountain. The regional archives possesses case files and some docket materials among its holdings for U.S. District Courts for Colorado and Utah, respectively. The case files usually contain less than a dozen pages each of routine court documents such as indictments, motions, and verdicts.[7] As of this writing exhibit materials for those cases have not been located.

RECORDS OF THE BUREAU OF RECLAMATION

The Heart Mountain camp was formally closed in November, 1945. Remaining at the site was a ghost town that had been home to nearly eleven thousand souls, the third largest community in Wyoming. Scores of barracks, administrative buildings, staff housing, a hospital, a power plant and many other structures were left behind. Administration of the site reverted from the WRA to the Bureau of Reclamation (BOR) and was opened for homesteading to returning veterans. Among the holdings of the regional archives are a series of photographs depicting the abandoned camp, removal of barracks and most other buildings, and clearing of the site. Also included are many scenes of the process of awarding homestead tracts and of families taking up residence on their new lots. One of the images shows a William O. White and his wife struggling to remove sagebrush from their tract. According to the caption, White was a "Japanese prisoner of war for 41 months" (American held prisoner by the Japanese) and moved to Heart Mountain from his home in Chicago to take up farming on one of the newly created homestead tracts.[8] The series include black and white prints, usually with accompanying negatives, and are found intermingled with photographs depicting work projects on the Shoshone Irrigation Project for the period 1945-50. Each item is captioned and dated.[9]

A related item has been recently received by the regional archives from the Bureau of Reclamation—Great Plains Region in Billings, Montana. It consists of audiotape recordings of a live broadcast originating in Cody, Wyoming in 1948. The broadcast was on the occasion of the awarding thirty-one homestead tracts on the Heart Mountain Division, drawn randomly from 490 applications of returning veterans. The tape also captures speeches given by dignitaries such as Wyoming Governor Lester Hunt and BOR Regional Administrator Kenneth Vernon prior to the drawing.[10]

OTHER RECORDS

Another collection of records documenting the closure of Heart Mountain, Topaz, and Amache appears in two related record groups–Record Group 270, Records of the War Assets Administration, and Record Group 291, Records of the Federal Property Resources Service. The records consist of real property case files which contain documents relating to the disposition of federal buildings and land, deemed surplus or excess, which had outlived their usefulness to the possessor agency. In the case of Heart Mountain (as well as Amache and Topaz), these case files contain primarily forms, property registers, land descriptions, property appraisals, final sales and disposition information, correspondence, and memorandums. The files for the Amache camp include maps and drawings of the camp layout and building dimensions. The case files are valuable for determining the final disposition of the many buildings that were removed from the camp sites, sometimes including itemized lists of structures that were transferred to other federal agencies, or sold to local agencies, organizations, or individuals. The files for the Topaz camp in the War Assets Administration records are especially thorough. Detailed finding aids to these records are available on request from the regional archives.[11]

HOW TO CONTACT THE NATIONAL ARCHIVES

The National Archives—Rocky Mountain Region is located in Building 48 of the Denver Federal Center, 6th Avenue and Kipling Streets, in Lakewood, Colorado. The research rooms are open from 7:30 a.m. through 3:45 p.m., Monday through Friday, except federal holidays. Written inquiries can be sent to P.O. Box 25307, Denver, CO 80225, or by e-mail to www.archives@denver.nara.gov. Telephone inquiries should be made to (303) 236-0817. Information about photocopy and reproduction fees is available upon request. Further information about the National Archives and Records Administration, including on-line access to selected records descriptions and digitized documents, is available at www.nara.gov.[12]

Notes

1. National Archives and Records Administration, *Guide to Federal Records in the National Archives of the United States* (1995) Vol. 2, Section 210-2. Written inquiries regarding these records can be sent to Archives I Textual Reference Branch (NWDT1), National Archives and Records Administration, 700 Pennsylvania Avenue NW, Washington, D.C. 20408. Information about non-textual records is available from the Archives II Textual Reference Branch (NWDT2), National Archives at College Park, 8601 Adelphi Road, College Park, Maryland 20740-6001.

2. Judge's Memorandum, June 26, 1944, Case File No. 4928, Criminal Case Files, 1890-1949, District of Wyoming (Cheyenne), Records of the District Courts of the United States, Record Group 21, National Archives and Records Administration, Rocky Mountain Region, Denver, Colorado (hereafter, records in the National Archives at Denver will be cited as RG_, NARA—Rocky Mountain Region).

3. Ibid.

4. Case File No. 2973, Transcripts of Records on Appeal, 1929-1954, Tenth Circuit (Denver, Colorado); Records of the U. S. Court of Appeal, RG 276, NARA—Rocky Mountain Region.

5. Case File No. 2973, Transcripts of Records and Briefs, Vol. 3, November Term 1945, Transcripts of Records on Appeal, Tenth Circuit (Denver, Colorado), Records of the U. S. Courts of Appeal, RG 276, NARA—Rocky Mountain Region.

6. Case Files No. 3076 through 3082, Transcripts of Records and Briefs, Vol 3, November Term 1945, Transcripts of Records on Appeal, Tenth Circuit.

7. Criminal Order Books, 1938-1948 and Criminal Case Files, 1931-1953, District of Utah, Records of the District Courts of the United States, RG 21, NARA—Rocky Mountain Region. Criminal Dockets, 1923-1969 and Criminal Case Files, 1912-1960, District of Colorado, Records of the District Courts of the United States, RG 21, NARA—Rocky Mountain Region

8. "William O. White and His Wife Prepare to Burn Sage on Their Unit #186," April 7, 1950, Photograph No. P26-600-5A, Photographs, Region 6, 1934-1954, Shoshone Project, Records of the Bureau of Reclamation, RG 115, NARA—Rocky Mountain Region.

9. Photographs, Region 6, 1935-1954, Shoshone Project, Records of the Bureau of Reclamation, RG 115, NARA—Rocky Mountain Region.

10. Audiotape, 1948, Bureau of Reclamation—Great Plains Region, Records of the Bureau of Reclamation, RG 115, NARA—Rocky Mountain Region.

11. Real Property Case Files, Records of the War Assets Administration, RG 270, and Records of the Federal Property Resources Service, RG 291, NARA—Rocky Mountain Region.

12. The author would like to thank Eileen Bolger for her assistance and Eric Muller, University of Wyoming Law Library, for sharing his archival research on the draft resistance movement at Heart Mountain, Amache and Topaz.

Part VII

Long Term Effects of Internment and the

Importance of Commemoration

Today the relocation center is gone. But Heart Mountain stands as a permanent reminder to former internees of what was once there, and how America
could turn on a group of its own citizens.

Illuminating the Shadows: Post-Traumatic Flashbacks from Heart Mountain and Other Camps

Gwenn M. Jensen

When Franklin Roosevelt signed Executive Order 9066 resulting in the incarceration of persons of Japanese ancestry in what he admitted were concentration camps, post-traumatic stress disorder (PTSD) was not even a part of the English language.[1] Recognized by the American Psychiatric Association in 1980, it was first applied to GIs who experienced "combat fatigue." One of the most distinguishing characteristics of PTSD, and one of the most unsettling, is reliving an event through a flashback. Trauma can lie forgotten or unacknowledged for years until the memory is jarred into life. Traumatic stress is defined as "an event that is outside of the usual human experience and that is psychologically traumatic."[2] The incarceration experienced by persons of Japanese ancestry during World War II was certainly that.

The traumatic experience began with the attack on Pearl Harbor and the Gestapo-like invasion of FBI agents into private homes in the days and weeks that followed. The uncertainty of the ensuing months was fraught with tension which was heightened by hysteria in the press and racist reactions of former friends and neighbors. The abrupt and unprecedented removal from homes, loss of property and possessions, and entry into makeshift detention centers further contributed to the burden of psychological stress. Incarceration in permanent quarters behind barbed wire and guard towers was a psychologically disturbing experience with detainees reporting such mixed emotions as blaming themselves for the imprisonment, to utter outrage at this illegal and unjust act.[3]

Those who chose to resettle in the interior of the country before the war ended reported occasional animosity and prejudice. In total, this unjust banishment lasted up to four years. Repatriation after the war to homelands in the formerly forbidden coastal states was not an easy transition. Early returnees were sometimes greeted with hostility or worse: outright violence. More than thirty acts of terrorism were documented when people returned to reclaim their lives.[4] Starting over, reestablishing lives and businesses, was a difficult process filled with hardship. A backdrop of traumatic stress hung over the Japanese American population for more than the official three years of exile.

Counteracting this burden of trauma were a blend of Japanese cultural norms and assimilated American ideals, although the latter was vastly circumscribed by the magnitude of the injustice inflicted upon citizens and residents by their own government. It is well known that feelings of powerlessness and lack of control are major stressors. The attitude behind the phrase *shikata ga nai*[5] helped combat these feelings by allowing people to focus on what they could control. The ideal of persevering through adversity, *gaman*, was another culturally fashioned coping device which helped those old enough to have learned these traits to control levels of stress which can have effects on health status.

However, as a pharmacist imprisoned in Poston said, "I am an American, I have never known anything else. This evacuation can't change me because *I am old enough* and will always be the same. But what about the children in their formative years? What will it do to them? [emphasis added]."[6] Social scientists know that cultural and social norms are inculcated in a progressive developmental process of socialization. It is a gradual acquisition of skills and values that takes years to accomplish. Thus, for the youngest of detainees, this process was incomplete. Because these coping mechanisms were not fully enculturated in the young, the children in camp were the most vulnerable to traumatic stress.

Amy Iwasaki Mass, a clinical psychologist, has written about the psychological effects of camps that she observed in herself and in her practice. She described various psychological responses including "repression, denial, rationalization, and identification with the aggressor."[7] In the course of my study on the health consequences of the mass incarceration, several people described their psychological reactions to the experience. One type was a delayed, classic flashback reaction, and another was a more immediate response. In this paper, three individuals describe flashbacks that occurred thirty to forty years after the trauma of internment. This dissociative response permits traumatized individuals to store the experience in safe, but eventually accessible, portions of the brain.

Of these reactions, there was a definite age correlation with the lingering effects of traumatic stress. The younger the person during the internment years, the more delayed the responses to the experience were. The following vignettes illustrate these responses. Narrations of flashbacks that arose unexpectedly were from younger individuals compared to those whose flashbacks were more consciously generated. Immediate responses, those that occurred at the time of incarceration and to those who were adults, generally did not lead to flashbacks in later life.

UNEXPECTED FLASHBACKS

Unexpected flashbacks are memories which arise when some kind of trigger spontaneously reactivates the memory. The trigger may be a smell, a sound, or other sensate function. According to Herman Sno and Don Linszen, "in principle, even the smallest fragment would give the complete picture, although the smaller the fragment the less sharp the picture would be."[8] Lenore Terr has found that "even those who were infants or toddlers at the time of their ordeals and thus were unable to lay down, store, or retrieve full verbal memories of their trauma, tend to . . . re-see highly visualized elements from their old experiences."[9] The following two experiences occurred to two Sansei women; one of whom had no conscious memory of trauma of the internment.

In a Day of Remembrance observance, the date Executive Order 9066 was signed in 1942, a panel discussion was held at the University of Colorado at Denver in 1990. Several former internees participated as panelists. June Kunatani,[10] an older Sansei and educator, was one of those panelists. This is the story of her unexpected flashback experience.

I was born in California and when the war broke out, I was a pre-schooler. My aunt was telling me that the biggest thing the family was concerned about was that they be able to stay together and go into the camps together as a family unit. My grandparents, I think, lived in Santa Ana, and we lived in the Boyle Heights area of Los Angeles, and then someone else lived in central Los Angeles. So what my aunts and my mother tell me is that they relocated and went to live at one of the Methodist churches in town. So that at least when the time came for them to go, they could move as a unit.

So our family went to Poston, Arizona. I was three or four, I can't really remember. But I thought that all of my memories about going were fun memories. It was the first time that I rode a train. We went as a unit so that my grandparents went with us. I didn't think that I really remembered a lot about it. And then . . . about 15 years ago, they had a student uprising when Nixon ordered the bombing of Cambodia. The students here sort of had a Woodstock West, is what they termed it. They camped out at the University of Denver where now the library is [located]. At the time, Governor Love called out the National Guard. And so they landed the National Guard in the arena, in the former football arena.

I was sitting in a building that was very similar to the barracks at camp. Tom, you probably remember all [inaudible]. But it looked like camp barracks. I was taking a stats class, and kind of looked out the window, and saw units of National Guardsmen walking by. They had their helmets on and the bayonets. And all of a sudden I jumped up, and I said, "Oh no, it's happening again." And then I ran out of the room.

Then I got to thinking, why did I say that? I mean, it didn't occur to me at the time. And then later I talked to a psychiatrist, and we were talking about memories that you may have had and probably what made the biggest impression on me then as it happened was that I work with pre-schoolers now. And that happened when I was three or four. I didn't think that I remembered. So somewhere along the line, I think when you're three or four, you don't have a language in order to express it. But the fear must have been there. So when I saw the National Guard walking by, I sort of had a flashback. And I did remember.

So since then, I've talked about it. It's been hard sometimes, but other times, again the biggest impact for me is that when I am working with pre-school children now that have been abused or whatever, it makes me realize it has a bigger impact on children than I first thought.

That's really about all that I remember about the camps. Most of the things I hear from my parents. The hardest thing, now that you've become a parent, you think back, what if you had, what was it, a month to get ready to pack. And you were a woman, and you had three school age children. And you can only take what you could carry. Plus what you needed to wear yourself and again relating back as a mother, what probably made a big impact on me is that the women that had young children must have really had a hard time. Because they were thinking not only of themselves, but of their kids.[11]

Irene Okazaki,[12] a Sansei woman who was born just after Pearl Harbor, called late one night in 1995 when I was in California conducting interviews for my dissertation. She started talking about redress and said that she did not realize it, but she had had a dislike for Caucasians for much of her early adulthood.

In many of the concentration camps there was a great deal of internal controversy between the detainees. The intensity of the debate peaked with the U.S. government's demands that each person over seventeen years of age declare their loyalty as a prelude to recruitment into the army's all-Nisei combat unit. In the early years the brooding anger of one faction focused on individuals thought to be too friendly with the War Relocation Administration. Irene's father was one of those singled out.

Irene related a story of an unexpected flashback which haunted her for years until she found someone that verified its inherent veracity.

> I denied it [my dislike for Caucasians] to myself, but it was an unconscious feeling. But after redress, it felt like having a weight lifted from my shoulders, a basket taken from my head. My attitude towards Caucasian people became more relaxed. I had unrealized resentment, bad feelings for Caucasians. I think I blamed them for the camp experience. But with apology and payment, "Cool, they're really okay." I thought it was something done to my parents, not me. But it may explain my concern with safety my hyperactivity with safety and protection issues. I have a pepper spray and an alarm thing on my car, also ammonia spray.[13]

Irene went on to describe a night several years earlier when she was staying at her parents' house and watched a zombie movie on television. When the zombie was heading toward a house, she had a physical reaction, "I got so afraid." That night she dreamt that "four or five people were going to break in and kill me and my parents." Waking from the nightmare, she reported, "I had an uncontrollable urge and ran into the closet; I stood in there for one hour; I couldn't move. Then it wore off."[14]

Irene continued, "Later on I found out that the incident really happened. People were looking for my father [in camp], and we were hiding in the dark[ened barracks]. When I started to whimper, my grandfather said, 'Sssh. Be quiet!'"[15]

The movie that triggered this memory occurred when Irene was in her late thirties or early forties. Prior to that night of nightmares, she had never heard the story about what had happened to her family in camp. Her parents had never spoken about either that particular experience or camp in general. It was several years after the zombie movie and the nightmare terror that she learned the story was true. She was shocked to learn how deeply this memory had been etched in her psyche as she was approximately one year old at the time. She was also astounded to find how much the incarceration had affected her life.

> My dad was forced to sell out before he left for camp. Within eighteen months after leaving camp, my parents and I moved nine times. I've always liked to have strict schedules, don't like to break promises, don't like to get into a situation where I don't feel in control. I had lots of nightmares when I was in elementary school. One recurring one about a big pressure is coming, looking at rooms, different rooms. All of a sudden in clearing, [I am] standing alone in clearing, holding a flower.
>
> I used to work for a major corporation. But I have a fear of flying. Last trip from Japan, the 747 stalled on takeoff, almost shook the plane to pieces, but flew okay afterwards. Ever since, I have had a fear of flying.[16]

Terr lists several well-known characteristics of childhood trauma which Irene described in her account, specifically "deliberate avoidance, panic . . . and hypervigilance."[17] She has determined that legal redress, ritual, and religion can be effective antidotes to a childhood trauma experience.[18] Irene described the effect the 1988 redress by the U.S. government had on her as "having a weight lifted from my shoulders." And she became more devout in her faith. Both of these responses continue to heal the psychic trauma she experienced.

In an equally frightening experience, Sachi Kaneshiro describes the terror she felt as an adult in a situation similar to the one young Irene Okazaki experienced. While living in a Poston barracks with a group of other single young women, Kaneshiro described how Maki Ichiyasu, one of her roommates who worked in an Administration office, did not hesitate to offer her opinion endorsing the enlistment of men in the all-Nisei combat unit.[19] This issue was similar to the "loyalty questionnaire" conflict in the way it divided the captive population of the camps. Many saw no reason to volunteer to fight a war when it meant leaving their parents and their families sitting in concentration camps. Indeed, contrary to popular belief, most young men of draft age in the general population did not volunteer.[20] They waited to be drafted.

After a brutal attack on one man, a Mr. Sato, who also favored the Nisei unit, Kaneshiro describes what happened next.

> Maki appeared as shaken as I had ever seen her. Two days went by, each of us becoming increasingly anxious. One morning, after Maki had left

for work earlier than usual, the three of us wondered aloud who would be the next victim. . . .

Five nights after the brutal attack on Mr. Sato, there was a loud commotion outside our closed door. I stood up to look out the window when a loud, strident male voice called out Maki's name and ordered her to come outside.

I turned to look at Maki. She seemed to be frozen in place. Again came the angry command for Maki to step outside. I watched anxiously as she took a step forward. Miss T reached out as if to stop her and whispered loudly, "Don't go!"

The dim lighting couldn't hide the apprehension on Maki's face "If I don't, they'll break in."

I remained standing just where I was, motionless, unable to think of how to prevent Maki from going outside. As she closed the door behind her, a man began shouting at her in Japanese:

"Onna-no-kuse-de! You stupid woman! Why are you trying to influence the people? What does a woman know about such things? Your country locks you up and you tell the boys to go out and fight for freedom? Don't you know they will be cannon fodder or latrine detail?"

The brutal tongue-lashing grew worse as other male voices joined in. "You're not married, you have no sons, what do you know? Stick to your women's work, your women's groups. Keep your nose out of the recruitment issue."

. . . There were more angry words spoken in Japanese. . . . I could hear Maki's unsteady voice as she tried to interrupt. "Listen to me, listen please." It was no use. They were not interested in what she had to say. . . . My stomach clenched with fear as I tried to imagine what we could do if this confrontation turned violent.

After what seemed hours . . . the shouting stopped and we could hear heavy footsteps moving away.

Maki came inside, pale and visibly unnerved. . . . Her voice was strained, diminished. "I don't want to drag any of you into this, it's really my problem. But I have a bad feeling they may come back."

We piled boxes in front of the door, but the four of us slept little that night. I lay curled beneath my sheet, unable to relax my tense limbs. My eyes remained wide open, as the dark closed in and every creak and rustle brought imaginings of a sudden attack. Listening to the soft sounds of my own breathing. . . .

The next morning an explosive racket made me jump. I looked up . . . to see Maki standing just inside the door. Baseball bats and football helmets tumbled out of a canvas bag she held upside down. I could not help breaking into a grin. . . .

"These are for our protection. After last night, I'm concerned those men might decide to come back. It's possible they may try to break in while we're sleeping. We've got to be ready. . . ."

For the next few nights, we stacked boxes against the door and went to bed wearing the stiff leather football helmets, each of us with a heavy baseball bat within easy reach. Straining to hear the approach of menacing footsteps, I slept little. The hours passed slowly as I stared into the dark, imprisoned by the stifling headgear.

At work, I found it difficult to concentrate or carry on normal conversations. I spent most of the time worrying about how I would react to a possible attack. On the third night . . . unable to drift off, I couldn't help thinking about the irony of the situation. Only six months earlier, we had been sent to this desert compound, supposedly to "protect" us from a hostile world outside. Now we were being threatened by people on the inside.

Here we were, wearing football helmets and clutching baseball bats, too frightened to go to sleep.[21]

When one learns of the terror felt by someone of Kaneshiro's age, it is readily apparent how intensely traumatic such a situation would be for a small child without the developmental skills for coping with such horror. It is not surprising under those circumstances to find that Irene Okazaki's fears persist to the present day.

CONSCIOUSLY-GENERATED FLASHBACK

In contrast to the unexpected flashback, the following experience illustrates a different way of triggering a memory. I define the consciously generated flashback as one that occurs in response to consciously conjured introspection and reflection on the trauma. Emmett Early explains that "abreaction, or the recollection of the trauma event" is one way to gradually incorporate the experience into the conscious mind and that it is a treatment modality for post- traumatic stress symptoms. Once the trauma is acknowledged and understood on a conscious level, its negative impact on one's psyche is diminished.[22]

One of the prominent differences between this consciously generated flashback memory and the former unexpected type, is the individual's age when the trauma occurred. Instead of the infant-toddler stage of development, the following individual experienced the trauma of the war years in his pre-adolescence. Even so, Early classifies this stage of development as a significant time of transition where the primary identity defenses are denial, dissociation, and repression. He further suggests that a trauma at this juncture "can alter the course of the survivor's development."[23]

Tom Higuchi,[24] a Nisei now in his sixties, was in junior high during his confinement at Heart Mountain. He describes in detail how that experience reverberated through his life until he was finally able to bring the trauma to consciousness and

223

effect a release from its control on his psychological well-being. Tom Higuchi, in his own words:

> . . . it was towards the end of Heart Mountain. They let a bunch of us school kids go into Cody, Wyoming. This is the town right outside Heart Mountain. I'd never been there, but we were on a school bus or something, and that was the first time. You know, I kind of looked forward to it. I mean first time I get to see outside. A little nervous . . . But it was sanctioned by whoever set it up so I figured, you know . . . And I think my mother gave me a dollar something, and I think we were all kind of looking forward to it. We'd get to see a real place [laughs] instead of camp.
>
> We got to Cody, and it was this real pretty town, small, a couple thousand people, well, maybe more. But very small, pretty, had a little park. I remember there's a statue or something of Buffalo Bill Cody. And then we drove down Main Street. And then all of a sudden I noticed these signs. They were on every door, every window, some of them had ten of them. They were all over Main Street, and said, "No Japs appreciated here." "Keep out, Japs." "Jap trade not solicited here." I mean, just *plastered*! It was such a tremendous feeling of rejection. We all slid down in our seats. I mean, I couldn't even look any more. I mean, I was just curious to see how many ways you can say it, but it was a horrible feeling. I hated that town.
>
> And then we got to Montgomery Ward, I think. We had a great old guy who was kind of our leader, and he was trying to take our minds off it, and he said, "Montgomery Ward, we'll be welcome there. You can buy winter clothing or . . ." He went on and on. We got to Montgomery Ward, and it was uneventful. But I was frozen. I was sure somebody was going to say, "Who let this Jap in?" you know, "these Japs in here?" I remember piles of clothing and stuff, and I was looking at something, and this saleslady came by and said, "Hello." And I was sure that was a sign that she was going to say, "Get out!" you know, "Get out of here! We don't want you."
>
> Anyway, when we got back to camp, I was so happy. [laughter] But Cody was like that. It was another icon. It was a place that I remember the people, the signs, you know, the whole thing. It was funny. I didn't know I carried that in my head. I mean, I thought of Cody every so often, and I'd have this, you know . . .
>
> Thirty years later, I'm in London. I'd been called over to do a job—a big job, big pay. I'd been hyped up, you know. There's this top American . . .
>
> I get to Heathrow [in the middle of a power blackout]. I get off, and I'm waiting for a welcoming committee or something, you know. And there's nobody there. [laughter.] And I've got rising panic, and I had a look around.

So I got there, got to the darkened hotel, and I went to registration, and I said, "I'm Tom Higuchi, and I'm expected here, but I don't know by whom or . . ." [laughter] And he said, "Oh, they're waiting for you." I said, "Who's they?" He says, "The group." I said, "What group?" He says, "Well, they just said the group is waiting for you." So I said, "I'll leave my bags, and I'll go straight up because it's getting kind of late." So I go up darkened halls, and I had to actually get up to the door to see the number.

I finally get to the right door, and I knock. And the door opens, and, it's a guy—a valet, a butler, you know. [laughter] A bow tie. And I said, "Uh, maybe I'm in the wrong place." Then the door swung open, and someone came out and said, "Come in, Tom." And so but I noticed in the crack that there is this silver service—really expensive silver service! I've never saw anything like it. I mean so old and expensive, you know, and had caviar and all this stuff. And I knew I was in the wrong place. Anyway the door opened. It's like a banquet, you know, like a big dinner. It's a table and must be thirty people sitting there all dressed up. Here I'm in my peacoat and jeans and tennis shoes. Cause I expected something else, you know, and I stood there.

And this guy was the Chairman of the Board, an international company, and says, "Hello, Tom, how are you? It's good to . . ." I didn't know the guy from Adam. I knew him by reputation.

Anyway, I walk into the room, and I can see the shock at the banquet table. All these people, men and women. John Havers says, "This is Tom." And I can see the look, you know, it was really terrible. Because I saw Cody. I can see the thought balloons over their heads. "My god, it's a Jap!" You know! "Supposed to be an American."

So anyway, the thought balloons, I can just see Cody. And, you know, after 30 years because this was 1970, I have this horrible reaction. I wasn't going to take it this time.

And something snapped in me, and I stared them all down, and I was saying, "You make the wrong move, and I'm walking out of here. Screw you!" I was ready to do it. John Havers and a big job, all this . . . I had just such, . . . it wasn't hate, it was hate. It was hatred. I wasn't going to take this crap . . . .

It turned out to be a real nice evening. The girls were wonderful, and they were as cordial as the English can be. [laughter] You're not sure if it's for real, but they were very nice. I talked with everybody, and then they said they were going to meet the next morning. The director came toward me, and he says, "And we'll dress like you, so you won't be embarrassed." [laughter] "We'll be very casual." I said, "Okay." In fact the next morning I wore a suit to the meeting. [laughter] And he said, "You bastard!" [laughter]

But anyway, it was a very pleasant thing. Then we all retired to our rooms, and the people at the hotel . . . While sitting in the room, I'm looking in the mirror, and I said, "Why in the hell were you so goddamn defiant? I mean so damn contentious, so pissed, cause . . ."

I mean my blood really boiled. I mean I looked, I stared them all down like, "You give me a move." I was really going to say something vile. "You look at me like that and screw you." I was ready to . . . You know I've had a temper, but I was ashamed of myself cause you know . . .

[It was such a strong reaction?]

Yeah, it was overpowering. I mean I hated this whole group. And I said, "Why in the hell did . . . ? What the hell got . . ." I was sitting there thinking. Then I realized that it was Cody. It was Cody. You know, all these people saying, "What are you doing here? You don't belong. Get out. You stinking Jap." I mean I just read it, I was so sensitive, you know, because when you become a certain kind of minority . . .

And, at Heart Mountain I remember, I had an epiphany.[25]

Some may protest, "There weren't that many signs." But there were enough to have been commented on by others. For example, Douglas Nelson writes: "A Methodist minister from Pennsylvania who visited Cody in the late summer of 1944, was struck by the extent of racial discrimination in the community. In a letter to Cody Mayor Raymond Howe, the minister complained of 'crude' signs reading 'No Japs,' which appeared in barber shop and hotel windows. He also criticized the policies of Cody restaurant owners who allegedly refused to serve Japanese."[26] In a television documentary, an unidentified Caucasian woman who had worked at Heart Mountain reported how she had driven detainees to Cody to shop. She described how she took widely circuitous routes to avoid passing by stores with anti-Japanese signs.[27] There seems to be total agreement on the presence of hostile and racist signs in Cody. It should be no surprise that they had a considerable effect on those who viewed them.

In conclusion, it is clear from published data and in this never before revealed testimony that traumatic stress had a significant impact on the lives of those who endured incarceration. It was especially traumatic for those who were unprepared: the youngest detainees. Economic and political effects of the concentration camps have been extensively reported. However, there is less information published on the mental health consequences, some of which included post-traumatic stress disorder. It takes a great deal of courage to recall such painful or disturbing memories, but by doing so, these individuals who told their stories here have given new insight into the health legacy of the mass incarceration. These experiences led some to midlife revelations where they were shocked to learn what a profound effect internment had on the course of their lives. Understanding the source of post-traumatic stress flashbacks can mean eliminating their power to haunt and can start the healing process.

Notes

1. This paper is a revised and shortened version of a chapter in my dissertation, Gwenn M. Jensen, "The Experience of Injustice: Health Consequences of the Japanese American Internment" (Ph.D. diss., University of Colorado, 1997).

2. Charles R. Frigley ed., *Trauma and its Wake. Volume II: Traumatic Stress, Theory, Research and Interpretation* (New York: Brunner/Mazel, Publishers, 1986), xvii.

3. Amy Iwasaki Mass, "Psychological Effects of the Camps on Japanese Americans," *in Japanese Americans: From Relocation to Redress*, eds. Roger Daniels, Sandra C. Taylor and Harry H. L. Kitano (Salt Lake City: University of Utah Press, 1986, revised, Seattle: University of Washington Press, 1991), 159-62.

4. Bill Hosokawa, *Nisei: The Quiet Americans* (New York: William Morrow and Company Inc., 1969), 437, reprinted, (Niwot: University Press of Colorado, 1992).

5. Translated as "it cannot be helped." It is defined as an expression of resignation and perseverance in the face of difficult or trying situations that are painful but inevitable." Brian Niiya ed., *Japanese American History: An A to Z Reference From 1869 to the Present* (New York: Facts on File, 1993), 311.

6. Alexander H. Leighton, *The Governing of Men: General Principles and Recommendations Based on Experience at a Japanese Relocation Camp* (Princeton: Princeton University Press, 1946), 43.

7. Mass, "Psychological Effects of the Camps," 160.

8. Herman N. Sno and Don H. Linszen, "The Deja Vu Experience: Remembrance of Things Past?," *American Journal of Psychiatry* 147(12): 1587-95, as quoted in Emmett Early, *The Raven's Return: The Influence of Psychological Trauma on Individuals and Culture* (Wilmette, Illinois: Chiron Publications, 1993), 1593.

9. Lenore C. Terr, "Childhood Traumas: An Outline and Overview," *American Journal of Psychiatry* 148 (1): 12.

10. A pseudonym is used to protect June Kunitani's privacy.

11. Author's interview with June Kunitani, February 19, 1990, Denver, Colorado.

12. A pseudonym is used to protect Irene Okazaki's privacy.

13. Author's telephone interview with Irene Okazaki, September, 1995.

14. Ibid.

15. Ibid.

16. Ibid.

17. Terr, "Childhood Traumas," 12.

18. Lenore C. Terr, "Family Anxiety After Traumatic Events," *Journal of Clinical Psychiatry* 50 (suppl. 11): 18.

19. Sachi Kaneshiro, "No Bitter Tears" (unpublished manuscript cited with permission).

20. Gene Amole, "The True Story of World War II," *Rocky Mountain (Denver) News*, April 20, 1997; Robert Famighetti ed., *The World Almanac and Book of World Facts* (Mahwah, New Jersey: World Almanac Books, 1997), 184.

21. Kaneshiro, "No Bitter Tears."

22. Early, *The Raven's Return,* 15.

23. Ibid., 12-13.

24. A pseudonym is used to protect Tom Higuchi's privacy.

25. Author's interview with Tom Higuchi, December, 1995, Los Angeles, California.

26. Douglas W. Nelson, *Heart Mountain: The History of An American Concentration Camp* (Madison: The State Historical Society of Wisconsin, 1976), 158.

27. Bob Nellis prod., *Winter in My Soul* (Casper, Wyoming: KTWO News, television documentary, 1986).

Public Memory, Commemoration, and the "Régime of Truth"

Scott L. Bills

> *"When I have to give up my life for democracy,*
> *I want to see the goddam thing first."*
> —*Jack Tono, Heart Mountain internee*[1]

The American reaction to the Japanese attack on Pearl Harbor in December 1941 "provoked a rage bordering on the genocidal," in the words of John Dower. The extent of the "crudely racist" character of that spontaneous and orchestrated public response was fully demonstrated by subsequent actions well known to readers of this volume—especially the relocation and confinement of Japanese Americans living on the West Coast. As Geoffrey Smith has pointed out, the systematic funneling of Issei and Nisei into ten concentration camps, located on desolate stretches of public land, was "the most broadly based and effective nativist crusade in American history." Certainly there was no national security justification for this mass incarceration of people. "Hatred directed at the suspected (and powerless) Asian adversary within," wrote Smith, "provided both a vicarious means of striking back at an expectedly awesome enemy and a source of unity and welcome consensus after the great foreign policy debate of 1941 [concerning the American role in a war torn world]."[2] The nation at large was mesmerized by the powerful symbolism of Pearl Harbor—an Asian power undercutting deep-seated assumptions about white Western cultural-technological superiority—and quickly acquiesced and adjusted to actions spurred by years of highly visible racism in California and neighboring states.

A sense of closure for the internees, the very public recognition of their unjust imprisonment and the payment of an indemnity, finally did come in the 1980s. Yet, larger questions about the contextualization of Japanese American relocation are still with us. We often have a profound ambivalence about recapturing those parts of our history that raise troubling moral questions about the character of our society, about our good intentions, about how we conduct ourselves at home and abroad. We prefer to think that injustices, if they have been committed at all, were brief, minor skirmishes that did not and could not tarnish our national drive for greatness. To describe ourselves, we like to invoke the old phrase, inherited from the Puritans, of a "city upon a hill": the image of a noble experiment rooted in innocence, consensus and freedom. It has been a favorite refrain of many presidents—viewing the United States, in the words of Joyce Appleby, as "the pilot society for the world."[3] As a people, we have been bathed in mythic discourse since the founding of the republic, though perhaps never more preoccupied with it than at the present moment when historical truth seems so elusive, layered with guilt, frustration, and complexity.[4]

Americans have been reluctant to accept the reality of the costs and judgments engendered by what Lloyd Gardner called the "politics of empire at home." This is because we have been reluctant to accept the notion of an American empire, one that extends back through the "manifest destiny" of continental expansion, then to the steady growth of U.S. influence overseas in the twentieth century. And this experience must be placed within the greater circle of global empires. As Anthony Wallace has written, "the removal of inconveniently located ethnic groups and their resettlement in out-of-the-way places is, and has been for thousands of years, a common phenomenon in the history of states and empires."[5] This analysis prefaced his description of the process of "Indian removal" pursued with such vigor by the administration of Andrew Jackson in the 1830s.

The so-called Five Civilized Tribes—the Choctaw, Chickasaw, Cherokee, Creek and Seminole—were targeted for relocation to lands west of the Mississippi River not because they were any longer a security threat, but rather because they occupied valuable, fertile land. In short, they were nonwhite and they were in the way. At the time, removal was presented as a fair and even merciful policy for a group of people who could not adapt to white society and thus faced, ultimately, corruption and collapse if left untended in their original lands. For the Cherokee, this forced march, carried out under the watchful eye of the army, became the "Trail of Tears"—resulting in the death of perhaps twenty-five percent of the tribe. The entire experience was rather easily ascribed to the growing pains of a robust democracy, and there was little public sympathy for the confinement of the Cherokee and many other Indian tribes onto lands that "became a vast, poverty-stricken concentration camp" for dispossessed peoples.[6]

Or we could speak of the hundreds of years of racial servitude that now seem like ancient history to the majority of Americans. The forced migration of millions of Africans to the Western Hemisphere was laced with a terrible cruelty that became institutionalized. The slave trade was ruinous as well for societies in West Africa and elsewhere on the continent. The further back we go, the murkier are the waters. This is the reality of empire.

The past lives in the present. If we forget its volatility, then current-day events, trends and prospects lose their meaning. For this reason, much has been written about the Americans' perilous insensitivity toward their own historical landscape. True, the past is never exactly replicated, but there are lessons to learn, mistakes to avoid, injustices to be remembered and incorporated into our collective consciousness. Sometimes, there can be redress and redemption, sometimes not. It is no coincidence that much of the literature about public memory has been spawned by crises of faith, conscience, and character. Loren Baritz, for example, in his study of U.S. intervention in Vietnam, wrote that Americans "are prone to unlearn experience. We are," he said, "the world's pastless barbarian . . . ."[7]

Similarly, Peter Carroll has warned us of the danger of events and narratives that are allowed to lie sleeping. "To live in history, by contrast," he said, "provides coherence. It offers the power to understand, and perhaps even to change, the course of time." In a book called *Democracy on Trial*, Jeanne Bethke Elshtain lamented the contemporary rupture of "democratic civil society" in the United States. "Culture changes," she wrote, "through the ongoing engagement between tradition and transformation."[8] We must live *in* history, and we must be collectively *engaged* in the production of a history that connects us to each other. We cannot afford to be spectators. We cannot afford to be numb consumers of history.

"In a democratic society," remarked Carl Trocki, "all people share the responsibility for creating their own history." But there is never one egalitarian history automatically assembled. Public memory, like personal memory, is highly selective. We prefer myths that exalt rather than facts that might demean. We like good wars, inspiring stories and happy endings. What John Bodnar has called "official memory" reflects this tendency to highlight moments of courage, ingenuity, persistence, dedication, sacrifice, triumph and victory. Ronald Reagan, as official storyteller, was certainly the best recent exemplar of the American style. Such triumphalism, as Thomas Paterson has pointed out, has meant that in the United States commemoration "often becomes celebration."[9] To put it differently, we find it difficult to conceive of commemoration as an activity other than celebration. But this is not why we recollect the experiences of Japanese Americans during the Second World War. We do not celebrate the fact that more than 110,000 people, for no good reason, lost their property, livelihood, and freedom through an arbitrary act of government. We do not celebrate the mass deprivation of constitutional rights.

Commemorations can also be forums on the past, on our public culture, articulating and explaining those experiences that do trouble us—or should trouble us. It is in this context and for this reason that we must remember and understand the source of conflict and struggle. What do we have to gain? Why dig up the messy past? In the process, we may reinvigorate a sense of *shared* national purpose and break the spell of a seamless present unfolding without reference points, without guideposts.[10] In the process, we may find an alternate path to the politics of hate and demonization that has become so pervasive in recent decades.

THE USES OF POWER

While the arbitrary power of the state certainly was the key precipitating force in the relocation of Japanese Americans in 1942, there are patterns by which power is diffused *through* society that help explain the ability of government to carry out such actions and retain legitimacy. That is, there must be widespread, active consent. In his studies during the 1960s and 1970s, focusing primarily on the character of power and the production of knowledge (or history), the French philosopher Michel Foucault noted, as have others before him, that dominant cultural values and assumptions are seldom *routinely* enforced by the state itself. Rarely is it necessary. Rather, those values and assumptions percolate downward to the level of the day-to-day, face-to-face interaction of citizens. That is, the most effective policing of social norms—which can be either positive (integrity, honesty) or negative (racism, ethnocentrism)—takes place spontaneously at the "extremities" of power: in our everyday activity amidst our families, neighborhoods and towns.

In this way, power is everywhere attuned to the regular reaffirmation of traditional narratives—those stories, true or false, that define us as a culture. This is what some writers call the master narrative (or metanarrative). Foucault termed it the "régime of truth"—the set of established assumptions about what is right and wrong, what is acceptable and unacceptable, what is worth remembering and what is not.[11] It is in this sense that historical "truth" is constructed (or contingent), that "knowledge" is transferred, that myths are reproduced and strengthened. This régime of truth exists, for the most part, below the surface of daily life, so much so that we are generally unaware of it. It becomes simply common sense, the will of the people, the law of the land.[12]

Public memory is driven by this intersection of official narrative and popular culture, shaped by the diffusion of power in society.[13] In this sense, it represents a ruling ideology, a set of shared assumptions defining the boundaries of legitimate behavior. The importance of ideological perspectives framing the interpretation of events first became clear to me as I worked on oral histories of the events surrounding the killing of four students, and the wounding of nine others, by National Guard rifle fire on May 4, 1970, on the campus of Kent State University.[14] The shootings took place after several years of rising societal conflict revolving around the Vietnam War. The immediate spark for nationwide campus uprisings that spring was the April 30 announcement by President Richard Nixon that U.S. troops in Vietnam were crossing into Cambodia. Deescalation seemed to have been abandoned in favor of a wider war. But also, and very prominently, youthful dissidents had forged a counter-cultural current that challenged established notions of authority, morality and social cohesion. This cultural struggle, far more than the antiwar movement itself, stirred public resentment against activist youth and gave government officials a weapon to use to marginalize dissenters in general. Often, the language of denunciation was quite harsh, as when Ohio Governor James Rhodes spoke in Kent, the day before the shootings, calling student antiwar demonstrators "the worst type of people that we harbor in America."[15]

There were four dead in Ohio—people, in the words of Michael Schwartz, a former president of Kent State University, "who hadn't really done anything."[16] In the aftermath of the shootings, for the most part, the students were blamed for what happened. If they had not been demonstrating against the war in Vietnam, it was argued—thus attacking the reigning régime of truth—then it would not have been necessary to import guardsmen to calm the campus and there would have been no shootings. The campus was closed. Local concern for the dead students was mitigated by a sense of relief that order had been restored. As resident Lucius Lyman Jr. put it, "immediately after the killings, not three or four days later, Kent was as calm as it ever was. . . . There was a normalcy in the community, in sharp contrast to what it had been on the days before."[17]

COMMEMORATION

While it may seem to be an elementary truism, we often forget that public memory is as selective as personal memory. Cataclysmic events like the Kent State shootings demonstrate convincingly that what and how we remember (our personal and collective "truth") is heavily influenced by our worldview. How, why and whether we choose, as a society, to remember dissonance is much influenced by our desire for a stable, triumphalist past. Hence, for at least a decade, students' annual commemoration of the Kent State shootings was a stormy affair. Neither the community nor the University wished to revisit that particular incident. For many towns-people and outside observers, commemoration was akin to celebrating the deeds of student radicals: those ill-clothed, long-haired, foul mouthed delinquents who had so spoiled the 1960s. For University officials, commemoration was a bothersome reminder of an event that had identified the institution with violence and disorder—threatening enrollment and endangering state funding. For student activists, however, the yearly commemoration was a means to assert the legitimacy of protest and ensure that what happened in May 1970 would not be forgotten and lose its historical vibrancy.

The 1970 activists and new subgeneration of students persisted in their mission; and ultimately they forced the University, step by step, to embrace a rapproachement with historical truth, to recognize that May 4th was a "pivotal" moment in the history of the institution and indeed the nation. This, I believe, is what freed the University to sponsor, for the first time, in 1995, its own symposium commemorating the Kent State shootings—gathering scholars and former political leaders without any fear about what they might say, of how critical they might be about the institution. In this way, I would argue, we have seen emerge a new style of commemoration: one that is less celebratory, more solemn, one that acknowledges mistakes, errors in judgment and injustices of the past in a way that offers an opportunity for public memory to come to terms with the complexity and ambiguity of history. We find this with the Vietnam Memorial in Washington—a long black wall that does not celebrate but rather encourages reflection, the experience of sorrow and loss.[18] We find this in the Civil Rights Memorial in Montgomery, Alabama, which lists the names of those who died for the struggle and invokes the rhetoric of Martin Luther King Jr.

This pattern of marking highly polarized and polarizing moments of the past was consciously adopted by the Kent State University Board of Trustees when its members approved construction of a permanent memorial for the campus in 1985. The booklet which outlined the design competition that followed made this very clear.

It is the hope of the University to create a memorial in relation to the site of the May 4th tragedy through which a person, tracing the path of the events of May 4, will gain a deep sense of the events of that day and thus arrive at a broader realm of feeling and understanding. The University hopes that a visitor's thoughts will be turned to the loss of the lives of four young students, the wounding of nine others and the emotional and moral injury to so many more. It is the hope of the University that a visitor's reflection will be elevated towards a probing comprehension of a trying moment in our nation's history; that all who experience this place with its memorial will be reminded of the essential tenets which unite us, pondering their delicate yet precious nature. The memorial must not be "accusatory" or "laudatory" or provoke "further dissension."[19]

The words inscribed on the official memorial—now completed, though on a smaller scale than originally intended—to the Kent State shootings are "inquire, learn, reflect." The words are aloof, yet they carry a subversive power for those who would genuinely inquire and learn.

REMEMBERING HEART MOUNTAIN

At Heart Mountain, Wyoming, the past lives in the present in a different way. Fifty-some years ago, Japanese Americans were systematically uprooted and imprisoned—people who hadn't really done anything. Thousands of families were forced to live in horse stalls, then later in ramshackle buildings in isolated parts of the country.[20] The Issei and Nisei were victims of the arbitrary application of state power. They were victims of a society where the diffusion of power accorded acceptance to harsh racial stereotypes, inflamed by official rhetoric. It is the issue of public memory that links the internment experience with broader themes in the American experience. Toyo Suyemoto Kawakami spoke eloquently about the "burdens of memory" in her account of life in the Topaz camp in Utah—memories that "Exposed to light, / Silently rough / And broken shards / Confront belief."[21] It was a burden that rested, during the war, upon individuals and families and an ethnic community at large, with concomitant tensions, some of which remain still unresolved. The relocation experience itself has been addressed elsewhere in this volume. My concern is with the larger burden, for contemplating broken shards is not a favorite American past-time.

What links my own studies of more recent events and the Japanese American wartime imprisonment is the self-conscious effort to correct official history, to produce a history that is more true. This the Nisei accomplished, at no small cost (despite the eventual cash indemnities awarded). What does it mean to commemorate the fiftieth anniversary of the closing of the Heart Mountain camp? It offers us the opportunity to remember and perhaps come to terms with the virulence of racism in American society. As well, and more subtly, the internment experience reinforces the view of Cornell West—who has written extensively about the black-white racial divide in U.S. society—that there is no morality inherent in a market economy.[22] Japanese Americans were cheerfully dispossessed not only by the government, but by their fellow citizens. Wartime ordinances in towns near Heart Mountain, restricting the movement of internees, were repealed at the insistence of local merchants wanting dollars and local farmers needing labor. Yet the use of terms like "Japs" and "Nips" continued unabated.

The Nisei struggled, as a community, for redress and redemption. Their achievement—expressed in the Civil Liberties Act of 1988—has reconfigured American history. That is, the narrative is now different. Textbooks have been rewritten in a way that more accurately describes the indignity and suffering of the wartime concentration camps. This struggle offers us an illustration of the rise of what Michel Foucault called "local criticism" prefacing an "insurrection" of "subjugated" knowledge. Here, "local" is not a geographical description, but rather designates a particular collective memory that once awakened, forces an adjustment in how we write about and remember our past.[23] Memorials themselves may or may not carry forward their message. Future generations may see them as little more than artistic expressions, as abstract artifacts. However, an open-ended commemorative tradition, attuned not to celebration and victory (for there may be no more victories) but instead to knowledge and reflection, may serve us well as a society. Commemorating Heart Mountain demonstrates that we have the courage to be something more than "pastless barbarians." To embrace historical truth in all its complexity: there is, I believe, no finer moment for any culture.

Notes

1. Quoted in John Tateishi, *And Justice for All: An Oral History of the Japanese American Detention Camps* (New York: Random House, 1984), 170.

2. John W. Dower, *War Without Mercy: Race and Power in the Pacific War* (New York: Pantheon Books, 1986), 36-37, 79; Geoffrey S. Smith, "Racial Nativism and Origins of Japanese American Relocation," in *Japanese Americans: From Relocation to Redress* , ed. Roger Daniels, Sandra C. Taylor, and Harry H. L. Kitano, rev. ed. (Seattle: University of Washington Press, 1991), 81.

3. Joyce Appleby, "Recovering America's Historical Diversity: Beyond Exceptionalism," *Journal of American History* 79, no. 2 (September 1992): 426.

4. See a brief, but perceptive, commentary by Michael Kammen, "History as a Lightning Rod," *OAH Newsletter* 23, no. 2 (May 1995): 1,6. He wrote, "Historians become notably controversial when they do not perpetuate myths, when they do not transmit the received and conventional wisdom, when they challenge the comforting presence of a stabilized past. Members of a society, and its politicians in particular, prefer that historians be quietly irenic rather than polemical, conservators rather than innovators" (p. 6).

5. Lloyd C. Gardner, "Lost Empires," *Diplomatic History* 13 (Winter 1989): 5; Anthony F. Wang, 1993), viii. See also William A. Williams, *Empire as a Way of Life: An Essay on the Causes and Character of America's Present Predicament Along with a Few Thoughts about an Alternative* (New York: Oxford University Press, 1980).

6. Wallace, *Long, Bitter Trail,* 11.

7. Loren Baritz, *Backfire: A History of How American Culture Led Us into Vietnam and Made Us Fight the Way We Did* (1985; reprint, New York: Ballantine, 1986), 336-37.

8. Peter N. Carroll, *Keeping Time: Memory, Nostalgia, and the Art of History* (Athens: University of Georgia Press, 1990), 147; Jean Bethke Elshtain, *Democracy on Trial* (New York: Basic Books, 1995), xii, xv. See also Elshtain's *Women and War* (New York: Basic Books, 1987).

9. Carl A. Trocki, "Why Remind Ourselves of the Vietnam War?" in *Vietnam: The Battle Comes Home* (Dobbs Ferry, NY: Morgan & Morgan, 1984), 11; John Bodnar, *Remaking America: Public Memory, Commemeration, and Patriotism in the Twentieth Century* (Princeton: Princeton University Press, 1992), chap. 1; Thomas G. Paterson, "Historical Memory and Illusive Victories: Vietnam and Central America," *Diplomatic History* 12 (Winter 1988): 1.

10. See Thomas Bender, "Wholes and Parts: The Need for Synthesis in American History," *Journal of American History* 73, no. 1 (June 1986): 125-26, and Michael H. Frisch, "The Memory of History," *Radical History Review* 25 (1981): 10-12. Frisch points out that there is a "pattern that can be found from popular culture to professional scholarship, a pattern wherein selective amnesia and artificial distance can combine to render even last month's history a two-dimensional caricature" (12). This is reminiscent of Douglas Coupland's term "ultra short term nostalgia" in his novel *Generation X: Tales for an Accelerated Culture* (New York: St. Martin's Press, 1991), 96.

11. Lecture, January 14, 1976, in Michel Foucault, *Power/Knowledge: Selected Interviews and Other Writings, 1972-1977*; ed. Colin Gordon; trans. Colin Gordon, Leo Marshall, John Mepham, and Kate Soper (New York: Pantheon Books, 1980), 97-98. Also important in terms of the enforcement of dominant cultural values is the work of Antonio Gramsci, *Selections from the Prison Notebooks of Antonio Gramsci*, ed. and trans. Quintin Hoare and Geoffrey Nowell Smith (1992; reprint New York: International Publishers, 1971). Gramsci used the term "hegemony" to describe how dominant elites manage "to win the active consent" of mass society (p. 244).

12. I am borrowing from Dick Hebdige, who stressed that the dominant ideology of society "thrives *beneath* consciousness." "It is here," he wrote, "at the level of 'normal common sense', that ideological frames of reference are most firmly sedimented and most effective, because it is here that their ideological nature is most effectively concealed." *Sibculture: The Meaning of Style* (London: Routledge, 1979), 11. Foucault, Power\Knowledge, 107 makes a similar point in his discussion of a "society of normalization."

13. See Bodnar, *Remaking America*, 14-15.

14. Scott L. Bills, ed., *Kent State/May 4: Echos Through a Decade*, rev. ed. (Kent, OH: Kent State University Press, 1988).

15. Transcript, Rhodes press conference, May 3, 1970, Box 63, May 4th Collection, Kent State University Archives. National polls at the time revealed that while the Vietnam War had become increasingly unpopular among the citizenry, so had dissenting youth. See, for example, *The Gallup Poll Index*, Report No. 58 (April 1970), Report No. 59 (May 1970), and Report No. 60 (June 1970); and Louis Harris, *The Anguish of Change* (New York: W. W. Norton, 1973), 67, 217.

16. "The Gym Controversy: 'a massive assault on this institution,'" interview with Michael Schwartz, October 10, 1980, in Bills, *Kent State/May 4,* 215.

17. "Town in Crisis: 'It's life, liberty, *and* property,'" interview with Lucius Lyman Jr., September 23, 1980, in Bills, *Kent State/May 4*, 73.

18. See Bodnar, *Remaking America*, 8-9, 20.

19. *Kent State May 4 Memorial, National Open Design Competition* (Kent, OH: Kent State University, 1985), 2.

20. The most recent history of the Heart Mountain concentration camp is Mike Mackey, "Heart Mountain Relocation Center: Both Sides of the Fence" (master's thesis, University of Wyoming, 1993).

21. Toyo Suyemoto Kawakami, "Camp Memories: Rough and Broken Shards," in *Japanese Americans: From Relocation to Redress*, 27-30. See also Estelle Ishigo, *Lone Heart Mountain* (Santa Clara, CA: COMMUNICART, 1972), for drawings depicting the stark character of life at the Heart Mountain concentration camp. Kent State activists of 1970 felt this same kind of burden; see comments by Bill Arthrell, in Bills, *Kent State/May 4*, 52-53.

22. Cornel West, *Race Matters* (Boston: Beacon Press, 1993), 17, 30.

23. Lecture, January 7, 1976, Foucault, *Power/Knowledge*, 81.

Index